The Dilemma
of Difference

A Multidisciplinary View of Stigma

PERSPECTIVES IN SOCIAL PSYCHOLOGY

A Series of Texts and Monographs • Edited by Elliot Aronson

THE BELIEF IN A JUST WORLD: A Fundamental Delusion
   Melvin J. Lerner

THE DILEMMA OF DIFFERENCE: A Multidisciplinary View of Stigma
   Edited by Stephen C. Ainlay, Gaylene Becker, and Lerita M. Coleman

HUMAN AGGRESSION
   Robert A. Baron

INTRINSIC MOTIVATION
   Edward L. Deci

INTRINSIC MOTIVATION AND SELF-DETERMINATION
   IN HUMAN BEHAVIOR
   Edward L. Deci and Richard M. Ryan

NONVERBAL BEHAVIOR AND SOCIAL PSYCHOLOGY
   Richard Heslin and Miles Patterson

THE PHYSICAL ATTRACTIVENESS PHENOMENA
   Gordon L. Patzer

REDEFINING SOCIAL PROBLEMS
   Edited by Edward Seidman and Julian Rappaport

SCHOOL DESEGREGATION
   Harold B. Gerard and Norman Miller

SCHOOL DESEGREGATION: Past, Present, and Future
   Edited by Walter G. Stephan and Joe R. Feagin

UNIQUENESS: The Human Pursuit of Difference
   C. R. Snyder and Howard L. Fromkin

A Continuation Order Plan is available for this series. A continuation order will bring delivery of each new volume immediately upon publication. Volumes are billed only upon actual shipment. For further information please contact the publisher.

The Dilemma of Difference

A Multidisciplinary View of Stigma

Edited by

Stephen C. Ainlay

Holy Cross College
Worcester, Massachusetts

Gaylene Becker

University of California, San Francisco
San Francisco, California

and

Lerita M. Coleman

University of Michigan
Ann Arbor, Michigan

PLENUM PRESS • NEW YORK AND LONDON

Library of Congress Cataloging in Publication Data

The dilemma of difference.

(Perspectives in social psychology)
Includes bibliographical references and index.
1. Stigma (Social psychology). 2. Social learning. 3. Social interaction. I. Ainlay,
Stephen C. 1951—   . II. Becker, Gaylene. III. Coleman, Lerita M. IV. Series.
HM291.D497   1986   302   86-15086
ISBN 0-306-42304-9

© 1986 Plenum Press, New York
A Division of Plenum Publishing Corporation
233 Spring Street, New York, N.Y. 10013

Printed in the United States of America

To the participants of the Summer Institute on
Stigma and Interpersonal Relations
from whence this dream arose
and for whom it now becomes a reality.

Contributors

STEPHEN C. AINLAY, Department of Sociology, Holy Cross College, Worcester, Massachusetts

REGINA ARNOLD, Department of Sociology, Sarah Lawrence College, Bronxville, New York

OSCAR A. BARBARIN, Department of Psychology, University of Michigan, Ann Arbor, Michigan

GAYLENE BECKER, Institute for Health and Aging, School of Nursing, University of California, San Francisco, San Francisco, California

LERITA M. COLEMAN, Department of Psychology, University of Michigan, Ann Arbor, Michigan

JENNIFER CROCKER, Department of Psychology, State University of New York, Buffalo, New York

FAYE CROSBY, Department of Psychology, Smith College, Northampton, Massachusetts

FREDERICK X. GIBBONS, Department of Psychology, Iowa State University, Ames, Iowa

NEIL LUTSKY, Department of Psychology, Carleton College, Northfield, Minnesota

LARRY G. MARTIN, Department of Administrative Leadership, University of Wisconsin, Milwaukee, Milwaukee, Wisconsin

RICHARD R. SCOTT, Quaker Oats, Chicago, Illinois

CAROL K. SIGELMAN, Department of Psychology, Eastern Kentucky University, Richmond, Kentucky

LOUISE C. SINGLETON, Institute for Research in Child Development, School of Education, San Jose State University, San Jose, California

HOWARD M. SOLOMON, Department of History, Tufts University, Medford, Massachusetts

MARK C. STAFFORD, Department of Sociology, Washington State University, Pullman, Washington

Foreword

The topic of stigma came to the attention of modern-day behavioral science in 1963 through Erving Goffman's book with the engaging title, *Stigma: Notes on the Management of Spoiled Identity*. Following its publication, scholars in such fields as anthropology, clinical psychology, social psychology, sociology, and history began to study the important role of stigma in human interaction. Beginning in the early 1960s and continuing to the present day, a body of research literature has emerged to extend, elaborate, and qualify Goffman's original ideas. The essays presented in this volume are the outgrowth of these developments and represent an attempt to add impetus to theory and research in this area.

Much of the stigma research that has been conducted since 1963 has sought to test one or another of Goffman's notions about the effects of stigma on social interactions and the self. Social and clinical psychologists have tried to experimentally create a number of the effects that Goffman asserted stigmas have on ordinary social interactions, and sociologists have looked for evidence of the same in survey and observational studies of stigmatized people in situations of everyday life. By 1980, a considerable body of empirical evidence had been amassed about social stigmas and the devastating effects they can have on social interactions.

At the same time that this was occurring, other developments were taking place in key behavioral science disciplines that have had a significant bearing on theory and research about stigma. In the fields of psychology, social psychology, sociology, and, to a lesser extent, anthropology, paradigms for analyzing interpersonal relations were developing and have now largely crystallized. Theory and research in these fields produced important new insights into fundamental social processes such as power relations, self-presentational styles, dynamics of social comparison, attribution and labeling processes, and processes of social control—insights that have been gradually melded into paradigms for analyzing interpersonal encounters of every sort.

These two developments—the burgeoning of research on stigma and the development of paradigms for analyzing interpersonal relations—began to come together a few years ago, resulting in a number of major new initiatives involving the subject of stigma. One of these, by no means the only one, was the Special Project on Stigma organized by the Center for Advanced Study in the Behavioral Sciences, Stanford, California. In 1980–1981, a group representing the disciplines of clinical psychology, social psychology, and sociology met at the center for the year to attempt a consolidation of research and theory in this area and to map out new directions for future research.

The Special Project, in turn, gave rise to the Summer Institute on Stigma and Interpersonal Relations that was held at the center in July and August of 1982. The authors of this foreword served as co-directors of the institute. Sponsored by the Andrew Mellon Foundation, the institute brought together 20 young scholars from a variety of behavioral science disciplines, including psychology, sociology, social psychology, clinical psychology, developmental psychiatry, education, history, and anthropology. Together they examined a wide variety of stigmas from a multidisciplinary perspective. The institute provided a forum in which investigators working on a variety of problems—including blindness, deafness, ethnicity, gender, criminality, physical illness, illiteracy, heresy and witchcraft, old age, mental illness, and mental disability—discussed research interests and explored the common and distinct aspects of the stigmatization attending different conditions.

Though the purposes of the institute were manifold, these did not include an obligation to produce a publication of any kind. Yet, following the conclusion of the institute, the summer scholars decided to write a series of essays reflecting the views of stigma that had evolved in their discussions. The essays, which make up this book, address a wide range of issues germane to understanding the phenomena of stigma. The ideas they present are not easily summarized. One can, however, identify a number of themes running through the essays that bind them together into a coherent framework from which future theory and research can proceed.

The authors of this book embrace a highly dynamic conception of stigma. They do not see stigmas as attributes that inhere in particular conditions or that persons automatically have because they acquire traits or qualities that may be discrediting. Rather, they view stigmas as products of definitional processes arising from social interactions between those who acquire potentially discrediting conditions and the individuals with whom they interact. The authors thus see the stigmatization process as highly problematic. Their focus, then, is on how stigmas develop, the intrapsychic and interpersonal forces that sustain them, and the forces that tend to diminish their power. Emphasis is placed on variability, change, development, and reversibility. Taken together, the essays of this volume compel us to view stigmas as emergent social constructs and require us to investigate how they came to be, what sustains them, and how they may change.

Inevitably, their view of stigma leads the authors to adopt a multidisciplinary perspective. In one way or another, each of the essays in this book prompts the reader to pay attention to context. In order to explain how stigmas emerge, to understand their variable character and their complex development over time, it is essential to understand the context in which evaluations and judgments are made about individuals who acquire attributes and qualities that are potentially stigmatizing. Some of the essays focus on the interpersonal context in which stigmas are embedded. Others show the significance of culture, social values, and norms in the creation of stigmas; still others remind us that we must locate these phenomena in their broader historical and economic contexts.

The essays in this volume go beyond simple assertions that context is important. They show how various factors interact to produce a range of social and psychological phenomena. Drawing on cultural, sociological, and historical materials, the authors formulate explanations of why certain conditions are stigmatizing and others not, why certain persons may be more vulnerable to the stigmatization process than others, why conditions that were once stigmatized no longer are, and why new forms of stigma emerge. Thus, the perspective is multidisciplinary in the best and most useful sense of the term.

Each of the chapters seeks to understand stigmatization from the point of view of a dominant body of theory and research within a given discipline. The way in which this is accomplished adds power to the analyses that are presented. In every case, the author or authors have made an effort to conceptualize stigma as an instance of a larger class of phenomena that scholars in their field have studied. In different chapters stigma is presented as a form of stereotyping, a consequence of social comparison and social learning, a form of social discrimination and inequality, a process of social control, or as an asymmetrical power relationship. This approach has two compelling virtues.

First, it makes the phenomenon of stigma far more understandable than it might otherwise appear to be. Stigmas are comparatively rare events in everyday life, and, because they are perceived as rare and somewhat odd, there is a tendency to attempt to understand them by recourse to concepts and theories that are themselves special or unique. The essays in this volume provide a much-needed counterbalance to this unfortunate tendency. By conceptualizing stigmas as special instances of ordinary processes of social learning and social interaction, we are able to grasp them more easily. In addition, we can begin to appreciate their affinity with other, more familiar, forms of social differentiation.

Second, this approach helps to point the way to future areas of research. Once we understand that stigmatization is a form of stereotyping, or that it is an expression of social control processes, or that it is a form of social comparison, or of attribution and labeling, we are then in a position to begin mapping out lines of research that may not have been previously apparent. We do this by identifying the kinds of questions that have been asked by researchers working in the "parent" fields and starting to ask these about stigmas. We can look at where these lines of work have led when they have been applied to other problems and what we can learn from them that may now be applied to the study of stigma.

As we read the chapters of this book, we are reminded once again of the value and the challenge of adopting a perspective that is multidisciplinary. We are also reminded of how far the behavioral sciences have come in this area since the publication of Goffman's book, and of how much further there is to go. Perhaps most reassuring is the fact that there exists a cadre of young and able researchers who are exploring the topic of stigma. It is with no small measure of pride that we may claim perhaps a modest role in having stimulated them to this important task.

ROBERT A. SCOTT
DALE T. MILLER

Stanford, California

Preface

The title of this book, *The Dilemma of Difference*, might just as well describe the coming together of social psychologists, sociologists, anthropologists, historians, and other social scientists to study stigma as it does the stigmatizing process itself. The rethinking of any problem from a multidisciplinary perspective, no matter how narrowly conceived, is made more difficult by specialization and antagonism between the disciplines. We believe, however, that the contributors to this volume have made a significant effort to transcend these divisions and to reexamine the problem of stigma. We are grateful to each of them for the time and dedication that this project required.

The names of the editors are listed alphabetically because the project was undertaken and carried out in a spirit of mutual endeavor. Each of us assumed a major role in keeping the manuscript moving along at various stages in the project's evolution. Trained as sociologist, anthropologist, and social psychologist, respectively, we made an effort to sustain the intellectual tension inherent in such a multidisciplinary enterprise throughout our editorial work. We voiced the concerns of other writers in our fields of study and called attention to the divergence in ideas when it seemed appropriate. Yet our disciplinary allegiances never led to conflict. In fact, we were amazed at how our viewpoints coincided time and again.

A special thank you goes to Lerita Coleman from her co-editors for overseeing many of the details related to final manuscript preparation while she was a Fellow at the Center for Advanced Study in the Behavioral Sciences—Stanford, California. Her efforts are greatly appreciated.

We also would like to acknowledge the assistance and support of many other people. The project would not have been possible without the generous assistance of the Center for Advanced Study in the Behavioral Sciences. The center provided not only the physical space but also the ambience in which disciplinary boundaries could more easily be crossed. A special note of thanks goes to Gardner Lindzey, director of the center, as well as to the entire staff, especially those who assisted in the editing, typing, and production of the manuscript. These included Margaret Amara, Muriel Bell, Lucy Johnston, Matt Fenner, Bruce Harley, Kay Holm, Deanna Knickerbocker, Beth Strack, and Anna Tower. Likewise, we are indebted to Dale Miller and Robert Scott, co-directors of the Summer Institute on Stigma and Interpersonal Relations, out of which the project emerged. A very special thanks must be extended to Lynn Gordon, our faithful, conscientious, and meticulous production editor for her invaluable assistance.

Finally, each of the editors received individual support, without which the completion of the volume would have been much more difficult. Stephen Ainlay would like to express his deepest gratitude to Judy Gardner Ainlay and James Davison Hunter for their continued support and substantive advice. He also extends his appreciation to the Committee on Professional Standards and the Committee on Research and Publications at Holy Cross College for their support. Gaylene Becker thanks her husband, Roger Van Craeynest, for his enthusiastic support throughout the project. Resources of the Institute for Health and Aging, University of California, San Francisco, were made available by Robert Newcomer, whose ongoing encouragement has been much appreciated. Thanks also go to Norton Twite for his cooperation in working on this project. Lerita Coleman wishes to acknowledge support from the John D. and Catherine T. MacArthur and Ford foundations, who sponsored her year as a Fellow at the Center for Advanced Study in the Behavioral Sciences. In addition, she is grateful to Damien Simon and Ruth Pearl Wilson for their re-lentless enthusiasm and continuous prayers.

The concerted effort of so many people has bolstered even further our conviction that much can be learned through a multi-disciplinary explication of the stigma concept and that the effects of stigma have the potential to be ameliorated to some extent through the application of new approaches to its study. This vol-ume represents an initial effort in this direction.

STEPHEN AINLAY
GAYLENE BECKER
LERITA COLEMAN

Contents

FOREWORD IX
    Robert A. Scott and Dale T. Miller

CHAPTER 1: STIGMA RECONSIDERED 1

    Stephen C. Ainlay, Lerita M. Coleman, and
    Gaylene Becker

        Social Science Contributions and Dilemmas in the
        Study of Stigma 2
        Stigma as a Social Construct 3
        The Impact of Stigma on the Individual 6
        Limitations on Conceptual and Analytic
        Categories 8
        Disciplinary Limits to Theory Building 9
        Developing a Multidisciplinary Approach 11

PART I. STIGMA AND SOCIAL MARGINALITY

CHAPTER 2: STIGMA, JUSTICE AND THE DILEMMA
OF DIFFERENCE 17

    Stephen C. Ainlay and Faye Crosby

Typification and Difference 20
Toward a Typology of Human Difference 23
Stigma and Justice 31
Stigma and Justice: Implications for Research 35

CHAPTER 3: STIGMA AS A SOCIAL AND CULTURAL CONSTRUCT .. 39

Gaylene Becker and Regina Arnold

The Universality of Stigma 40
The Cultural Basis of Stigma 41
Stigma in Sociohistorical Perspective 43
Stigma and Societal Assumptions 44
Stigma and Structural Inequality 45
Individual Experience of Stigma in a Sociocultural
    Context 48
Stigma and Social Change 51
Destigmatization 52
Conclusion 55

CHAPTER 4: STIGMA AND WESTERN CULTURE:
A HISTORICAL APPROACH 59

Howard M. Solomon

Corporeal Imagery 61
Stigmatization of Heretics, Homosexuals, and Jews 64
Structural Similarities in Stigmatization 68
Conclusion 75

CHAPTER 5: STIGMA, DEVIANCE, AND SOCIAL CONTROL:
SOME CONCEPTUAL ISSUES 77

Mark C. Stafford and Richard R. Scott

Definitions of Stigma 78
An Alternative Definition: Stigma and Deviance 80

Measuring Stigmas 84
Social Control 87
Summary and Conclusions 90

PART II. THE STIGMATIZING PROCESS

CHAPTER 6: STIGMA AND THE DYNAMICS OF SOCIAL COGNITION   95

Jennifer Crocker and Neil Lutsky

Introduction: Cognitive Approaches in the Study
    of Stigma 95
The Origins of Social Thought about the
    Stigmatized 101
Functioning and Consequences of the Social
    Cognition of Stigma 106
Changing the Cognition of Stigma 114
Conclusions: Cognitive Approaches in the Study
    of Stigma 120

CHAPTER 7: STIGMA AND INTERPERSONAL RELATIONS 123

Frederick X. Gibbons

Stigma and Morality 124
Relationships between Disabled Persons and Others
    129
Relationships among Stigmatized Persons 132
Peer Support Groups 140
Conclusion 143

CHAPTER 8: STIGMA: A SOCIAL LEARNING PERSPECTIVE 145

Larry G. Martin

Introduction 145
The Social Learning of Stigma 147

The Social Learning of Stigma across the Life Cycle   150
The Development of Beliefs, Attitudes, and Values ..   153
Social Learning and Stigma: A Multidisciplinary
    Perspective   159
Conclusion: The Perpetuation of Stigma in Society .   160

CHAPTER 9: FAMILY EXPERIENCE OF STIGMA IN CHILDHOOD
CANCER   163

Oscar A. Barbarin

Introduction   163
Childhood Cancer as a Form of Stigma   164
Stigma and Family Functioning   169
Stigma as a Family Experience   171
Altered Status of the Child in the Family   172
Altered Status of the Child in the Community   174
Stereotypes of Children with Cancer   175
Childhood Cancer as a Master Status   176
Self-Perceptions of Stigmatized Persons   177
Reactions to Social Encounters with Stigmatized
    Persons   178
Altered Family Relations and Functioning   180
Altered Status of the Family in the Community   181
Conclusion   183

CHAPTER 10: STIGMATIZATION IN CHILDHOOD: A SURVEY
OF DEVELOPMENTAL TRENDS AND ISSUES   185

Carol K. Sigelman and Louise C. Singleton

Developmental Issues   185
Developmental Theory and Stigma   187
The Early Origins of Stigmatization in Infancy   191
Developmental Trends in Stigmatization over
    Childhood   193
Reactions to Physical and Mental Disabilities   199
Summary and Implications   204

PART III. STIGMA, CONTINUITY, AND CHANGE

CHAPTER 11: STIGMA: AN ENIGMA DEMYSTIFIED 211

Lerita M. Coleman

    The Dilemma 212
    The Origins of Stigma 216
    Stigma as a Form of Cognitive Processing 218
    The Meaning of Stigma for Social Relations 221
    Fear and Stigma 225
    Conclusion 227

References 233

Index 257

CHAPTER 1

Stigma Reconsidered

Stephen C. Ainlay, Lerita M. Coleman, and Gaylene Becker

This is an era of specialists, each of whom sees his own problem and is unaware of or intolerant of the larger frame into which it fits.

—Rachel Carson

This book is about stigma, a topic that is both elusive and perplexing. Yet stigma is an everyday phenomenon, partially known to everyone who even temporarily slips beyond the bounds of social acceptability. Stories of the stigmatized and indeed the stigmatizing process itself are as close as a newspaper on the doorstep. Furthermore, the concept of stigma elicits numerous adjectives that testify to its ephemeral quality. In this chapter alone, for example, we speak of the paradoxes of stigma, its ambiguity, its variety, and the polarities it engenders. Even while attempting to define stigma, we will tell you that such a task is difficult because notions of stigma are bound by culture, time, and society. What is more, we discuss the general misconceptions social scientists have about stigma, how much has been overlooked, and how little is yet known.

In this first chapter, we purposely raise more questions than we or anyone else could possibly answer, even in a lifetime of effort. Our aim, in keeping with our goal for the rest of the volume, is *not* to find solutions to the stigmatizing process. Our purpose is much more modest: to stimulate thinking in the study of stigma so that other scholars will be intellectually seduced by the subject matter. Accordingly, all the essays in this book have an emergent quality. The contributors to this volume were brought together in the first place by a mutually held interest in stigma. Yet the chapters that appear here bear the mark of interdisciplinary dialogue. We have had our ideas and our respective disciplinary viewpoints challenged by one another in the quest for answers to two major questions: (a) What is stigma? and (b) why does stigma persist?

We hope this outpouring of questions, criticisms, and the like will not deter readers but instead will spark their imaginations and that this book will be used to shape ideas, develop research, and teach others. We view the study of stigma, if not exactly with religious fervor, then at least with a conviction that this is a critical and much-neglected construct in the social sciences, one that is sorely in need of a multidisciplinary examination.

SOCIAL SCIENCE CONTRIBUTIONS AND DILEMMAS IN THE STUDY OF STIGMA

Few books have more eloquently addressed the topic of stigma than did Erving Goffman's classic *Stigma* (1963). No one before or since Goffman has been more self-consciously concerned with defining the phenomenon of stigma. Drawing primarily on sociological, social psychological, and clinical studies, Goffman examined a variety of stigmatizing situations in which individuals were denied full social acceptance. Through descriptions and anecdotes, he posed a series of provocative questions and in the process designed an eclectic blueprint that prepared the way for the study of stigma.

Since Goffman's study, numerous works have addressed the subject of stigma (e.g., Jones, Farina, Hastorf, Markus, Miller, &

Scott, 1984; Katz, 1981; Schur, 1980), usually from a particular disciplinary vantage point. Nevertheless, nearly all students of stigma accept the basic components of Goffman's definition of the phenomenon: that stigmatized persons possess an attribute that is deeply discrediting and that they are viewed as less than fully human because of it (Goffman, 1963).

In fact, Goffman may be the only social scientist who has attempted to explicitly define stigma (Katz, 1981). The absence of any further significant development of the concept is probably due, in part, to the originality of Goffman's insights. It is also due to the equivocal nature of stigma. Which attributes people find discrediting and the intensity of their beliefs and reactions vary so much that devising a single definition proves difficult, if not impossible. The failure of social science to answer the lingering, often nagging question—why does stigma persist?—is therefore less surprising.

STIGMA AS A SOCIAL CONSTRUCT

The contemporary connotations of the word *stigma* are not really much different from its original meaning (Goffman, 1963). For the Greeks, stigma referred to bodily signs that called attention to some moral failing on the part of the person bearing them. Signs, often cut or burned into the body, were intended to cause other people to avoid the bearer—the slave, traitor, or criminal. Today, stigma involves the same sense of moral disapproval, denigration, and avoidance.

Yet the meaning of stigma has often been difficult to pin down, precisely because what is stigmatized is bound by culture and epoch. Some of the particular attributes that disqualify people from full acceptance vary between cultural realms and across historical periods. Other stigmas, such as the stigma associated with incest, seem to be particularly durable, but few stigmas are interminable.

By its very nature, stigma is ambiguous. What is perceived as stigma may be quite different from one social context to the next—so different that at times we strain to see any similarity. As much as we might like to draw up an exhaustive list of stigmatizing attributes, any such attempt would inevitably fail because the list is endless and reflects ongoing cultural and historical change. Given these considerations, defining stigma becomes more difficult.

Each society creates hierarchies of desirable and undesirable attributes and sets rules for the management of such attributes—the use of avoidance, for example, to reduce contact with stigmatized persons. Different stigmas elicit various reactions from a nonstigmatized individual, ranging from sympathy to homicidal assault. Between these two poles, responses include avoidance, ambivalence, and abandonment. Stigmas are remarkably varied in nature. For example, some stigmas elicit similar responses across time and culture, as in the case of specific behavior that conflicts with basic social rules. Other stigmas seem to be created to meet the particular needs of society at a given point in time. The zeitgeist, or cultural framework of a society—whether it is politically conservative or liberal, hunting-gathering or industrial, autocratic or democratic—also helps determine what is stigmatized.

Of course stigmas evolve as cultures and societies change. At the same time, as members of society, we perpetuate our conceptions of stigma and ways of responding to stigmas by passing them on to succeeding generations through social learning or socialization. Conceptualizations of stigma thus go hand in hand with the continuity of culture.

Stigma is a social construct—a reflection of culture itself, not a property of individuals. As Goffman insisted, the "normal" and the "stigmatized" are not persons but perspectives (1963). There is nothing inherent in the attributes of any persons that qualify them for stigmatization. Instead, people qualify as stigmatized only within the context of a particular culture, historical events, or economic, political, or social situation. Being a Christian in 1985 is very different from being one in A.D. 4, and being a Christian in the United States differs from being one in the Middle East. Likewise, people in the United States may not distinguish between Moslems and Hindus, but this distinction becomes a basis for stigma in India.

Many components of stigma evolve along with society, including efforts to "destigmatize" certain groups or traits. Historical development can change the course of a stigma, altering descriptions and categories of stigmas, the stigmatization process, and the consequences of stigmatization. Discontinuities abound even in this approach to understanding stigma. As we become more knowledgeable about stigma, further inconsistencies in public attitudes and feelings become apparent. The AIDS epidemic, for example, may well be short-circuiting the gay liberation movement's attempts to destigmatize homosexuality. Consequently, homosexuality today may be once again as stigmatized as in the past.

It further appears that the destigmatization process is asymmetrical. That is, current developments may bring an immediate halt to the destigmatization process by reawakening and reinforcing old negative stereotypes and attitudes. Deinstitutionalization and halfway houses for the mentally ill, for example, have gained some public support in the last 10 years, yet some segments of the population refuse to allow such attempts at "normalization" to operate in their neighborhoods. Destigmatization as a whole is a gradual process, taking years and sometimes decades to raise people's consciousness and to erase negative attitudes. In some cases, it is never complete. Stigmas do persist tenaciously, although perhaps more strongly at certain times and places than at others.

In some ways, social scientists may have legitimized stigma by suggesting that it is only human, if not "natural," to perceive and rank differences between ourselves and others. Such an understanding suggests that people cannot change and may excuse them from feeling that they should try. Additionally, inferences made from such observations may lead to the dehumanization of both stigmatizer and stigmatized. Are our perceptual systems "wired" or constructed in this manner? What do such explanations mean for those who are being stigmatized? Are we programmed to perceive a *them* and an *us*? We know that what appears to be "figure" to some is "ground" to others, and vice versa. Regardless of how we perceive and order our personal worlds and the extent to which we accept or disown stigma, it remains and in doing so colors everyone's existence.

As our explanations of how stigma operates become more subtle, we develop equally subtle ways to stigmatize. For example, people with certain stigmas may not be refused employment, yet neither are they promoted. We allow ourselves to have social relationships with stigmatized people, but these relationships are often not egalitarian because our perceptual system or set of categories will not permit us to envision a stigmatized person in a category comparable to our own. The many communities where stigmatized people are tolerated but not fully accepted provide an example of these perceptual incongruities and the pervasiveness of stigma in society. Reactions to those who are stigmatized, whether subtle or blatant, have a dramatic impact on stigmatized persons over the long term.

THE IMPACT OF STIGMA ON THE INDIVIDUAL

We have no cognitive explanation about why a stigma becomes a "master status"—that is, one in which the defining attribute eclipses all other aspects of stigmatized persons, their talents and abilities (Goffman, 1963; Kanter, 1977, 1979). Stigma creates dependence, and thus stigmatized persons may become engaged in a bondage to sources of power despite a desire for independence from them. Stigmas may place once-powerful people in powerless positions. For example, a stigmatized condition acquired late in life may force the individual to relearn her or his own sense of relative prestige and authority. Conversely, persons previously denied the ear of political leaders may experience an increased sense of power through membership in self-help groups—initiating a sense of collective action made possible by their newly acquired stigma. In still other cases, stigma allows powerless people to feel a sense of superiority or power over others who are more severely stigmatized. Finally, stigma may also give the demarcation of power greater clarity so that everyone knows who has control over whom. The social-control function of stigma appears to be especially highlighted in times of scarce economic resources.

Stigma creates discontinuities for people over the course of their lives. Despite the elusive nature of stigma, it follows us through the life cycle. Although feelings about the stigmas of others may be passed from one generation to the next, change in perceptions of stigma across our lifetimes is always a possibility, especially if we acquire a stigmatized condition (for example, cancer, physical disability) or experience the stigma of a close friend or relative (Goffman [1963] labels this a "courtesy stigma"). Looking at the two extremes of the life course continuum—early childhood and old age—it may be that children and elders have very different notions of what constitutes stigma and react differently to it as well. If we think of the experience of stigma as occurring over the life course, we may better understand the significance of stigma for personal development, how it waxes and wanes in salience at the individual level. Yet even when stigmas no longer continually tug at the individual in daily routines, they linger as memories, reflections of culture that alter people's behavior and their lives.

The consequences of stigma can be paradoxical because they have the potential to be both dehumanizing and inspiring. The experience of social exile, whether literal or figurative, may result in the development and maintenance of low self-concept for some individuals, yet be the catalyst for the emergence of a new and vibrant self in others. Some individuals who experience stigma gradually come to see it as a social process whose onus they repudiate. Knowledge of the arbitrary nature of stigma may ultimately free individuals from the mantle of responsibility they carry. When this process occurs through social movements, the burden of stigma is shifted elsewhere—onto society itself.

Individual transcendence of stigma is dependent on many factors, such as cultural beliefs, social status, individual personality, economics, physical environment, and education. No one disciplinary perspective is adequate either to explain the components of a given stigma or to make predictions or suggestions about altering the experience of those who have a given stigma.

Factors such as those enumerated previously all affect individual capacity to adapt to stigma and to function effectively in life.

LIMITATIONS ON CONCEPTUAL AND ANALYTIC CATEGORIES

Barriers to the study of stigma relate not only to obstacles inherent in the phenomenon of stigma but also to the nature of social scientific discourse to date. The place of stigma research within various fields of study, for example, contributes to our failure as social scientists to adequately address the concept of stigma. Typically, stigma has been relegated to the level of a subtopic within a subfield of a particular discipline. Sociologists, for example, have usually treated stigma as a special instance of deviance, posing questions about stigma in terms of deviations from society. Deviance, in turn, is not even a principal area of study for sociologists, despite its perennial presence in course listings at colleges and universities. Similarly, for social psychologists, stigma has been of interest only insofar as it sheds light on prejudice, stereotypes, cognition, and the like. Anthropologists have discussed stigma primarily in terms of in-groups and out-groups or in terms of social control in various cultural settings. Until recently, stigma simply has not been a relevant interpretive filter for historians; to find research on stigma in historical studies, we must extrapolate from examples embedded in other discussions. Regardless of disciplinary affiliation, then, research on stigma has been on the fringe of academic thought.

Additionally, those researchers dealing with stigma within each discipline have typically ignored related work in other fields of study. The effort to develop a greater understanding of stigma has been hampered by this discipline-specific approach for several reasons: (a) conceptual and analytic categories are often limited to one disciplinary perspective; (b) discipline-specific theory building about other concepts fails to address the stigma concept; and (c) ignorance of cross-disciplinary research limits theory building. These points demand further consideration.

Those who have been interested in the stigma phenomenon have usually applied a single conceptual framework to it, based on their disciplinary perspective. These frameworks have ranged from psychoanalytic theories about the self to models of cognitive processes, from structural-functional analyses to phenomenologically based theories. In utilizing single conceptual and analytic tools, researchers have retained a narrow view of the stigma concept and thus failed to uncover the paradoxes and trends embedded in stigma that a multidisciplinary perspective reveals. The uncritical use of a single theory leads to contrasting one view with another rather than synthesizing and integrating differing perspective. There has been little critical analysis of how the various theories differentially affect the nature of research or the findings that are reported.

What is more, divergent conceptual categories lead to multiple levels of analysis. We are not suggesting that such variation is necessarily bad. On the contrary, we believe that the greater the variation in the conduct of research on stigma, the better. Knowledge of other disciplinary and conceptual points of view can, however, only enhance such diversity. From one disciplinary vantage point, for example, researchers are easily enticed by the study of the interpersonal dynamics of stigma and thus lose sight of its cultural and historical specificity. Similarly, it is easy to become intoxicated by the magnitude of paradigmatic arguments and forget that stigma also involves life dramas, with the corresponding pain and triumph of real people.

DISCIPLINARY LIMITS TO THEORY BUILDING

The definition of research problems within the constraints of a single disciplinary perspective has characterized nearly all areas of social scientific inquiry, and is by no means restricted to research on stigma. Our training often prevents us from comprehending the significance of findings from other disciplines, however, if they are couched in a theoretical framework unfamiliar to us. As social scientists increasingly are encouraged to read and publish only within their own disciplines, ignorance of other fields deepens. Findings have been both duplicated and contradicted, resulting in the emergence of competing conceptual models. Opportunities to discuss and debate such inconsistencies in stigma research rarely occur and are frequently overlooked when they do.

What is learned by studying stigmatized groups is often applied, not to an understanding of stigma, but to other concepts—such as deviance, social control, and stereotyping—within specific disciplines. Refinement of such concepts reflects the special interests of certain disciplines but not the concept of stigma itself. A greater awareness of the significance of the stigma concept could foster discussion between disciplines, stir creativity, and bring about greater conceptual clarity—both for stigma and for theories within specific disciplines.

Social scientists live in the world as well as study it. In studying stigma, researchers are "culture-bound," restricted by the prevailing cultural biases as to what constitutes normality. They may find it difficult to shed the social baggage of values and norms that reflect cultural background and recent history. Stigma, nevertheless, is sometimes studied as if it were a concept that is timeless, without cultural interpretation outside society. Without some awareness of stigma as a dynamic yet ever-present phenomenon, cultural myopia may significantly affect our ability to understand the nature of stigma and the reasons for its persistence.

When increased cross-fertilization does occur between disciplines, it creates a greater pool of social scientists who are attuned to the topic and who may combine their ideas. The work that is generated from such endeavors not only will lead, we hope, to theory building, greater conceptual clarity, and increased conceptual creativity but will ultimately affect the real-life situations of individuals who experience stigma.

Those of us who conduct research on stigma from particular disciplinary perspectives are no more or less susceptible to a danger that all investigators face—that of forgetting we are uncovering only one piece of a much more complex whole. A multidisciplinary view of stigma is useful not only because of its holistic approach but because it may lead to areas of inquiry that might otherwise be overlooked in the planning and conduct of research. Only by understanding the nuances of stigma as well as by revealing the whole, can we really hope to advance the conceptual development of work in this field.

DEVELOPING A MULTIDISCIPLINARY APPROACH

A major goal of this book is to stimulate social scientists to consider the concept of stigma in new and creative ways and to utilize these ideas in the conduct of social research. Perhaps stigma is a social artifact that social scientists will someday use to tell future generations something unique about social stratification, social interaction, identity, language, political thought, economic conditions, and cultural change, as archaeologists have used the tools of earlier peoples to describe various aspects of culture.

The chapters in this volume are a first attempt to step beyond our disciplinary boundaries and to broaden the applicability of certain constructs in the study of stigma. To do this, we must question the existence of stigma itself and its profile of characteristics. The chapters in the first part of the book, "Stigma and Social Marginality," all raise questions about the nature of stigma. They ask: What signals does stigma give us about culture? About the nature of social life? About the nature of social change? Ainlay and Crosby ask questions about how individuals fit their experiences into some interpretive scheme, how we routinize our lives and strive for predictability in life. Because difference, epitomized by stigma, wreaks havoc with predictability, Ainlay and Crosby ask how we reconcile the dilemma of difference, thereby posing one of the key questions of the book.

Becker and Arnold, in their chapter, "Stigma as a Social and Cultural Construct," focus on what is considered stigma and the ways stigmas change with time, place, and context. In his chapter, "Stigma and Western Culture: A Historical Approach," Solomon continues this theme, calling our attention to the myriad interacting phenomena that create the ways stigma is addressed historically and culturally. Stafford and Scott, in their chapter, "Stigma, Deviance, and Social Control: Some Conceptual Issues," take a different approach and examine the ways in which societies have attempted to regulate the population by defining difference as deviance and by controlling it through various structural means. These chapters all point to the stability of some stigmas and the modifications that have occurred in attitudes toward other stigmas. They all address the question of whether the handling of stigma in a particular time or place is a barometer of social change, and thus they highlight the ephemeral, often paradoxical, nature of stigma.

Stigma is not only a reflection of culture, however; it is a cultural process. In the second part of this book, "The Stigmatizing Process," the authors describe and discuss various aspects of the stigmatizing process, moving from a general discussion to particular examples. Crocker and Lutsky describe the development of stereotyping and attitudes that affect the perception of stigma, whereas Gibbons addresses the specific social and psychological components inherent in interactions between those who are stigmatized and those who are not. Martin introduces the concept of social learning and examines the process by which we learn stigma socially. He describes how stigmatization is a cultural artifact that emanates from social learning to be exhibited in our social relationships. The study of social interaction will undoubtedly continue to be one of the chief vehicles through which research on stigma is conducted, and the chapters in this part of the book provide some insights into how such research can incorporate the broad perspectives we are fostering in this volume.

The far-reaching nature of stigma suggests not only that we need to conduct research on stigma itself, but also that research on topics not directly related to the study of stigma can benefit from reference to the stigma concept. For example, the chapter by Barbarin demonstrates how the stigma concept can be applied in studies of family life. As a construct, stigma can be studied either as the primary research problem or as part of a range of topics that are best addressed together. What is more, although research may not specifically address the topic of stigma, stigma may be an important explanatory factor in the findings on another topic. For example, the research reviewed by Sigelman and Singleton was not all conceived as stigma-related, yet it is stigma-related by virtue of what it tells us about the development of stigmatization in childhood.

In the final part of the book, "Stigma: Continuity and Change, we consider issues of continuity and change in relation to stigma. Social research should contribute not only to a greater understanding of stigma but to positive social change as well. Although some social scientists desire to understand the social environment without tampering with it, this seems to us neither feasible nor desirable. Social scientists interact with other people, and the very nature of these interactions necessarily changes the environment. In the final chapter, Coleman draws conclusions about the multidisciplinary view of stigma and its implications for the study of stigma and for the potential for change to occur as a result.

The central importance of the stigma concept to the way we view ourselves and others suggests that although social change may occur that reduces the impact of stigma, stigma will always be part of the human condition. For example, the 1960s and 1970s witnessed the transformation of two traditionally stigmatized categories, blacks and women, in changes that permanently altered the fabric of American society. Yet the harsher economic conditions of the 1980s have in some ways limited the extent to which the stigmas associated with race and gender have been reduced, so that other stigmatized categories such as "unemployed," "physically unfit," and "elderly," to cite only a few, have evolved in addition to the former categories.

A growing awareness of the dynamics of stigma in society has fostered a variety of responses among the public, from movements that attempt to counter social oppression to support groups for a wide variety of stigmatized conditions. Even though we will not succeed in completely eradicating stigma from society, effective use of the concept in social science endeavors may enable us to better understand ourselves and our social environment, which may in turn make possible individual efforts to move beyond the experience of stigma.

PART I

STIGMA AND SOCIAL MARGINALITY

CHAPTER **2**

Stigma, Justice, and the Dilemma of Difference

Stephen C. Ainlay and Faye Crosby

What has stigma to do with justice? On the face of it, the answer is obvious: little if anything. Stigma involves situations where one individual or group treats another individual or group as less than fully human. Justice involves the fair distribution of outcomes and the procedures by which distributions are arranged. The conceptual overlap looks slight, at first blush. It seems hardly surprising, then, that scholars rarely mention the two terms in the same breath except, perhaps, to note that societies stigmatize some lawbreakers or to comment on the injustice of some stigmas.

Scratch beneath the surface, however, and much of this conceptual disparity vanishes. Stigma and justice present ideas that are richly and complexly interrelated. Both "stigma" and "justice" imply interpersonal relations; neither really has meaning apart from the judgments of social actors as they confront one another. Both are products of the human need to bestow meaning upon experience. That is, both help to provide individuals with an ordered sense of the world around them. Finally, both concepts

The ordering of the authors' names is alphabetical.

center around "normative" issues, which involve what "ought" and what "ought not" to be.

Thus, the words *stigma* and *justice* are not simple cognitive concepts that tell us "what is." Stigma involves much more than the fact that people are different, whereas justice involves much more than organizational proscriptions for legal order. In making this statement, we anticipate the major points that our chapter seeks to address. By way of introduction, let us consider these in somewhat greater detail.

First, although stigma and justice can be approached as societal and/or institutional abstractions (we can talk of a "just society" or we can discuss stigma as an "instrument of social control"), one must never lose sight of the fact that such "macro" observations are processually bound with the interactions of social actors. It is thus imperative that we understand the ways in which people conceive of the just distribution of punishment, rewards, misfortunes, and the like. It is likewise important that we account for people's sense of normalcy by examining those human differences that are routinely processed and those that prompt revulsion or avoidance. How do such conceptions of stigma and justice affect the nature and quality of interpersonal relationships? Having addressed these issues, we can better entertain questions as to the societal disparities that such relationships betray. Furthermore, their resolution will demonstrate the close ties between stigma and justice.

Second, all societies evolve legal systems, but the nature of the systems varies. Stigma is also a feature of all societies, but societies differ in what they stigmatize. Both legal systems and stigmatizing processes bespeak, by their very existence, of a need for order. They attest to the central feature of human experience: people's ongoing struggle to achieve some meaningful ordering of themselves as well as their social and physical environments. These ordering activities are certainly not limited to stigma and justice but also manifest themselves through cultural attributes, such as rules of grammar, etiquette, and religious belief systems. Nevertheless, thinking of stigma and justice in terms of their ordering character will help reveal their conceptual and empirical overlap.

Finally, both stigma and justice tell us much about how people think the world does and should operate. Some of their assumptions may be part of the foundation of legal systems. People usually act as if the laws they obey are not simply arbitrary conventions. Laws are lent natural, social, or even cosmic significance. Furthermore, people are able to distinguish between these sources of legal legitimation. They speak of the laws of nature, the laws of man, and the laws of God. Correspondingly, they discriminate between crimes against nature, crimes against humanity, and crimes against God. Yet behind every violation of law lies a concern with volition. Did the person intend to violate a law? Volition constitutes an important aspect of morality. The need to believe in a just world disinclines us to believe that individuals suffer blamelessly.

This same concern with "justice" informs people's confrontations with persons who carry stigmatized "marks" as well. Our essay argues that assumptions that underlie legal systems are also at play in the stigmatizing process. A person's encounter with the blind person, the facially disfigured, the mentally retarded, and members of other "out-groups" triggers ordering activities. Stigma involves a process by which people catalog differences. It also raises the same issues of volition, morality, and blame that are embedded in legal systems.

To justify the assumption that an impulse toward order underlies both the creation of a justice system and the stigmatizing process, this chapter will explore the ontological underpinnings of both justice and stigma. The exploration concentrates on what we call the "dilemma of difference." Perceptions of difference arouse us, promising to simultaneously please and distress us. Unending sameness deadens the human spirit, but differences produce stress.

By supplementing such social philosophical insights with the devices of other investigators, we can arrive at a more adequate assessment of stigma, justice, and their overlap. For example, psychologists and sociologists offer clues to the interactive character and societal consequences of the two phenomena, whereas anthropologists and historians shed light on their rich cultural and historical variability.

This chapter takes its form from its purpose. In the next section, we discuss the dilemma of difference. We ask: How do people deal with difference when they encounter another human being or think about other human beings? What differences excite interest and what differences excite alarm? At what point and under what conditions do differences result in hierarchies? In the final portion of the chapter, we return to the concepts of stigma and justice. We point out commonalities in the ways scholars may approach the two topics—searching empirically for Platonic ideals. Whether or not one can discover universals in what people punish (legally or through stigma), one should understand the making of laws and the creation of stigmas as facets of the human need for order.

TYPIFICATION AND DIFFERENCE

A basic premise of our discussion is that human life is characterized by ongoing efforts to fit experience into some interpretive scheme. As Berger, Berger, and Kellner (1973, p. 63) have suggested: "To be human means to live in a world—that is, to live in a reality that is ordered and that gives sense to the business of living." We can term the attempts of people to give their world and lives meaning and order (as does Berger), "nomos-building activity." All such activity involves the process of what phenomenologists have called "typification" (Schutz, 1971). In Andrew Weigert's terms (1981, p. 101), "It seems to be an inescapable feature of human living together that we routinize our lives to some degree. These routines, then, become the basis for our living in a world which is a typical world, that is, knowable and predictable." This knowability and predictability of the world is accomplished through "recipes" (Schutz, 1971). Recipes allow us to place things, settings, and/or people (and even ourselves) into meaningful categories. According to Schutz (1971, p. 8), "What is experienced in the actual perception of an object is apperceptively transferred to any other similar object, perceived merely as to its type. Actual experience will or will not confirm my anticipation of the typical conformity with other objects."

Maurice Merleau-Ponty expresses much the same idea in his discussion of our organization of the perceptual field. In Merleau-Ponty's terms (1963b, p. 104), we use "forms" to organize our perceptions of both physical and social environments. As he further specifies, these forms do not operate in a mechanistic fashion. On the contrary, they are "symbolic" (as opposed to "amovable")—that is, they can be readily transferred to new experiences, new situations, and new objects that we confront, including other people. In other words, the process of typification involves an ongoing comparison between the recipes or types we carry with us and the things we experience around us. Furthermore, recipes or forms can, and will, be modified to accommodate novel encounters.

Difference is an essential part of the process of typification. Put most simply, differences are variations between or within types. When we encounter a chair, we know it to be a chair because it corresponds to our recipe for chairs (legs for support, flat surface for sitting, etc.). Most of us can, using such a typification, readily distinguish the chair from a telephone (which has its own recipe). Thus, we somewhat routinely and casually distinguish between types. We can also note differences within types. We know a telephone by its receiver, dial (more currently, its touch-tone keypad), and cord. Yet when selecting a telephone, we become quite aware of differences within the type: trimline versus wall phone, versus standard desk phone. We even allow for certain departures from our preconceived recipe, as in the case of the cordless phone. Difference both between and within types is, therefore, central to the process of typification.

Some differences will be highlighted; others will be suppressed. The former are part of our perceptual foreground and are what we might term "salient," whereas the latter become part of our perceptual background. Whether or not we notice differences may depend, in large part, upon what we consider relevant. That is, depending upon our priorities in a given situation, we may bring into focus various definitional qualities of a thing, event, or social actor and force others into the background, summoning some greater similarity. Phenomenologists have observed that we all confront a "horizon" of possible perceptions. From this horizon, only some will be called to our perceptual foreground. What is relevant to the observer (which is clearly context-specific) determines which things remain in the horizon and which come to the foreground of our attention. Alfred Schutz (1971, pp. 59–60) whimsically discussed this process with regard to his dog Rover:

> There are mountains, trees, animals, dogs—in particular Irish setters and among them my Irish setter, Rover. Now I may look at Rover either as this unique individual, my irreplaceable friend and comrade, or just as a typical example of "Irish setter," "dog," "mammal," "animal," "organism," or "object of the outer world." Starting from here, it can be shown that whether I do one or the other, and also which traits or qualities of a given object or event I consider as individually unique and which as typical, depends upon my interest and the system of relevances involved—briefly, upon my practical or theoretical "problem at hand."

To use an earlier illustration, when people are fatigued, a chair will most likely be typified as an object for sitting. Here the difference between a chair and a sofa will not seem great, but the difference between a chair and a ladder will. By contrast, when people seek objects that are out of their grasp, that same chair may be used to extend their reach. In this situation, the difference between a chair and a sofa will seem great, but the chair will seem similar to a ladder. The perception of the chair can thus vary, depending on which of its characteristics are seen as relevant to a given situation.

Both recipes themselves and the system of relevances we use in their application to the world around us often fall into the social domain. They are social in at least two ways (Schutz, 1964, p. 121): (a) They are socially approved; and (b) they are socially distributed. By the first, we mean that recipes and even relevances are often shared by the actor with fellow social participants and define what is correct procedure and conduct as well as what is good and natural in a given society. By the second, we mean that recipes and relevances are passed on to actors by those who have preceded them in human experience (especially teachers and parents), and they are exchanged by contemporaries (especially consociates—

persons with whom we have a particularly close association). We know the chair to be an appropriate place for sitting (and not the table) because of recipes that are given to us through socialization and interaction with others (who would likely register their disapproval if we chose to sit on the table). This is not to say that all recipes are pregiven or that unique recipes are precluded. On the contrary, recipes can be modified to handle the unexpected. The majority of recipes are, however, handed over to the individual and become "taken for granted until further notice."

It is worth noting that the typification process is not free of error. One need only recount the familiar story of the person who drinks from the finger bowl in a Chinese restaurant or imagine a person who fails to distinguish a communion wafer from a cookie. In other words, it is possible that a person will fail to make note of appropriate differences. Likewise, a person may ascribe differences where distinction is inappropriate.

All that we have said about the process of typification, generally, and the notation of difference, specifically, can be said to be true of our perceptions in both the physical and social worlds. That is, we apply recipes, make distinctions between and within types whenever we confront physical objects around us or experience various settings, as well as when we interact with other people.

It is the typification of human differences that interests us most in our discussion of stigma and justice. We will therefore turn to this area in greater detail.

TOWARD A TYPOLOGY OF HUMAN DIFFERENCE

How do we decide that a person is "different?" What do we intend when we arrive at such a conclusion? From what has been said before, it can be anticipated that human differences are derived from recipes, but what are the sources of these recipes? These and other questions must be addressed if we are to understand the special place of stigma and justice in the typification process.

Difference is as ubiquitous a part of interpersonal experience as is typification. Various philosophers have insisted that the processing of human differences is integral to the recognition of others as autonomous social actors. This argument is central, for example, to Husserl's discussion (1970) of "appresentation." How is it that we come to view other people as independent actors not of our own creation? Husserl answers this question with a three-part process of interpersonal perception.

Husserl notes that people do not directly perceive others as egos. At first, we only perceive the physical body of another person. Yet there is a sort of "coincidence of meaning" that takes place when we see other bodies (not when seeing other objects, like chairs). We are predisposed to view another body as having consciousness. The other body becomes a sign of a mind analogous to our own. The typification of one's sense of self suggests a body inhabited by consciousness. This first stage of interpersonal perception is what Husserl called "appresentational pairing."

In a second stage, people become further aware of a sense of sameness because the other's body fulfills certain expectations. This is to say, the other's body performs various movements and activities that we are familiar with via the experience of our own bodies. Therefore, we further assume that the body of the other appresents a corresponding consciousness.

In the last stage of Husserl's model, the other person's body engages in activities and behaviors that deviate from people's experience of their own bodies. In such a way, it becomes apparent that the other is not an exact duplicate of oneself. Through a process of empathy, the "I" in the situation recognizes the other as "Other" (difference gives significance to the capitalizing of the term). In other words, it is difference that demonstrates to us the autonomy and independence of other social actors.

Beyond this sort of philosophical anthropology, we can say that the processing of difference affects the nature and quality of our interaction with other people. As Robert MacLeod (1958, p. 45) suggested some years ago, "the way in which we apprehend the other person is basic to the dynamics of interpersonal relations, to the group-structure of the world of people as we see it, and, very practically, to the way in which social tensions develop and are resolved." We do not restrict ourselves here to the differences one perceives in the makeup or manipulation of another person's mere physiological presence. Our concern with difference extends beyond these to perceived personality traits and membership in groups as well.

Obviously, people do not treat all differences equally. In this chapter, we term those differences that go unnoticed in our interaction with others *background differences* and those that are routinely accounted for as we "size up" fellow social participants we call *foreground differences.* These are not, of course, static categories but rather are subject to historical and cultural variation.

Seen but unnoticed human differences form a sort of perceptual horizon from which we select those differences that are salient to a given situation or moment. Merleau-Ponty (1963a, p. 68) describes this delimiting aspect of perception by noting, "I direct my gaze upon a sector of the landscape which comes to life and is disclosed while the other objects recede into the periphery and become dormant, while, however, not ceasing to be there."

A brilliant maple tree during fall foliage will prompt observers to direct their attention away from the more mundane and contextual landscape that frames it. Similarly, in our perception of other persons, we routinely dismiss information about potentially identifiable differences that seem irrelevant to our interaction. These background differences do not disappear any more than does the mundane landscape, but they are not salient to our determination of the course of interaction nor to our conclusion regarding the character of the other person. These background differences are hard to grasp, precisely because they are seen but unnoticed. To illustrate, one really needs to look for other cultures and other historical periods where differences we ignore are brought into salient relief or where differences that we highlight are suppressed. Consider, for example, the reported practice in ancient Rome of taking an emetic so that one could continue eating more food. If this practice were commonplace, it would be hard to imagine the ancient Romans bringing into relief some of the behavioral oddities associated with bulimia in our contemporary society.

The noting of some foreground differences may, however, be

inherent as evidenced by some studies of attention and the visual system. Researchers studying the attention of infants, for example, have argued that even newborns bring certain differences to the foreground on the basis of contour, contrast, and movement. Furthermore, as Kagan (1970, 1972) notes in his "discrepancy hypothesis," by the second month of life, children already bring to the foreground of their attention stimuli that differ moderately from those that are already part of their attentional schemata. Kagan also observes that, by the end of the first year, children attempt to interpret and understand unusual events. The nomos-building process thus begins in early human development. Yet the physical cues that develop sensory schemata in infants are only antecedent to complex, socially distributed recipes that direct our attention toward certain foreground human differences and away from others—and furthermore specify the way in which we channel our response to those differences.

Like all perceptual phenomena, differences between humans are noticed or suppressed depending upon our relevances and projects of action. Where does the interaction occur, for how long, with what intensity, and with what intended consequence? We are, after all, "situationally embedded" creatures. This is so central to human experience that Douglas (1970, p. 37) speaks of the "principle of the integrity of the situation"—that is, "that concrete human events are always to some degree dependent on the situational context in which they occur and can be adequately explained only by taking into consideration that situational context." This is certainly true of the cultural and historical context of differences, and also of the interactional context of the immediate moment.

Our valuations of foreground differences are not uniform. Some foreground differences are evaluated in more or less neutral terms. We can differentiate persons on the basis of hair color, yet (despite our sometime cultural fascination with blondes) we generally use this as a mere means of describing and/or recognizing others. In these terms, hair color is a foreground difference—we do notice it—but it carries little consequence for the social actor.

Many foreground differences, however, are either positively or negatively evaluated. They transcend mere differentiation and involve stratification or some hierarchically arranged valuation. In our society, we prize certain physiological characteristics, mannerisms, and group identifications. We find obese persons, for example, to be almost revolting (Millman, 1980). We applaud the person who maintains direct eye contact in a conversation (attributing sincerity, honesty, and other positive traits to such physiological manipulation), and avoid or curtail interaction with those who do not (Scott, 1969). Even the most cursory review of the literature on socioeconomic variations in income, education, housing, and health care will suggest that "white" versus "nonwhite" is a key issue in the opportunities we accord people in the modern world.

Our encounters with human difference in social interaction do not always lead to ready typification. In some instances, difference may prompt a sort of intermediate stage that comes before either negative or positive evaluation. This intermediate stage has been characterized as "disorientation." As Lofland (1969, p. 178) points out, people will sometimes come across things, events, or other people who "fall outside of or between actors' existing cognitive categories for rendering reality coherent and understandable." In other words, the situation is both outside their typificatory scheme and novel. In such instances, we are not initially sure how to categorize the difference. Goffman (1967, p. 97) would argue that such disorientation often leaves us embarrassed—a symptomatic response to confronting something that lies outside our typificatory scheme. What he describes as a sort of "orgasmic flush" characteristic of embarrassment may well be our initial response to truly marked differences in others. Ultimately, however, our predisposition toward order dictates that disorientation give way to categorization. Either we find a recipe (not immediately apparent) that can be expanded to accomodate the situation, or we develop an altogether new one.

Those foreground human differences that are negatively evaluated form the basis of stigma. As Goffman (1963, p. 3) observed in his classic study, a stigma may be quite simply defined as "an attribute that is deeply discrediting." Other writers have since varied the terminology. Schur (1984), for example, substitutes the word *devaluated* (more in line with the labeling tradition in sociology and its stress on the evaluation process) for *discredited*. Others (Jones, Farina, Hastorf, Markus, Miller, & Scott, 1984) substitute *mark* for stigma (feeling the latter too "melodramatic"). In any case, the central point remains clear. Stigma is a special case in the typification of difference; that is, one that is very much in the foreground of our attention and is negatively evaluated. Like Goffman (1963, p. 4), we would include here human differences involving what he calls "abominations of the body" (various physical deformities), "blemishes of individual character" (various signs of "weak will," such as unnatural passions, dishonesty, addiction, homosexuality), and "tribal stigma" (differences of race, nation, and religion).

Given that a difference is devaluated, how and why is it brought to the foreground? Jones *et al.* (1984) have identified six "dimensions of stigma" that seem to influence this outcome. Their review of the literature suggests that the stigmatizing process is affected by (a) "concealability" (Is the condition hidden or obvious?); (b) "course" (How does the condition change? What is its ultimate outcome?); (c) "disruptiveness" (Does it block or hamper interaction?); (d) "aesthetic qualities" (Is the condition repellent, ugly, or upsetting?); (e) "origin" (Is the person responsible for the condition?); and (f) "peril" (Is danger posed by the condition? If so, how imminent and how serious is the threat?). These six dimensions guide our typificatory scheme of differences that are negatively evaluated. Having said this, however, we should also note that each can be placed on some continuum and so the question remains of "at what point" each prompts a negative evaluation. The answer varies by both time and place—in other words, by social-historical context.

It is imperative that we remind ourselves that both recipes of human difference and the relevance structure that focuses our attention on some differences and directs it away from others are, by and large, socially distributed and maintained. This is certainly true of what we negatively evaluate or stigmatize. It is also true of what differences we notice in the first place. This is, of course, most easily demonstrated by the abundance of cultural and historical diversity regarding what is viewed as acceptable and unacceptable difference. There are many illustrations in the anthropological literature, but one of the best with regard to stigma can be found in Collin Turnbull's classic study of the Pygmies (1962, pp. 184–187). Therein, he discusses cultural variations in the typification of menstrual blood between the Pygmies and the neighboring BaBira. For the latter, menstrual blood carries negative connotations:

> Blood of any kind is a terrible and powerful thing, associated with injury and sickness and death. Menstrual blood is even more terrible because of its mysterious and regular recurrence. Its first appearance is considered by the villagers as a calamity—an evil omen. The girl who is defiled by it for the first time is herself in danger, and even more important she has placed the whole family and clan in danger. She is promptly secluded, and only her mother (and, I suspect, one or two other close and senior female relatives) may see her and care for her. She has to be cleansed and purified, and the clan itself has to be protected, by ritual propitiation, from the evil she has brought upon them. At the best, the unfortunate girl is considered a considerable nuisance and expense.

Ultimately, Turnbull concludes, the menstruation affair in BaBira culture is "a rather shameful one in the eyes of the villagers, as well as a dangerous one. It is something best concealed and not talked about in public. The girl is an object of suspicion, scorn, repulsion, and anger. It is not a happy coming of age." By contrast, Turnbull describes the Pygmies' view of menstruation:

> For the Pygmies, the people of the forest, it is a very different thing. To them, blood, in the usual context in which they see it, is equally dreadful. But they recognize it as being the symbol not only of death, but also of life. And menstrual blood to them means life.

Correspondingly, the reaction among the Pygmies is quite different:

> So when a young Pygmy girl begins to flower into maturity, and blood comes to her for the first time, it comes to her as a gift, received with gratitude and rejoicing—rejoicing that the girl is now a potential mother, that she can now proudly and rightfully take a husband. There is no mention of fear or superstitution, and everyone is told the good news.

Such anthropological considerations lead us to conclude that all societies stigmatize human differences, but clearly they vary in what is stigmatized.

This observation raises, of course, the issue of cultural uni-

versals. We cannot hope to resolve in this chapter an issue that
has stirred so much controversy. Nevertheless, we would suggest
that the processing of some human differences is universal.
Gross distortions of normally taken-for-granted body image must
prompt a universal need to order the differences. (Such a response is hinted at in the research into children's reactions to
radical changes in the arrangement of human facial features. See
Maurer & Barerra, 1981, for their review of this literature.) Furthermore, we would suggest that all societies share a negative
evaluation of certain differences—all societies stigmatize. This
may well be necessary for the coherent definition of group boundaries, the establishment of *we* versus *they*, and the specification
of what it means to be "normal" in a given culture or historical
period. Yet which differences come to be negatively evaluated,
hence altering the quality of interaction with others, is likely to
vary by place and time. Jones *et al.* (1984, p. 302) observe that
stigmas can lose their negative valence with time and changing
historical circumstance.

The relevance structure that determines people's response to
differences is both shared and personal in nature. As noted earlier, what we notice as well as what we think is important can be
generated as original responses to novel situations. This is certainly true in the processing of human differences. We can even
reasonably assert that typifications of stigmatized conditions are
"in the eye of the beholder." We each have a unique biographical
hold on the world, with our own personal goals, biases, and prejudices. Thus, individuals may find themselves in biographical situations that leave them with an acute idiosyncratic distaste for
certain physiological or behavioral traits in other people.

But individual relevance structures do not exist completely
apart from categories that are socially approved and derived. If
nothing else, our style of response to those with what we determine to be a negative difference is probably socially derived. The
member of BaBira society "knows" how to respond to menstruation and can apply this same typified response to characteristics
and behavior that are personally annoying. Avoidance, discrimination, and the like are socially distributed solutions to negatively
evaluated differences and are available to individuals for channel-

ing both their socially shared and personally relevant distastes and dislikes. We would assert that even the most private recipes are bound up in this fashion with those that are socially shared. Similarly, we should not reify social recipes to the point that we lose sight of their human construction. Negative evaluations of human difference do not exist apart from the actors who hold, share, and perpetuate them. We suggest that the processing of human differences involves both privately held and socially shared relevance structures (although, again, the two are related and inform one another).

It is shared negative evaluations of human differences that are central to stigma. Individually held biases do not carry the weight of socially designated (hence shared) negative evaluations of difference. For the person with some negatively evaluated difference, this is obvious because the former can be escaped whereas the latter cannot. Beyond this, we would note that societal devaluations are powerful because they cannot be dismissed as the ravings of some idiosyncratic bigot. Instead, they form part of a socially shared sense of "reality." This characteristic of devaluations is essential for one's very humanness to be questioned (by stigmatizer and stigmatized alike), and as such, these devaluations can be passed on to succeeding generations and woven into the institutional fabric of society.

Having said all this, we can now suggest a typology for viewing the typification of human difference (see Figure 1). Our typology must necessarily account for private and social relevances (although, again, they are interrelated), background and foreground differences, and various subtypes of the latter (positively, neutrally, and negatively evaluated), Perhaps most important, our typology takes note of the special place of stigma within this framework. As our discussion clearly implies, although we can set up a model of the typification of difference, the content of each cell is epoch-bound or culture-specific.

STIGMA AND JUSTICE

It is ironic that the same ordering process that makes the world intelligible and attracts our interest in its comings and

Relevance Structure	DIFFERENCES (Attributes, Behavior and Membership)			
	Background Differences (Seen but Unnoticed)	Foreground Differences (salient)		
		Positively Evaluated	Neutrally Evaluated	Negatively Evaluated
Private (personally relevant)				
Shared (societally relevant)				Stigma

* Interrelated

FIGURE 1. A typology of human difference.

goings, so severely disrupts, curtails, and even precludes our interaction with others. This is the nature of stigma. Justice becomes pertinent to this discussion because it also expresses the
need for order. M. Lerner (1980, p. vii) anticipates the importance
of this typificatory nature of justice by opening his preface to *The
Belief in a Just World* with this observation: "The belief in a just
world is an attempt to capture in a phrase one of the ways, if not
the way, that people come to terms with—make sense of—find
meaning in, their experiences." The essential characteristic of the
just world—the "essence of justice," in the words of Perelman
(1977)—is that like be treated alike and different be treated differently. Deciding what is alike and what is different involves not
only judgments of kind but also judgments about which attributes ought to be considered relevant to which outcomes. It is
easy to recognize that men and women are of different genders,
for example, but it is another matter to determine whether or not
gender should be considered as a "relevant" attribute when deciding the nature of one's work or the amount of one's recompense
for work.

The problem of justice is an issue of *legitimation.* We use this
term, as Berger does (1967, p. 29), to mean "socially objectivated
knowledge that serves to explain and justify the social order." Why
do some people come to possess positively evaluated differences
that set them apart from others? Why do other people become the

objects of the stigmatizing process? Justice legitimates such inequities and by so doing makes inequity tolerable. This is most clear in the case of "divine justice," whereby inequities are bestowed with an ultimately valid ontological status. (When justifications are lent a divine or religious character, students of religion often refer to this, more specifically, as the problem of "theodicy.") It is also true of "natural justice" and even "human justice." The effectiveness of the former is attested to by the dominance of "natural law" in recent intellectual history (Hofstadter, 1955). "Human justice" may be the most fragile of the three, but it, too, serves to legitimate the unequal evaluation of differences.

The key to success for all legitimations is the ability to disguise their socially constructed nature. How much easier it is to bear the apparent suffering heaped on the urban poor when it is a matter of divine justice or natural law. Suffering as somehow part of the divine plan or evolutionary law removes the burden of responsibility that, in fact, underlies all social recipes. This is why, of course, human justice is the most fragile typificatory scheme. We can insist that the distributions are made by persons with some special insight, but ultimately it is still humans that are accountable. Hence the questions of "why me?" or "why not them?" may seem more pressing, and the answers do not enjoy the same ontological validity as do answers based on natural or divine insight.

We need to consider the issue of volition here in greater detail. Such popular expressions as "he deserves his lot" betray our intolerance of random events. Do we mean, however, that the person who possesses some negatively (or positively) evaluated difference has done something to deserve the same? For some differences, we mean precisely this. The person with venereal disease possesses a negatively evaluated difference. The condition certainly prompts the avoidance, revulsion, and disgust associated with stigma. Further, we hold that person accountable for his or her sexual indiscretion and view his or her physiological plight as "just deserts." Do we hold the blind person, paraplegic, or dwarf responsible for her or his differences in the same fashion? We certainly have done so. For example, the belief that masturbation leads to blindness was once widely held (Monbeck,

1973, p. 16). More frequently, however, we view such persons as being on the losing end of the grand divine or natural plan. For example, Truzzi (1968, p. 202) reports that even the parents of dwarfs view the birth of such children as a punishment or an act of God's wrath. Justice, in this sense, is not bound to the judicial system's preoccupation with *mens rea* (the ability to form intent). Thus, although Freidson (1966) understandably divides deviance into that for which people are held to be willfully responsible and that for which they are not, his typology only makes sense in terms of justice more narrowly conceived than it is here.

Our discussion thus far by no means exhausts the overlap between stigma and justice. Interpretive schemes include both "cognitive" (what is) and "normative" (what ought to be) constructs. Neither stigma nor justice is merely descriptive. Rather, both are prescriptive. They tell people something about how the world ought and ought not to be. With regard to stigma, foreground differences are negatively evaluated because they somehow disrupt what we understand to be the recipe for being "fully human." Justice tells us something about why differential outcomes with regard to the possession of salient differences should exist in the first place. As M. Lerner observes (1980, p. vii):

> We do not believe that things just happen in our world; there is a pattern to events which conveys not only a sense of orderliness or predictability but also the compelling experience of appropriateness expressed by the implicit judgment, "Yes, that is the way it should be."

Recipes that are considered critical to our maintenance of a shared sense of reality are often imbued with a moral significance (Berger & Luckmann, 1966). We accordingly tend to interpret departures from these recipes as having immoral overtones. Again, this speaks to the normative nature of both stigma and justice. We not only negatively evaluate other persons who somehow deviate from our typificatory scheme but, as if to add greater weight to their violations, we often attribute moral failings to them as well. This makes the problem of justice manageable, by making sense out of the distribution of stratified differences among people. Thus, we have historically dispensed with the problem of blindness by considering it a punishment for some

wrongdoing (Monbeck, 1973), and the problem of poverty by viewing it as the product of moral inferiority in the lower class (Ryan,
1971). Stigma typifies these conditions as situations to be avoided. Justice typifies our desire to avoid persons who fail to do so,
and also provides a recipe by which their life difficulties seem
understandable, if not almost merited.

This is not to say that our conceptions of justice make the
typification process altogether easy. As Davis (1964) reports, our
belief that people deserve the differences that set them apart can
cause interpretive problems for us as well. He notes that one of his
informants (in his study of visibly disabled persons) reported that
people frequently remarked, "How strange that someone so pretty
should be in a wheelchair." Such discord in the distribution of
differences can leave us perplexed or even disoriented, but we are
perplexed or disoriented precisely because of the close relationship between the stigmatizing act and our notions of justice.
The two typificatory schemes are, in other words, intricately
entwined.

Finally, we would again note that, like all interpretive
schemes, stigma and justice are normative constructions that are
"taken for granted until further notice." In other words, we do not
mean to imply a static model of either stigma or justice. We have
been careful to point out that salient differences that are negatively evaluated change over time and between situations. We are
therefore cautious about universal stigmas. We would be equally
leery of notions of ultimate justice. M. Lerner (1980, p. 23) notes
that although we assume that we live in a just world, we do not all
live in the same world. Justice, stigma, and social actors themselves are all situationally embedded.

STIGMA AND JUSTICE: IMPLICATIONS FOR RESEARCH

Our observations about the parallels between justice and stigma hold implications for conducting research as well as casting
theory. During the last 20 years, social scientists have become
increasingly active in the empirical pursuit of justice, and the
number of empirical studies of justice behavior has grown geo-

metrically within the last decade. We believe that stigma research can profit from the insights that have been generated by justice research during this period.

For centuries, investigations of justice have centered around the question: What is just? As an abstraction, the question defies an answer. Some, like Kant, have appealed to intuition. According to the Intuitionalists, certain social arrangements appear just intuitively, whereas others appear intuitively unjust. The problem comes in deciding whose intuition counts. Any dissent undermines the Intuitionalist claim to universal rules, so that ultimately for thinkers like Kant, "there is no way to get beyond the plurality of principles" (Rawls, 1971, p. 41).

A different type of response has come from Utilitarians such as Bentham and Mill (Wolff, 1977). These thinkers could call *just* that system that brings the greatest happiness to the greatest number of people. Yet, without quantitative measures of happiness, the Utilitarian formula remains little more than a platitude. On the other hand, to quantify something as qualitative as happiness is surely to engage in a practice that Gould (1981) labels the "mismeasurement of man."

Contemporary justice scholars have moved beyond both the Utilitarians and the Intuitionalists. Rather than simply changing the answer, they have rephrased the question. No longer do researchers ask: What *is* just? Now they query: What do people *think* is just? Posing the question in this fashion rapidly leads one to a middling level of specificity, and the question becomes: What do certain people in certain situations find just or fair? Investigating the associations between various principles of fairness and various social arrangements has become a major focus in current work on distributive justice. Both Melvin Lerner (1980) and Morton Deutsch (1985) have examined the link between justice values on the one hand and social context on the other. Deutsch (1975) distinguishes between the principles of equity, equality, and need. The equity rule states that everyone's outcomes ought to be in proportion to inputs. Equity tends to be used as the guiding fairness principle in commercial relationships. Equality states that outcomes ought to be divided equally among all participants. Equality tends to be used as the fairness rule among friends. Finally, distributing outcomes on the basis of need is the principle used most often in assymmetrical relationships where one party has responsibility for another party. Such research prioritizes the situational embeddedness of justice systems.

Following the lead of the justice researchers, stigma researchers might profitably prioritize the situational embeddedness of the stigmatizing process, turning their attention to the link between social arrangements and stigmatizing processes. Although labeling theorists in the social sciences have recognized that it is important to understand how people define situations, persons, and events as problematic, they have concentrated on the consequences of labels for the person bearing the stigmatized characteristic—their world view, their self-image, and the like. Where researchers have examined the attitudes of the stigmatizer, they have not adequately explored the ways in which the situation qualifies the stigmatizing process. What circumstances make people prone to notice differences among themselves? What circumstances allow differences to be relegated to the seen-but-unnoticed category? What social arrangements—indeed, what physical conditions (cf. Sanday, 1981)—make people arrange differences along a continuum, and what arrangements permit people to notice differences among themselves without denigrating those who do not resemble them? Answering these questions will require that researchers transcend their own disciplinary boundaries. Most notably, cultural and historical variations in the stigmatizing process need to be examined more thoroughly.

How likely is it that stigma researchers will move along the path we outline? Prediction is hazardous, but the signs seem encouraging. Current work shows a shift away from viewing individuals in isolation and toward a more interactionist view (Jones et al., 1984), a shift that echoes developments in the justice literature. Yet much remains to be done to unveil the situationally embedded process of categorization that is involved in both stigma and justice. Only with a fully developed interactionist approach that focuses on *both* the stigmatizer *and* the stigmatized, can scholars deal adequately with the complex web of observations surrounding the concept of stigma.

CHAPTER 3

Stigma as a Social and Cultural Construct

Gaylene Becker and Regina Arnold

Much of the sociological and psychological literature on stigma focuses on the individual as the central unit of analysis, with little if any discussion devoted to the sociohistorical context or the cultural milieu within which the individual experiences stigma. With this focus, however, an important key to understanding the puzzle of stigma is omitted. It is our contention that modes of analysis that begin with the social, cultural, and historical contexts of stigma provide a necessary framework from which to view the individual. In this chapter on stigma, we address the gap in the literature by presenting three levels of analysis: the sociostructural, the cultural, and the individual. Our aim is to reveal the social and cultural backdrop against which stigma occurs, including who disqualifies whom from social acceptance and the nature of the interactions between stigmatized persons and non-stigmatized persons.

The concept of "tribal" stigma described by Goffman (1963), in which an entire racial group is stigmatized, illustrates the need to ground theoretical problems of stigma in their social, cultural, and historical contexts. If we assume that societal values, beliefs, and mores are dynamic and are especially so in rapidly changing societies, then we may also assume that interactions between blacks and whites will be affected by such sociocultural shifts. Without empirical testing, we cannot necessarily assume that interactions between blacks and whites will remain the same regardless of social climate or historical period. Broad sociocultural and historical forces play critical roles in the way stigma is interpreted by the individual, and the dynamics of a social group's response to a stigmatized status are affected as well.

THE UNIVERSALITY OF STIGMA

The concept of stigma is apparently universal. Every society has norms and values that define acceptable attributes and behavior for its members. What is more, each society has mechanisms of social control to ensure that the majority of its members conform to these norms. Persons who do not conform or who break cultural taboos are sanctioned by society.

Broad views about what constitutes stigma are generally shared by members of a society. They will hold common beliefs about both the cultural meaning of an attribute and the stigma attached to it. These beliefs about stigma dictate the nature of a stigma, the specific attitudes people hold about a given stigma, and the responses of stigmatized persons. These factors will also greatly affect the way in which a stigmatized individual is integrated into a social group or kept marginal to it.

Although the concept of stigma is universal, perceptions of what constitutes stigma vary from one society to another. This is due to differing cultural norms, values, and structures. A system of cultural beliefs is guided by a template of culture that individuals carry with them, underlying thought and action. It shapes and patterns beliefs in a systematic manner. As individuals, we are often unaware of this process; we seldom stop to ask *why* we think and behave in the way we do because culture is by and large an unconscious process. Stigma is defined in the context of this cultural process and is thus a reflection of culture. Regardless of what attributes or characteristics are identified as stigmatizing in each society, a stigma connotes a "moral taint" that is deeply discrediting to the individual (Goffman, 1963). For example, the incest taboo exists in most societies, and stigma is usually associated with it (Fox, 1980).

THE CULTURAL BASIS OF STIGMA

Although some behaviors or attributes appear to be universally stigmatized because of their perceived harm, other behaviors and attributes are stigmatizing only in specific cultural contexts. Among the Trukese, for example, drinking and aggressive behavior are considered culturally appropriate, even expected, conduct for men and are not stigmatized (Marshall, 1979). In the United States, however, when such behavior is carried beyond the cultural norm—for example, when it affects one's job and family life—it may be stigmatized (Ablon, 1981c), even though the moral taint associated with drinking alcohol may have lessened with time (Gusfield, 1975).

The cultural meaning ascribed to an attribute or behavior defines how it will be viewed in its cultural context. For example, mental illness is viewed in many societies as a stigma (Edgerton, 1976). In some societies, persons whose behavior is aberrant are thought to be possessed by demons and are incarcerated or even killed (Halifax, 1982). Yet in other societies, such behavior is cause for elevation to a special rank such as healer or shaman, and magical properties are attributed to the individual (Halifax, 1982). Ideas about what constitutes mental illness and how it fits into the social scheme of a given culture vary, however, because mental illness is itself a cultural construct (Estroff, 1983). The cultural meaning of mental illness is related to the cultural definition of certain behaviors and beliefs about their cause, treatment, and effect on society (Edgerton, 1976). These factors are all closely tied to the stigmatization of any given condition.

In the United States, for example, there is a high incidence of congenital hip disease among the Navajo. This condition affects a person's daily functioning, causes pain, and limits mobility. A team of health workers went to the Navajo reservation to plan a program that would improve health and offered to set up screening and treatment for children with congenital hip disease. Because the Navajo did not view the condition as either stigmatizing or disabling, they rejected the offer (Rabin, Barnett, Arnold, Freiberger, & Brooks, 1965).

The underlying cultural basis for the perception of stigma may thus have profound consequences for the nature of stigmatization and the individual's experience of it. Comparison of deafness and epilepsy in ancient Greece demonstrates how beliefs foster stigma and how the stigma takes different forms, depending on the beliefs that surround it and the measure of control others believe they have over the condition.

The Greeks believed that deaf persons were harmless but lacked a basic ingredient of health, namely speech. They viewed deafness as having a natural cause. Viewed as inferior, deaf persons were to be protected for their own good and the good of others. The Greeks conceived of deafness primarily as a legal problem (Bender, 1960). This attitude imputed mental disability and a dehumanized quality to deaf people, a notion that has been maintained through the centuries. The stigma of deafness continues to carry with it an assumption of mental inferiority (Becker, 1981).

In contrast, epilepsy was called the "sacred disease" because people feared it, and those who suffered from it were outcasts (Pasternak, 1981). Epilepsy was viewed as having a supernatural cause, and consequently the fear of epilepsy was rooted in the belief that the epileptic could harm others. The epileptic was thus perceived as dangerous, and legal measures were considered insufficient to control the individual. This element of potential harm has continued to be present in beliefs about epilepsy throughout much of subsequent history. In the Middle Ages, for example, epileptics were classified as potential witches (Scheerenberger, 1983).

STIGMA IN SOCIOHISTORICAL PERSPECTIVE

Cultural perceptions shift over time, fed by social and historical changes. They determine how we organize and categorize experience.

The social and medical management of asthma historically illustrates these changes in perception. Persons with asthma were stigmatized in the past because their daily functioning was often severely impaired. In 19th century Paris, Proust, an asthma sufferer, hosted large social gatherings late in the day, at which he would make only cameo appearances when he was most likely to appear "normal" (Bree, 1966). In a historical study of the treatment of asthma, Gabbay (1982) concluded that the definition and treatment of asthma in Western medicine were not only dependent on changing concepts of disease but were directly related to the values, social attitudes, and political prejudices of the era in which people lived.

Efforts to conduct research on alcoholism from a complex, multidisciplinary vantage point provide another example of the value of a broad sociocultural and historical framework in the study of stigma. Such efforts have resulted in an increased understanding of alcoholism in relation to a given society. In the United States, this increased understanding has contributed to a cultural shift toward viewing alcoholism as a disease. The significance of viewing alcoholism in its historical context is described by Gusfield (1975, p. 96–97):

> For most of the nineteenth century, the chronic alcoholic, as well as the less compulsive drinker, was viewed as a sinner. It was not until after Repeal (1933) that chronic alcoholism became defined as illness in the United States. Replacement of the norm of sin and repentance by that of illness and therapy removes the onus of guilt and immorality from the act of drinking and the state of chronic alcoholism. It replaces the image of the sinner with that of a patient, a person to be helped rather than to be exhorted.

Cultural shifts within a society such as that described for alcoholism usually affect attitudes toward stigmatized persons positively and may affect social interaction as well.

In some cases, cultural perceptions remain remarkably stable over the generations. In China, for example, disabled and female children were stigmatized and were often killed or cast out of the family home (Chinn, 1982). Although attitudes may have vacillated toward greater leniency or harshness over time, depending on famine, war, and other historical events, basic attitudes about these stigmatized populations were perpetuated for centuries in religious beliefs that dictated social behavior.

Designations of stigma have histories, and the public definition of deviant behavior is itself changeable. Interpretations of stigma, as illustrated by the examples given before, are open to reversals of political power, twists of public opinion, moral crusades, and the impact of social movements. What is stigmatized in one social and historical period may be viewed as the norm in another (Gusfield, 1975).

STIGMA AND SOCIETAL ASSUMPTIONS

The overall structure of society is determined not only by its cultural attributes such as norms, values, and religious beliefs but also by the nature of its social organizations and its political and economic structures. These factors contribute significantly to the way in which the concept of stigma is used and how it is viewed in society.

The literature on stigma, when it departs from a social interactionist perspective, tends toward a structural-functional analysis of norms and deviance, thereby limiting the discussion of stigma. In most instances, assumptions about stigma in a given society remain vague. These assumptions are not explicitly stated nor are the implications for the analysis of stigma within that society made clear. Analysis of stigma in a given society will differ greatly, however, depending upon the societal type—for example, a folk society versus an urban-industrial complex.

In small, homogeneous societies that share a set of values and have a cohesive structure and considerable social stability, the degree of consensus about what constitutes stigma will be high. This is particularly true of small tribal and agricultural societies in which social change occurs slowly. Ostracism or death may be unequivocal for persons who have violated norms considered critical to the continued social functioning of the group. In such cases, the stigma is perceived as so great that to allow the stigmatized person to continue living in the group would challenge societal norms. For example, in some social groups punishment for adultery is carried out by consensus, as with the stoning of a woman who had committed adultery in *Zorba the Greek* (Kazantzakis, 1952).

Shared perceptions of stigma are much less common in large, complex societies with numerous social and cultural groups and in societies where social change has been rapid. What is perceived as stigmatizing varies considerably within such societies. A society characterized by heterogeneity, conflict, and change and by broad variations in values will be characterized by disagreement regarding attributes that may be deeply discrediting.

Heterogeneity in complex societies implies that stigmatized individuals may sometimes reject stigmatization, whereas stigmatized individuals in small homogeneous societies are more likely to share negative perceptions of their stigma with others in the society. Refusal to accept a stigmatized label is best exemplified in the work of sociologists who have studied out-groups such as H. S. Becker (1963), in some of the literature on social protest movements (Lomax, 1962), and in some of the work of researchers who are themselves members of frequently stigmatized groups, such as blacks and women (Ladner, 1973).

STIGMA AND STRUCTURAL INEQUALITY

In all societies, some persons have greater power than others, even in those societies that espouse equality as a major value. The social structure and belief system of a given society usually defines who will hold the power and what the nature of that power will be. Power may be defined as prestige, affluence, or the ability to maintain social control over others. Or power may be defined through religious means. Power may be held by a chosen few or by a larger group of persons defined by their high status. Those in control in a society have the power to impose their norms, values, and beliefs on people who are powerless. Social stratification thus dramatically influences the process of stigmatizing certain individuals. Vested interests of those in positions of power and authority are maintained through the institutionalization of stigma, which entails denial of access to economic, political, educational, and social institutions.

Social inequality may be directly related to stigma, or it may be indirect. In highly stratified societies, such as advanced capitalist societies, where inequalities of class and prestige predominate, certain groups will experience greater stigmatization. Those with the power and authority to influence legislation and court decisions, for example, create stigmatized groups by assigning particular attributes such as race, sex, and class a negative value and applying sanctions against them. For example, in the United States, blacks and prostitutes have been stigmatized historically by those in control of the legal arm of the society. In the 18th century, Maryland lawmakers restricted the application of vagrancy laws (first used in 14th century England and applied to laborers in general) to "free" Negroes. Also during this period, New York explicitly defined prostitutes as a category of vagrants (Chambliss, 1964).

The individual's place in the social hierarchy profoundly affects the degree to which the individual will experience stigma. Class differences are of primary importance in whether stigma occurs and how it is experienced. For example, Hindus in India consider physical disability a sign of moral pollution, but the extent to which this sense of pollution is carried by the individual is directly related to social class. In his description of growing up blind in India (1982), Ved Mehta's experience of blindness and the stigma attached to it was filtered by his high caste. His wealthy family sheltered him from society's view of his condition, and his opportunities in life were very different from those of most blind persons in India who become beggars.

Any individual or social group may be stigmatized on the basis of ascribed attributes such as age, sex, race, and class. In the United States, there are many stigmas associated with such attributes. Historically, we have witnessed discrimination and oppression that have effectively reduced the opportunities and life expectancy of individuals in the stigmatized groups. Of these social inequities, H. S. Becker states, "differences in the ability to make rules and apply them to other people are essentially power differentials and distinctions of age, sex, ethnicity, and class are all related to differences in power" (1963, p. 17). For example, class, status, and racial distinctions account for why some women who deviate from social norms are labeled criminals and others are not, why some women who behave oddly (usually outside of their appropriate gender roles) are committed to hospitals and others are not, and why some women with no visible means of support are charged with vagrancy and others are not. The difference between those who earn a deviant title in society and those who do not is largely determined by the way the community interprets and codes the many details of behavior that come to its attention (Erikson, 1966).

Stigmatization based on ascribed attributes is compounded by the subsequent impediments that are created through the institutionalization of stigma. For example, in the United States, black women who receive welfare are highly stigmatized (Valentine, 1978). In this society, it is considered a mark of disgrace and a stigma to be poor or unemployed, and to be black in a white-dominated culture and female in the male-dominated culture is considered deviant by definition (Schur, 1984). Thus, such individuals experience multiple stigmas.

The plight of illiterate people epitomizes the institutionalization of stigma and the effects of structured social inequality within society (Martin, 1985). Functional illiteracy continues to be widespread in the United States. Although illiteracy is specifically related to the inequities of the educational system, and more specifically to class inequalities, individuals (usually from poorer socioeconomic classes and from certain ethnic groups) bear the blame for what are essentially systemic and institutional problems (Martin, 1985; W. Ryan, 1971). When educational inequities become institutionalized in a society that values education, the stage is set for lack of education to be stigmatized. This complex of factors creates a vicious circle for the illiterate person, who is highly stigmatized and is prevented from functioning effectively in our society. Unable to obtain employment or to take advantage of other opportunities in life, such individuals are further penalized by denial of access to the social institutions of society.

INDIVIDUAL EXPERIENCE OF STIGMA IN A SOCIOCULTURAL CONTEXT

The experience of stigma for individuals arises from social attitudes that are both subtle and pervasive. Nevertheless, individuals with a stigma quickly become aware of the way that others view them. Although face-to-face interaction is a major factor in continually reminding the individual of his or her stigmatized status, it is by no means the only conveyor of social attitudes about a given stigma. In the United States, for example, we are bombarded by the media, a key conveyor of mainstream American cultural values, in which we receive constant messages about many stigmas, such as being old, disabled, or poor.

Failure to possess attributes viewed as important by a social group is experienced as stigma. A child born without arms may experience stigma, just as a person jailed for a felony does. Such stigmas may be attributed to the violation of society's rules, if not by oneself, then by one's parents or ancestors. In China, for example, a birth defect in a child was traditionally viewed as a result of the child's parents' having broken some moral or religious rule, thereby causing displeasure to the gods (Chinn, 1982). Individuals experience such culturally dictated stigmas as failures to conform to society. They may consequently experience a deep sense of personal responsibility for their stigmas.

The feeling of personal responsibility for stigma is often passed from one generation to the next (Freidson, 1966). Children are socialized by their parents to internalize negative attitudes about certain stigmas, even when these are directed against themselves. For example, a child who is sent to a camp for overweight children experiences the stigma of obesity in a variety of ways: through parental attitudes and actions, through segregation from other, "normal" children, and through the regimen of the camp (Millman, 1980). Stigma may thus be permanently internalized in a negative body image.

The very fact of exclusion from part or most of American life can be a continued reminder of one's stigma. Black men and women who are excluded on the basis of race from living in certain areas, from attending certain schools, and from becoming members of certain social clubs experience a lifetime of stigma. The same is true for the disabled person who is sent to special schools in childhood and later on as an adult cannot find employment.

Stigmatized individuals find themselves in a continual struggle with negative attitudes and with the devalued status that accompanies them and must constantly develop strategies for dealing with the stigma. Some female prisoners handle their stigma by verbally rejecting the label of "criminal." This rejection is based on their own view of their situation—economic need, unemployment, lack of skills and education, and other institutional barriers (Arnold, 1979).

The degree to which the individual feels stigmatized, the degree to which the stigma is shared with others in society, and the degree to which the stigma can be "normalized" will all affect the process of adaptation that the individual undergoes in dealing with the stigma. MacGregor (1979) cites the case of a young woman whose face was disfigured when she was a European freedom fighter during World War II. She initially experienced little stigma. Her disfigurement was a symbol of her bravery in fighting for her country and was acknowledged by others. In addition, she was only one of many people who were disfigured. When she emigrated to the United States a few years later and entered new social roles and a new environment, the context of her disfigurement was not recognized. People stared at her. No one else knew the history of her "hideous" scars. The stigma she experienced profoundly affected her ability to carry out her roles with equanimity, and she began a quest to change her appearance through plastic surgery.

In this example, the changes in the social and historical context in which the woman lived clearly affected her perceptions of her condition and her ultimate reaction to it. Changing one's appearance is one of many ways to cope with stigma. For most persons with visible stigmas, however, such change is not possible. For these persons—ethnic minorities and those with physical disabilities—and for all the persons with "hidden" stigmas, coping with the stigma is a process of individual adaptation.

The cumulative life-course experience of individuals shapes their perceptions of themselves as stigmatized. What is done to them because of the stigma and what they do to themselves to counter it are a direct reflection of the broad social and cultural context in which people live. The individual who tries to cover up a history of convictions for child molestation is doing more than minimizing the effect of the stigma on social interaction. That person is, in effect, attempting to circumvent the impact of the stigma on his or her entire life. A person convicted of a felony has little hope of leading a regular life with work, family, friends, and hobbies if knowledge of the stigma is widespread. Mankoff (1971) states:

> The stigmatization which typically accompanies having a criminal record and being punished by the legal system makes it difficult for persons so labeled to become reintegrated into the community. Employers are reluctant to hire people with criminal records, political rights such as voting are often lost and social ostracization may also occur.

Even if the individual succeeds in concealing the past, a sense of stigma is kept alive by the knowledge of cultural beliefs about such behavior as well as by the need to be secretive (Goffman, 1963). Hidden stigmas may thus profoundly affect identity, as they engage the individual directly in the broader sociocultural context while completely sidestepping social interaction.

A similar phenomenon can be identified for leprosy. Although leprosy has been on the wane since the 14th century (Rubin, 1974), the stigma attached to leprosy has only begun to abate in the last 100 years or so. Deinstitutionalization is occurring only now (Gussow & Tracy, 1968). The profound stigma of leprosy motivates those who are afflicted by it to keep it a hidden stigma, if possible, and to normalize it whenever it does become public knowledge (Gussow & Tracy, 1968).

Stigmatized individuals may undergo a complex process of normalization at the level of personal experience. Normalization describes the way in which stigmatized individuals adapt themselves to society by attempting to reduce their variance from cultural norms. The concept of normalization has been used to describe how deaf persons (G. Becker, 1980) and dwarfs (Ablon, 1984) make their lives ordinary to themselves over a lifetime in order to explain away cultural differences created by their condition in everyday life. The ability to normalize oneself in relation to cultural norms positively affects conceptions of self.

As the stigma is integrated into identity, sometimes as a positive attribute, it may move from the foreground, where it occupies much of the individual's thoughts, to the background, where it is a tangible but nonintrusive aspect of daily life (Beisser, 1979). This allows the person's life to once again become routinized. The stigma thus becomes less salient and less negative. It is here that social interaction is especially relevant, as social interaction may call up the stigma more vividly than anything else. For example, when an individual with severe allergies that are chronic in nature encounters a toxic environment, the hidden stigma becomes visible, and the individual is "discredited" (Goffman, 1963).

Normalization covers a broad area of behavior. It occurs on all levels of consciousness over time and affects one's world view as well as one's behavior. Normalization can occur with any disenfranchised group set aside by deviance or social marginality. It is likely that the larger the group, the younger the people, and the greater their shared sense of uniqueness, the more thorough the process will be. In a group such as the elderly deaf, where the members have developed a shared value system, have a common language, and perceive an ever-present threat from the outside world, normalization becomes a group phenomenon (G. Becker, 1980). This process is a strategy for survival for various stigmatized minorities and has been described for many populations, including black communities (Stack, 1974; Mithun, 1973) and tramps (Spradley, 1970).

STIGMA AND SOCIAL CHANGE

Social protest movements play a major role in social change. Social movements involve public affirmation of pride in oneself and solidarity with others who have been socially and culturally downgraded, stigmatized, or otherwise victimized in the social system (Merton, 1972). The examination of such movements provides insights into how stigmatized individuals and groups manage and reconstruct their stigmas, and hence their identities.

The development of group identification and strong communal feelings is critical to the emergence of social protest movements. As individuals become increasingly conscious of their personal stigma, they often become aware that the stigma encompasses more than themselves alone. As they begin to make contact with others like themselves, a change takes place in their perception of their stigma as well as in their behavior in interaction with others (Zola, 1979). What they previously considered to be a personal problem has become a social issue.

These personal changes may gradually become a collective experience. Behavioral and attitudinal changes among a significant number of persons with similar stigmas may ultimately lead to the formation of groups struggling to legitimize themselves. If their numbers and collective voice are sufficiently large, an atmosphere may be created to foster legislative and other changes at the institutional level.

Such changes in personal and collective behavior often go hand in hand with the process of normalization described earlier. Association with others who share a stigma may positively reinforce one's sense of self. The disparity between reality as one knows it and as others apparently know it is reduced because meaningful social interactions with nonstigmatized persons may be increasingly limited. This phenomenon occurs with repeat offenders for whom crime has become a way of life. It is a dynamic that has been observed among many stigmatized groups (G. Becker, 1980) and is a central factor in social protest movements (Toch, 1965).

Social protest movements are formed and grow when persons who are members of a specific stigmatized population identify with the movement and are won over to its thinking, leading to greater solidarity and strength (Toch, 1965). For example, the "sisterhood" often referred to in the women's movement of the 1960s and 1970s stood for all women, even though all women did not accept the precepts of feminism. The sense of belonging that derives from involvement with a stigmatized social group may significantly alter the way one perceives and evaluates oneself in relation to those outside the social group. Members of social movements may reject others' evaluation of them and reflect this change in attitude in their interactions with those who are not stigmatized.

Changes in attitudes about a stigma occur at both an individual and group level. Reinforcement of newly positive attitudes is often carried out through symbolism in the stigmatized group. For example, when the black power movement emerged in the 1970s, the raised fist became a powerful symbol of group identification among blacks. It particularly came to symbolize the collective struggle against black oppression through protest. So powerful was this symbol that it was adopted by other ethnic groups and stigmatized minorities as well. In the transformative process such symbols become a means of self-affirmation and at the same time reinforce the collective nature of the stigmatized group (G. Becker, 1981).

The reinterpretation of a stigmatizing attribute to the level of a political public issue is a sign that its "moral" status is at stake. Legitimacy for the stigmatized group thus becomes a possibility (Gusfield, 1975). Even when the group is a small and politically powerless one, it may nevertheless attempt to protect itself by influencing social and political processes.

The legitimation of a stigma may occur in league with powerful groups in society, such as social workers, medical professionals, and university professors. For example, prostitution, historically considered a crime, has been reinterpreted by radical feminist criminologists as a question of economic survival. The prostitute is viewed as a victim who is faced with financial insecurity, stigmatized by arrest, and vulnerable to drugs (Klein & Kress, 1976). Because her partners are not implicated, the gender-related stigma of her position is all the more clear.

DESTIGMATIZATION

Protest movements that began in the 1960s are representative of individuals and groups reacting against being stigmatized and consequently oppressed and denied access to social institutions. Because of such movements, we are witnessing a certain "destigmatization" in American society. A dramatic shift is occurring in cultural values, trends, and perceptions of social groups that experienced much greater stigma in the past. For example, we have seen a shift from a view of male life as the norm, with women considered deviant and therefore stigmatized, to a view of women as normal, and female life as at least one-half of the norm (Chodorow, 1978; Gilligan, 1982; Miller, 1976). Examples of destigmatization elucidate the central nature of the stigma construct in American life, as they relate to the family, race, and health.

Changing norms and values surrounding the family, the role of women, and the place of children are due in no small part to the women's movement and have led to a lessening of stigma. Consequently, women and children are increasingly viewed as victims of oppression rather than as responsible for their plight (Schur, 1984). For example, the long tradition that discredits the testimonies of women and children when they speak out about sexual assault is undergoing tremendous change (Brownmiller, 1975; Herman, 1981).

Changes in the tribal stigma of race can to a large extent be attributed to the civil rights struggles of blacks and whites on behalf of blacks as a group. During the 1960s and 1970s, barriers to social institutions were lowered sufficiently to allow some blacks to gain access. We see the fruits of these changes in the increasing numbers of blacks in the middle class. The stigma of race persists, however, being manifested differently in different historical periods and mediated by socioeconomic class (Wilson, 1980).

The independent living movement, composed of persons with severe health problems, gained its momentum from the civil rights movement and the women's movement and has dramatically expanded the options for disabled persons. At one time almost totally isolated from the general population, disabled people are today more visible and often live in the mainstream of American society. One purpose of this social movement has been to look beyond the particulars of specific disabilities to the commonalities experienced by all disabled people and their experience of stigma. Consequently, some of the stigma attached to physically disabled people as a group has lessened, and individual self-esteem has improved as well.

CONCLUSION

Stigma is a concept imbued with cultural meaning. It is not a property of the individual but is related to social, cultural, and historical phenomena that reflect the individual's experience of stigma. Although relationships between individuals are a major component in understanding stigma as a construct, these relationships occur in a sociocultural and historical context that shapes the nature of such relationships. Thus, to comprehend the nature of stigma, we must take a close look at culture, the social structure, and the historical period within which stigma exists.

Social change is a by-product of culture. By its very nature, culture must change, whether intentionally through the efforts of individuals, or unintentionally through the sheer dynamic interaction of social, historical, and economic forces. Just as culture changes, so does stigma. Even when stigmas no longer carry the potent force of a cultural proscription, such as tuberculosis in the 19th century or leprosy in the Middle Ages, they linger on until their viability as stigmas is superseded by the cultural imperatives of a new era. Only when a stigma is no longer of value for a given society does it dissipate.

Because stigma is a social and cultural construct subject to the vagaries in interactions between historical forces, social institutions, and cultural beliefs, the nature of stigma is arbitrary, changing from one culture to the next. Yet, as a reflection of society, stigma is modeled to closely fit a specific cultural "recipe." This fit between stigma and its social and cultural context contributes to its perpetuation in society.

The nature of stigma is responsive to society in yet another way, however, that has to do with individual potential for effective functioning despite the cultural constraints that stigma imposes. Intracultural variation in what constitutes a stigma is great, as is

the diversity of human experience in facing and coping with stigma. As we have seen in this chapter, some stigmas do not severely
hamper the individual's adaptive potential, whereas others effectively hamstring the individual and inhibit adaptive behavior.
Social inequities are created in this process that are detrimental
to all of society, not just to those who are stigmatized. Thus, in
some societies stigmatized persons fulfill social roles that utilize
their abilities and integrate them into society, yet in other societies stigma is deepened by the failure to adequately integrate
stigmatized individuals into the social fabric. Not only does stigma remain, it has more devastating consequences for the individual in some societies than in others.

Despite the gradual demise of tribal society, cross-cultural
variation in stigma will continue to be significant, as will intracultural variation. Stigma is not only a cultural universal but has
universal importance cross-culturally. Stigmatization in one society may have shock effects that ripple through other societies.
When the cultural meaning of certain stigma-related actions
eludes observers from other cultural groups—or when it is all too
clear—the stage is set for conflict. The potential effects of these
phenomena are staggering because they have been responsible in
the past for conflicts both within and between societies. For example, the scenario of one nation trying to control or intervene in
the actions of another nation perceived as stigmatizing portions
of its population repeats itself with predictable regularity. Social
scientists have a role in these sometimes subtle, sometimes cata-
clysmic forces—to tease out the critical factors in understanding
stigma, both cross-culturally and intraculturally, and to develop
tools with which to better understand our own and other
cultures.

The dynamic interactions between the forces of society,
culture, history, and the individual are highly complex. Thus, the
multidisciplinary perspective has much to contribute to the study
of stigma. As social scientists, we need to look within, between,
and beyond our own social group, culture, and historical era.
Although sociologists could benefit from the comparative approach of anthropology, for example, anthropologists could benefit from applying what they learn in other cultures to broad politi-

cal and structural issues within our own culture. Moreover, temporal issues related to stigma need to be addressed more carefully by all social scientists. Greater attention to the element of time would give us a better understanding of the dynamics surrounding stigmas in our midst that will soon become part of history. Efforts to understand the nature of stigma must be addressed with this complexity in mind, so that we may apply ourselves to the work of ameliorating the effects of stigma on the individual.

CHAPTER 4

Stigma and Western Culture
A HISTORICAL APPROACH

Howard M. Solomon

Until recently, history has told the story of the winners. Within the last two decades, however, a new kind of social history has emerged. The stigmatized—beggars, criminals, homosexuals, heretics, and the mentally ill—have driven kings, generals, robber barons, and bishops from the traditional center of historiographic attention. Even though contemporary historians are now concerned with historically stigmatized groups, much of their research remains unknown to scholars in other disciplines.

Social psychologists and sociologists by and large assume the importance of individual motivation and behavior in the stigma process. Contemporary social historians, on the other hand, are less interested in the particular actor, or the discrete event, per se, than in the deeply ingrained, slowly moving conditions underlying historical change. As Fernand Braudel, the most influential proponent of this approach, has put it, an appreciation of long-term structural conditions is more important to historical understanding than is a simple examination of the "conjuncture" of events (Braudel, 1980; Hexter, 1972; Stoianovitch, 1976; Stone, 1979).

Much of the historical community's ignorance of stigma research in other disciplines seems rooted in methodological prejudice predating the current popularity of social history. The historiographic mainstream, as the shifting fortunes of family history and the history of sexuality show, remains leery of applying clinically derived (to say nothing of Freudian) insights to earlier historical contexts (Bizière, 1984; Stone, 1981). This particular prejudice seems all the more troublesome, given the usual enthusiasm with which historians borrow from economists, anthropologists, art historians, and demographers.

Historians do not choose their subjects randomly. Movers and shakers fascinate us. Like geologists, we are more drawn to the fault lines and fissures of the past than to the regularity of even, unbroken terrain. And when we examine a subject and develop its story, we essentially widen those fissures. Our attention marks historical actors with a power that continues to separate them from their less extraordinary contemporaries, even generations after they have died.

Technique and "objectivity" aside, the essential nature of what historians do today is little different from what Stone Age storytellers did. Storytellers in oral cultures employ parallel construction (X did this, but Y did that) and an agonistic tone (praising X while damning Y) to order events and impress their listeners. The drama of struggle—of good over evil, order over chaos, definition over ambiguity—is usually the underlying script. Remembering and retelling history, in other words, is a violent and self-serving act, a way of marking boundaries between *us* and *them*. The tongue is as mighty as the sword: Like physical combat, public speech has traditionally been man's work (Ong, 1981, 1982).

This sense of polarization and conflict does not disappear with the appearance of writing. Far from it. Since classical times, historical language has carried this underlying rhetorical structure. Men have been the subjects and practitioners of history, public behavior, and power; except as dramatic foils, the feminine, the private, and the dispossessed have been discredited or absent. In fact, the more that "objective," "scientific" historiography has freed itself of an explicitly moral and theological vocabulary, the more pernicious have the hidden structural messages become. Not surprisingly, feminists and deconstructionists have been much more sensitive to problems of language and conceptualization than have mainstream historians (Culler, 1982; Kelly-Gadol, 1976; Keohane, Rosaldo, & Gelpi, 1982; Ryan, 1982).

We must go beyond the important work of writing the specific histories of homosexuals, of the illiterate, the physically disabled, and the aged. We must recognize that stigmatization—marking · actors with positive and negative qualities, separating them from their fellows, reducing a myriad of social characteristics into one or two overarching traits—may be inseparable from the structure of historical discourse itself. Exploring that inseparability, along · with discussing the status of stigma research in the field of premodern European history, is the purpose of this essay.

This chapter, therefore, offers illustrations of the role historians can play in understanding stigma. The first two parts of the chapter will trace the development of corporeal imagery in the medieval church and its role in the stigmatization of heretics, homosexuals, and Jews. The third part of the essay will analyze the features that these and other historically stigmatized groups have in common: (a) their functions as social intermediaries; (b) their associations with filth and corporeality; and (c) their roles, when institutionalized, as public figures.

CORPOREAL IMAGERY

The human body provides a natural symbol for conceptualizing about social identity (Douglas, 1970). Regardless of how much contemporary research focuses upon the symbolic and social aspects of stigma, we must never forget its original, limited meaning: "bodily signs designed to expose something unusual and bad about the moral status of the signifier" (Goffman, 1963, p. 1). Discussing stigma in historical perspective, therefore, begins with examining the social uses of corporeal imagery.

Monastic orders were the first group within Christian Europe to be set off from the general population; they accomplished this through a process of self-stigmatization. Their history and the central importance of corporeal imagery to their culture provide the model for subsequent forms of stigmatization in Western history.

Maintaining the vestiges of Christian culture in the face of political collapse and barbarian invasion, European monastic communities were first established in the isolated countryside or on the margins of populated areas: on mountain passes (Monte Cassino), on tidal coasts (Mont St. Michel), or on the islands of distant Britain and Ireland. With the restoration of political order in the 10th and 11th centuries, dozens of monasteries appeared throughout western Europe. Their hard-won successes in clearing land and raising crops eventually attracted civilian populations. Nevertheless, not until the advent of the Franciscan and Dominican friars in the 13th century did European religious orders actively turn their attention to the urban arena. Lester Little's important work (1978) on monastic poverty and the profit economy analyzes the tension between those inherently antithetical values.

As Peter Brown (1971) has argued, the early church much more resembled an archipelago of isolated believers than the single, homogeneous continent of belief and practice that we have come to view it as. No wonder, then, that issues of discipline and practice—conformity to external, easily verifiable standards of ritual behavior, clerical appearance, proper conduct—occupied church administrators much more than did issues of internal, personal spirituality (Bynum, 1982; Vauchez, 1975).

Precise rituals marked the passage from civilian to religious life: having one's head shorn, putting on distinct clothing, answering to a new name—becoming redefined in the eyes of the community. These rituals were concrete reminders of the vows of chastity, poverty, and obedience, physically setting the religious apart from his civilian contemporary. But they also simultaneously marked the elevated status of religious life, as medieval clerics enjoyed political, fiscal, and legal privileges denied to others. Indeed, the stigmas of clerical dress and appearance and the larger issue of what the sacrament of ordination meant became particularly important in the 12th century, as agricultural growth and urbanization increased clerical contact with lay society.

Lay people participated in, and were identified by, a host of social entities (towns, parishes, confraternities, guilds) embodying collective dignities greater than their own. The very word *corporation* (*corpus* is Latin for "body") tells much of the story. From a legal point of view, corporations acted as individual physical bodies writ large. Civil and religious society itself was described in corporeal terms ("the body of Christ," "the body politic").

Past studies (Bynum, 1982; Steinberg, 1984) have analyzed how the high medieval church transformed Christ into an approachable, loving deity. This transformation had immense dimensions. The Mass, representing the sacramental reenactment of the Crucifixion, was receiving increasing doctrinal and ritual attention. Artists, from the mid-13th century on, portrayed Christ in humane terms, unlike early depictions as a deity sitting in heavenly judgment. Other phenomena, such as pilgrimages, the veneration of relics, the concept of Purgatory, and, above all, the burgeoning Virgin Mary cult, brought new attention to Christ's wounds (certainly the most important stigmas in Western culture) and to metaphors about the human body (Finucane, 1977; Rothkrug, 1980; Sumption, 1975; Weinstein & Bell, 1982).

Religious transformation does not happen in a vacuum. These changes were directly related to the increasing importance of commerce and capital in medieval life. Personal profit, churchmen argued, took wealth out of circulation and thereby corrupted the healthy functioning of the body of Christ. Profit was viewed as a form of idolatry, with money as the devil's tool, and avarice was a deadlier sin to moralists of this period than pride had been to their predecessors (Little, 1971, 1978). Artists portrayed avarice as a constipated humanoid, all appetite but no circulation, his swollen moneybags looking very much like grotesque testicles (private wealth = privates) or intestines (Little, 1971). Precisely as Christianity was being likened to the life-giving, orderly functions of the upper body—the heart, the head, and Christ's blood, non-Christian forces were being likened to the corrupting, disorderly functions of the lower body—the sexual organs, the anus, and feces.

These religious metaphors counterpointed the lives of ordinary women and men. Their bodily appearances recorded the cru-

elties of disease, malnutrition, and unreliable health care. Leprosy, whose symptoms earned a central place in the popular
imagination,represented the ambiguity inherent in all disease—a
curse but also perhaps a sign of special grace (Brody, 1974; Mundy, 1955; Sontag, 1979). Like other preindustrial cultures, medieval Europe stigmatized butchers, barbers, leatherworkers, prostitutes, surgeons—those who worked with hair, flesh, leather,
and blood (Dumont, 1970; Legoff, 1980). Premodern European
folk wisdom, in which princesses were invariably fair-skinned,
knights strong-armed, and peasants dirty, stunted, and deformed, upheld a common belief system: The physical body reflected moral and social status (Darnton, 1984; N. J. Davis,
1983). Clothing and bodily appearance carry much more symbolic
meaning in "traditional" cultures than in cultures with high literacy (Bourdieu, 1977; Ong, 1982; Solomon, 1982). Hence these
cultures are particularly concerned with sumptuary laws, with
disguise and masking, with visual distinctions between people of
different estates, and with transvestism (Warner, 1981).

STIGMATIZATION OF HERETICS, HOMOSEXUALS, AND JEWS

The Christian stigmatization of heretics, homosexuals, and
Jews in the 12th and 13th centuries resonated with bodily imagery. The simultaneous introduction of inquisitorial and patri-
archal values profoundly influenced the subsequent stigmatization of such persons.
The earliest conflicts between heresy and orthodoxy took
place within a narrow social arena: a handful of administrators
and intellectuals, arguing the most theologically pressing and intellectually rarefied issues. Such debate enabled the early church
to establish its doctrinal center and mark the limits of acceptable
choice for its adherents ("heresy" from *haerisis*, Greek for
"choice"). Early heresies were associated with important individuals of relatively equal status and were primarily a clerical,
rather than a lay, phenomenon (Russell, 1965). In early monastic

communities, conflicts of doctrine were resolved, by and large, by the participants themselves.

This approach to conflict typified other small-scale, face-to-face medieval communities. Members of a clan, a village, a frank-pledge (12 or 15 men organized for purposes of public order, taxation, and justice), or a monastery shared considerable information about their fellows. The social values and identities of such communities, as Pierre Bourdieu (1977) argues, were embodied in speech, actions, tools, and living and working spaces, rather than in formalized, written laws guarded by professional lawyers and judges. Disputes arose and were resolved locally. Honor and shame, rather than appeals to external authority, monitored behavior and reputation. In such communities, falsely made accusations violated the social order as surely as did the offenses of criminals.

From the 8th century onward, heresy broadened its social context, mirroring the church itself. Laymen and laywomen increasingly became its proponents as streets and markets became its arena, rather than cathedrals and cloisters. The research of scholars who have examined heresy in the High and Late Medieval periods (Kieckhefer, 1979; R. E. Lerner, 1972; Russell, 1965) indicates a number of common threads: the authority of scripture over church tradition, a devalued role for the ordained priesthood, and the importance of an active, world-centered Christian life. As heresy grew, church response grew in severity as well. Widescale burnings replaced admonition and penance, and, by the 12th century, face-to-face, accusatorial debate gave way to inquisitorial justice imposed from outside and above.

Inquisitorial justice values the needs of the state above those of its individual members: crime violates not only individuals but justice itself. The word *inquisition* means "inquest"—when authorities invite allegations, arrest witnesses, and collect information, creating a dossier (Langbein, 1974, 1976). The medieval Inquisition assumed, a priori, that where there is smoke, there is fire; for every known heretic, there were others waiting to be uncovered. It was therefore unnecessary to make specific, discrete charges of wrongdoing to initiate the process. After 1254, the

Papacy even prohibited inquisitors from informing those who were arrested of the identity of their accusers. Michael Foucault (1965, 1978, 1979) and Thomas Szasz (1970) have argued strongly that the assumptions underlying the inquisitorial method continue to underlie modern institutional psychiatry.

The 13th-century Inquisition reflects the administrative sophistication of the medieval church. Paradoxically, however, it also reflects a xenophobia, a crisis of confidence about its mission. Muslim infidels in Iberia and the Holy Land might threaten Christian Europe from outside, but those who corrupted the body of Christ from within were viewed as even worse (Senac, 1983; also see Davies, 1982; Lauderdale, 1976). Christian Europe questioned the integrity of its physical boundaries (its epidermis) and the vitality of its ritual and doctrine (its heart) and found, instead, behavior it defined as pathology within itself. That pathology included not only heretics but sexual deviates and Jews as well (Boswell, 1980; Davies, 1982).

Recent studies are forcing a reconsideration of homosexuality in premodern Europe (Boswell, 1980; Bray, 1982; Bullough & Brundage, 1982; Burg, 1980; Davies, 1982; Trumbach, 1977). As Boswell (1980) has persuasively argued, early moral and legal sources are remarkably tolerant of homosexuality. Classical writers differentiated between chaste and unchaste, romantic and unromantic relationships, but the distinction between heterosexual and homosexual relationships was absent from their discourse. Same-sex relationships were well known, and until A.D. 342, homosexual marriages were legally recognized. Similarly, Jesus and St. Paul confined their opinions on sexuality to issues stemming from the breakdown of heterosexual marriage: the role of women, raising children, and the concerns of orphans. They said little about same-sex relationships, to which such issues did not apply. Particular churchmen might express themselves regarding homosexual behavior, but not until the Third Lateran Council in 1179 did a general church council concern itself with homosexuality. Christian intolerance of homosexuality, then, must be attributed primarily to social and economic change, rather than to the theological origins of Christianity.

Following the breakdown of Roman, urban society (2nd to

4th centuries A.D.), and the eventual development of feudalism and manorialism—rural-based political and economic systems— issues of generativity and kinship increasingly colored discussions of sexuality. This "ruralization" of social values had dramatic and far-reaching impact upon the treatment of the stigmatized later in history.

The agricultural economy of the High Medieval period, venerating the productivity of the soil and the holy fecundity of the Virgin Mary, had little tolerance for nonprocreative sexual practices. As population growth and economic change threatened to fracture many noble and bourgeois family holdings, medieval lawyers looked to Roman law for principles of patrimony and primogeniture to protect their clients' property.

Roman law provided economic and political elites with powerful legal tools. Everywhere vertical and hierarchic modes tended to replace patterns of property and kinship in which responsibility was horizontally and communally distributed. Increasingly, for example, fathers headed households in which title to property passed to the eldest son, where political authority and professional justice were imposed from above (Goody, 1983; D. Hughes, 1978; Stone, 1981). Dynastic monarchies, urban oligarchies, and the Papacy itself (papacy = "papa") all enthusiastically exploited Roman law and its overarching glorification of hierarchy and patriarchy.

The church's relatively benign treatment of homosexuality during its first millennium parallels its treatment of Jews to some degree. Some early Christians, like St. John Chrysostom, associated Jews with animallike, runaway sexuality; others in the 5th and 6th centuries prohibited Christian-Jewish relations, fearing the possibility of Christians converting to Judaism (Poliakov, 1965). Nonetheless, Jews and Christians generally enjoyed peaceful relations during this time, more indicative, perhaps, of the weakness of the early church than of any basic doctrinal tolerance.

The 9th century liturgy separated Jews from pagans and believers, as unworthy of Christian prayer. (The Good Friday missal read, "Don't genuflect to the Jews.") In the next two centuries, as the metaphors of Christian purity and Christ's unpolluted body animated crusader and preacher, theologian and monarch alike, the condition of European Jews deteriorated precipitously. In the 1140s, Jews in England and the Rhineland were accused of ritual murder and profaning the Host. By the 1340s, they were accused of poisoning town wells. These accusations, with their connotations of abnormal sexuality, satanism, and pollution, forged the stereotype of the Jew in late medieval culture (Cohen, 1982; Oberman, 1984; Poliakov, 1965; Prager & Tellushkin, 1983; Rothkrug, 1980).

From these separate historical threads of heresy, homosexuality, and Jews was woven a single portrait: the stigmatized, non-Christian Other, against which Christian institutions of the High Medieval period defined themselves.

STRUCTURAL SIMILARITIES IN STIGMATIZATION

Behavior and characteristics ascribed to heretics, homosexuals, and Jews often seem to distort or invert those of the clerical orders. There are structural similarities in terms of (a) the functions they perform as social intermediaries; (b) the corporeal characteristics attributed to them; and (c) the means by which they were institutionalized. These shared similarities apply to other stigmatized groups such as witches, the insane, criminals, and the poor.

SOCIAL FUNCTIONS

As Victor Turner and others have shown (MacAloon, 1984; Turner, 1973, 1977), liminal spaces, and the actors who inhabit them, play important roles in the social process. Margins, borderlands, and thresholds defining different social areas are charged with ambiguity and power. The historically stigmatized often function as social intermediaries, such as translators, healers, traders, and magicians, and occupy ambiguous, multivalent terrains. Indeed, their positions as intermediaries make them particularly vulnerable to the stigmatization process.

Jews were merchants within Christian Europe and, until the

emergence of Genoese, Venetian, and Florentine traders in the 12th and 13th centuries, were largely responsible for European trade with Islamic Iberia, North Africa, and the Levant. Landowning and craft restrictions forced Jews into moneylending just as church moralists were touting avarice and usury as the deadliest of sins (Little, 1971, 1978). Jewish loans, as well as Jewish service as tax collectors (especially in Iberia), were often connecting links between Late Medieval monarchs and their increasingly overtaxed subjects. Likewise, Jewish translations brought Christian scholars in contact with Arabic and classical sources.

Research on heresy and witchcraft suggests similar relationships between economic activity and the vulnerability to stigmatization. Heresy and the textile industry had important connections with stigma. Public authorities took for granted that itinerant textile workers lived dangerously on the edge of law and order (Geremek, 1976). The woolen industry tied isolated rural shepherds and cottage weavers to the urban world of bankers, workshops, and international commerce. Traveling journeymen worked at the interstices of different markets, crafts, communities, and cultures, the conditions of their work making them peculiarly vulnerable to foreign ideas and to fluctuations in foreign markets (Geremek, 1976; Lis & Soly, 1979). Similarly, the working conditions of shepherds and millers seemed to predispose them to being receptive to new and threatening ideas (Ginzburg, 1980; LeRoy Ladurie, 1978).

Witchcraft connected the natural and supernatural worlds. Witches, like heretics and Jews, performed a host of functions as cultural and economic intermediaries. Those accused of being witches tended to live at the interstices of rural and village life and—contrary to the stereotype—not as recluses or hermits. A number of studies (Demos, 1982; Larner, 1981; MacFarlane, 1970; Monter, 1976; Thomas, 1971) have shown that certain persons were cultural intermediaries, who in turn became likely targets of suspicion. For example, cunning men and midwives were intermediaries between health and sickness; beggars were intermediaries for the circulation of charity; and tavernkeepers were intermediaries for the spread of information and of hospitality. The elderly, who played a crucial role in spreading information, socializing children, finding lost tools, and remembering how and why people died (Bever, 1982), also became the objects of accusations.

The European witch craze, from the middle of the 16th to the middle of the 17th century, was coterminous with the Protestant and Catholic reformations and the scientific revolution. Protestant theologians desacralized the marketplace and the calendar, rejecting the concept of usury and the saints' days of traditional Catholicism (Agnew, 1979; Burke, 1978; Monter, 1983). Regions of liminality—markets, the boundaries of church property, pilgrimage routes, Carnival—and those who formerly occupied them—Jewish moneylenders, penitents, magical healers—lost their privileged roles. Space and time were becoming homogeneous, to be mastered by the rationality and capital of the merchant class.

The witch's role as intermediary was threatened just as other mystical intermediaries such as saints, angels, and magical explanations for misfortune were being displaced from religion and natural science. The impact of printing and economic change upon society diminished the role of gossip, which became simply the unimportant tattlings of noisy old women (Ong, 1982; Rysman, 1977). The growing power of lawyers as well as the professionalization of medicine and the appearance of regional and national medical licensing similarly threatened the autonomy of local communities in healing their own social and medical ills (Bowsma, 1973; Thomas, 1971).

Social mediation, even with the bourgeois appropriation of the domains of liminality in the 16th century, remained a powerful, dangerous, and inherently ambiguous game (Agnew, 1979). The Italian expression *traduttore, traditore* may sum up our distrust of those who mediate: Translators are traitors.

ATTRIBUTED CHARACTERISTICS

Sociologists have long been aware of the tendency, in the study of stigmatization, to reduce numerous and sometimes contradictory characteristics into categories of master and subordinate status, where a single distinguishing trait becomes dominant (Becker, 1963; E. Hughes, 1945). Attributions of bodily filth and unnatural sexuality become the primary characteristics for the groups we are examining.

Characteristics attributed to one stigmatized group were applied to others. For example, *Ketzer,* the German word for "heretic" (derived from *Cathar,* heretics of southern France), was often synonymous with "sodomite" and "witch." "Bugger" was synonymous with "sodomite" in 13th-century English. By the 16th century, this word was also associated with "witch," originally derived from *bougre* ("Bogomil" or "Bulgarian"), referring to heretical ideas of Eastern origin. The word *synagogue,* a meeting place of Jews, was applied to groups of witches and heretics and was often interchangeable in the late Middle Ages with the word *brothel.* The underlying thread of these symbols was in their attributions of unnatural sexuality and bodily filth.

Dietary and sanitary codes were crucial to Jewish self-identity (Davies, 1982; Douglas, 1966). Turned upside down and inside out, those practices provided the idiom for the stigmatization of Jews. Accusations of ritual murder and defiling the Host, for example, inverted the reality of *Kashreth* (kosher laws) in the preparation and storage of foods. The accusation of poisoning Christian wells inverted the reality that sanitary practices and personal hygiene were more developed among Jews than within the general population, whereas accusations of extraordinary sexuality inverted the reality of Judaism's rigorous prohibitions of homosexuality and marriage to non-Jews.

Similar inversion occurred in the case of heresy. By the end of the 12th century, it was commonplace to link heresy with fornication (Lerner, 1972). This linkage occurred as discussions of clerical obedience and chastity, including sexual purity, and issues of money were becoming preeminent in church debate (Boswell, 1980; Bullough & Brundage, 1982). These issues were especially related to the sacraments of ordination, marriage, and penance. It is true that some later heretics did advocate polygamy and unbridled sexuality, taking literally St. Paul's statement that "everything is pure to the pure in heart." But the mainstream of medieval heresies—and especially the Albigensian and Waldensian movements, whose popularity in the late 12th and early 13th centuries prompted much of this debate—were notoriously ascetic.

Issues of sexuality run throughout the witchcraft persecutions. Continental witches, under torture, confessed to participating in orgiastic sabbaths and black masses, where kissing the devil's ass and eating human flesh inverted elements of the Mass and the clerical vows of chastity and obedience. Accusations initiating the trials were considerably less sensational in content and tone but still had a sexual character. Witches were typically accused by their neighbors of poisoning wells, drying up cattle, ruining crops, and spoiling the fertility of newly married couples. In a sense, all of these accusations involve the theft of sexual and generative power (Demos, 1982). Throughout Europe, menopausal and postmenopausal women, crossing the threshold to widowhood, poverty, and altered sexual activity, were disproportionately represented in the statistics of witchcraft. The stereotypic old witch that book-educated lawyers and theologians had long taken for granted (Cohn, 1975; Kieckhefer, 1976) here intersected with the actual conditions of women's lives in preindustrial Europe (Bever, 1982).

Premodern science was highly dependent upon analogy and metaphor; the behavior of animals low in the hierarchy of Creation "explained" their human counterparts. Homosexuals were associated with rabbits, hyenas, and weasels, all of which, according to standard bestiaries, had "unnatural" breeding habits (Boswell, 1980). Jews were identified with pigs (proscribed to Jews, according to the kosher laws) and (along with witches) with goats, animals evocative of satyrs, devils, and forest behavior (Russell, 1977, 1981). Belief in the principle of spontaneous generation—that vermin (rats, insects, frogs, worms, etc.) grew from corrupted matter—provided scientific support for theological and political assumptions that deviants fornicated unnaturally and uncontrollably. The current, common prejudice that social freedom spontaneously creates sexual or political perverts carries traces of this historical belief structure.

Premodern scientific language, as Lucien Febvre's classic work (1982) on Rabelais argues, was ill-suited for empirical accuracy. More recent studies indicate that the consistent use of rhetorical tropes of inversion and reversal made evil, witches, and monsters virtual linguistic necessities in 16th- and 17th century intellectual discourse (Clark, 1980; Park & Daston, 1981; also see Vickers, 1984). Linguistic and semantic patterns, in other words, may have been as important historically as cultural or economic patterns in determining the treatment of stigmatized individuals.

It would be wrong, however, to see relationships of language structure and stigmatization as historically or culturally limited. Much of contemporary critical thought confronts extremely broad issues bearing on such relationships.

Theoreticians of communication, for example, wonder about the effects of semantic structures underlying modern scientific discourse. Proponents and opponents of deconstructionism argue over whether every act of thought automatically and irremediably displaces and disenfranchises its subject.

For the student of stigmatization, these discussions raise some humbling questions. Are we culturally locked into a dialectical predilection for rendering all social reality into mutually exclusive categories of either/or, us/them, good/bad? Is it possible for individuals, or groups, to define themselves without first creating an external Other? If human language (all language, and not only the language of the socially powerful) is inherently a process of "putting down," excluding, absenting, and dismembering the subject, is stigmatization inherent in what it means to be "human?"

For a long time, we have turned to anthropology (Dumont, 1970; Turner, 1973, 1977) and comparative religion (Eliade, 1959; Otto, 1957) for discussions of the "Other," the "Awful," and the "Different" in the social process. We must now also look to literary critics like Jacques Derrida (1981), René Girard (1977), and Julia Kristeva (1982) for insights into the Other, the Awful, and the Different as problematic to language itself. Their work should be better known to stigma researchers. A number of useful introductions discuss these and other relevant issues of contemporary humanist criticism (Culler, 1982; Norris, 1982; Ryan, 1982; Wilden, 1972).

INSTITUTIONALIZATION

The existence of the homosexual, the Jew, and the heretic, like that of the monk, testified to the unchanging truths of a Christian, agricultural, feudal society. Institutionalization of the stigmatized, therefore, had a simple imperative: to render more obvious the differences between them and Christian society. This was accomplished by (a) marking them with special clothing or branding, and (b) displaying them in public places. These methods often appear as inversions of similar methods used to mark members of the religious orders.

Erving Goffman (1961) pointed out how important standardized clothing is to the functioning of "total institutions" (prisons, mental hospitals, armies, etc.) in contemporary society. An analogous process was at work in premodern Europe. Convicted witches, relapsed Christians, degraded clerics, heretics, and criminals were routinely forced to appear in public, and often executed, wearing a nondescript shirt. Whether their own undergarment or a special penitential chemise (the Spanish Inquisition's *sambenito*, the Italian Inquisition's *habitello*, or sheets kept by English archdeaconal courts, for example), this ritual dress was a common feature in the treatment of the stigmatized. The chemise symbolically obliterated all marks of private personhood and made the stigmatized a quintessentially public figure. The absence of identifying decoration signified the presence of ambiguity, that most dangerous and powerful quality (Solomon, 1982).

Thirteenth- and 14th-century Spanish and French Jews as well as repentant heretics and (later) beggars and common criminals were obliged to wear distinctive patches on their clothing. Like the chemise, these patches were functionally similar to those that clerics and pilgrims wore. Authorities forced Jews and heretics to wear special hats (flat and round for Jews, pointed for town gossips) and endure public humiliation (parading through the market, public execution, listening to sermons or rigged debates), rendering them easy targets for ridicule and abuse. Physical marking and ridicule remained important in unofficial, popular treatment of village cuckolds, promiscuous women, and sexual deviates, even as public authorities, by the 17th century, were

increasingly applying economic and carceral forms of punishment (Burguière, 1980; N. Z. Davis, 1971, 1984; Garfinkel, 1956;
Thompson, 1972).

Once identified and marked, the stigmatized were perambu-
lated around the parish and/or displayed in the marketplace.
Convicted criminals were expected to beg public forgiveness on
church doorsteps and the threshold of the gallows. The bodies of
executed criminals were displayed on bridges, town walls, or
along highways. The common feature of these rituals was that
they all took place in public sight, in those spaces—thresholds,
markets, boundaries—culturally charged with ambiguity and
liminality.

Clothing and ritual sharpened the distinctions between the
stigmatized and Christian society. Like the creation of Jewish
ghettos, for example (as well as monasteries and leprosariums),
they served less to isolate the stigmatized from the nonstigmatized than to render their differences more visible and for-
malize their contact (Boswell, 1977; Mundy, 1955; Pullan, 1983).

"It is . . . not cleanliness or health that causes abjection but
what disturbs identity, system, order. What does not respect bor-
ders, positions, rules" (Kristeva, 1982, p. 4). The necessity of
protecting Christian society from the danger of ambiguity created
a simple therapeutic—it made the stigmatized visible, inimitable,
public, and inseparable from the stigma itself.

CONCLUSION

Economic and social revolution, intellectual and political
change in the 17th and 18th centuries combined to destroy for-
ever the institutions of medieval society. The unusual and different were removed from the centers of public life, institutionalized
instead in prisons, mental hospitals, and clinics. Clerics no longer monopolized the process of stigmatization, and religion, which
had long colored its language, was superseded by a babel of new
vocabularies—of medicine, therapy, social science, criminal justice, and political reform (Foucault, 1965, 1975, 1978, 1979).

It was superseded, but not silenced, for religion and morality are still at work in the stigma discourse. Like our forebears, we remain fascinated by the Ambiguous, the Disorderly, the Hidden, the Different. Unlike them, however, we pretend to live in a rational and secular age, unaware sometimes of how heavily history, and language, weigh upon us. Historical study, exploiting the work of humanists and social scientists, can uncover the structural underpinnings of our thinking about stigma and give us the freedom—if we choose—to go beyond.

CHAPTER 5

Stigma, Deviance, and Social Control
SOME CONCEPTUAL ISSUES

Mark C. Stafford and Richard R. Scott

One reason why it is difficult to approach the study of stigma with much confidence is that there are so many kinds. Consider just a short list: old age, paralysis, cancer, drug addiction, mental illness, shortness, being black, alcoholism, smoking, crime, homosexuality, unemployment, being Jewish, obesity, blindness, epilepsy, receiving welfare, illiteracy, divorce, ugliness, stuttering, being female, poverty, being an amputee, mental retardation, and deafness. One of the few common denominators of these characteristics may be that all of them generate ridicule and scorn. However, there is another, more important reason why the study of stigma must be approached cautiously. Conceptualization and use of the term have been so vague and uncritical that one may reasonably ask: What is a stigma? To many, the answer is simply a "flaw," "shortcoming," "blemish," or "taint," but that answer does little except to imply that stigmas are opprobrious.

Then consider the notion that stigma is synonymous with deviance (in the sense of a norm violation) and involves efforts at social control. That notion is at once conventional and controversial—conventional in that stigma is more likely to be linked with deviance and social control than with any other concepts (e.g., Elliott, Ziegler, Altman, & Scott, 1982), but controversial in that very few discussions of deviance and social control cover as wide a range of phenomena as listed above. We will argue that much can be gained from such a notion, but considerable work is needed since, in many ways, "deviance" and "social control" are no less primitive terms than "stigma."

DEFINITIONS OF STIGMA

Goffman (1963) notes that the ancient Greeks used the word *stigma* to refer to bodily marks or brands exposing the bearers as persons to be avoided (e.g., slaves, criminals, or sinners). "Today," according to Goffman, "the term is . . . used in something like the original sense, but is applied more to the disgrace itself than to the bodily evidence of it" (pp. 1–2). Stigma is equated with an "undesired differentness," of which there are three types: (a) physical deformities; (b) "blemishes of individual character" such as homosexuality and unemployment; and (c) "tribal" stigmas of race, nationality, and religion (Goffman, 1963, pp. 4–5).

The following definitions illustrate other ways of conceptualizing stigma:

> We . . . reserve the concept of stigma for outcomes of a discrediting process, where the target person is viewed as morally flawed and arouses revulsion. (Jones, Farina, Hastorf, Markus, Miller, & Scott, 1984, p. 297)

> In brief and in theory, stigma denotes one's morally spoiled identity, one's social undesirability. (Pfuhl, 1980, p. 202)

> Stigmatized persons . . . are little valued *as persons.* (Schur, 1983, p. 31)

> [When it comes to stigma,] we are discussing the entire field of people who are regarded negatively, some for having violated . . . rules, others just for being the sort of people they are or having traits that are not highly valued. (Birenbaum & Sagarin, 1976, p. 33)

> Stigma . . . conjures up images of blemished selves and discredited bodily or moral attributes that automatically exclude the bearer from

the competitive game by assigning labels of inferiority. (N. J. Davis, 1980, p. 207)

[Stigmatized] individuals . . . have attributes that do not accord with the prevailing standards of the normal and good. They are often denigrated and avoided—openly in the case of known criminals and other transgressors, or covertly and even unconsciously . . . when the disdained person is an innocent victim of misfortune (e.g., a paraplegic). (I. Katz, 1981, p. 1)

Inspection of these definitions reveals one fundamental point of agreement. All of them suggest in one way or another that stigma involves disvaluation of persons (see, e.g., Pfuhl's 1980 definition). All of the definitions, however, are ambiguous in that they leave unanswered all manner of questions. For example, even if we assume that stigma has something to do with disvaluation, whose disvaluation is relevant? Must the disvaluation be of a certain intensity before we can say that there is a stigma? If so, how intense?

Schur (1983) suggests that others respond to stigmatized persons as members of disvalued categories (e.g., the blind, the unemployed, the deaf) rather than as individuals. Virtually any discussion of stigma is likely to emphasize this or some similar process (variously termed *categorization, typification, objectification, inferiorization,* and the like). The problem lies in this question: How is disvaluation to be inferred? Arguing that being female is a stigma, Schur (1983, pp. 35–36) points to such factors as social and economic inequality as evidence of the disvaluation of women. Granted, highly valued persons are not likely to be relegated to the lower echelons of society as women have been. However, we assume that women experience inequality *because* they are disvalued. If we identify disvaluation in terms of inequality, it is tautological to speak of the former as *influencing* the latter.

Jones *et al.* (1984) point to "outcomes of a discrediting process" as a criterion for identifying stigmas. They do not specify what constitutes such a process, however, and specification is not realized by referring to a response such as revulsion. Must the revulsion be overt? Suppose that an individual expresses revulsion by denouncing a person in clearly derogatory terms to another person but without the matter going any further. Would the revulsion denote a stigma? Or does the process entail direct action or interaction with the person being discredited?

Like Jones *et al.* (1984), N. J. Davis (1980) associates stigma with particular outcomes except that she emphasizes exclusion and the assignment of labels rather than revulsion. In this case, does it matter whether persons resist or object to the exclusion? If not, what is the significance of unquestioned acceptance of exclusion (e.g., when Christians are denied membership in B'nai B'rith)? As for assigning labels of inferiority, an illustrative list might include "fag," "nut," "hood," "nigger," "pervert," "head," "broad," "con," "lush," "moron," and "crip." Here the question is: How can labels, by themselves, be used to identify stigmas when any particular label may not have the same meaning in all social contexts (e.g., the term *hood* may be pejorative in some social circles, laudatory in others)?

AN ALTERNATIVE DEFINITION: STIGMA AND DEVIANCE

Whatever else stigma may entail, two features loom obvious: First, it is a relative phenomenon, meaning that what is a stigma in one social unit (family, company, nation) may not be so in others. For example, obesity is condemned in contemporary Western societies, but Clinard and Meier (1979, p. 530) point out that "fattening houses" were used formerly in certain parts of Africa to produce beautiful women. Similarly, whereas old age may be dreaded in one society, it may be accorded considerable prestige in another. A second feature of stigma is its collective (i.e., social) quality. Persons who are disvalued by one member of a social unit will also tend to be disvalued by other members. The task, then, is to define stigma to recognize these two features but in such a way that problems raised with other definitions can be avoided.

Consider this alternative definition: *Stigma is a characteristic of persons that is contrary to a norm of a social unit.* The characteristic may involve what people do (or have done), what they believe, or who they are (owing to physical or social characteristics).

Given that "norm" is the key concept in the definition and

that a norm is often treated as a synonym for a *rule* or *standard,* the definition may appear to be a restatement of the definitions of Birenbaum and Sagarin (1976) and I. Katz (1981) given previously. There is justification, however, for emphasizing norms rather than rules or standards because only the notion of norm recognizes both the relativity and collective nature of stigma. Rules or standards recognize only the first feature. There may be nothing collective about rules or standards in that they can be formulated and imposed by an individual (Meier, 1981).

The definition closely resembles what is commonly taken as a definition of deviance—that deviance consists of norm violations. As previously indicated, however, few discussions of deviance cover as wide a range of phenomena as is usually associated with stigma because deviance has been conceptualized more or less exclusively as behavior, and many stigmas have little to do with behavior (e.g., ugliness, paralysis, cancer).

The heart of the issue (i.e., how narrowly or broadly we conceptualize stigma and deviance) lies in the question: *What is a norm?* The following definition is fairly representative: A norm is a shared belief that persons ought to behave in a certain way in certain circumstances (Blake & Davis, 1964; Gibbs, 1965; Homans, 1961; Morris, 1956). The focus on behavior explains the relatively narrow meaning usually assigned to deviance. In contrast, we argue for a broader concept of norms, involving not just behavior but also characteristics such as race, gender and physical well-being. This more general conception seems to be what Goffman (1963, pp. 126–130) has in mind when he speaks of "identity norms." These are depictions of "ideal" persons, shared beliefs as to what individuals ought to be (behaviorally and otherwise). Goffman suggests that in the United States the ideal is a "young, married, white, urban, northern, heterosexual Protestant father of college education, fully employed, of good complexion, weight, and height, and a recent record in sports" (p. 128). Persons who fail to match any of these characteristics (e.g., *all* women) will tend to be disvalued to some degree.

It is this broader conception of a norm that we use in defining stigma and that justifies treating stigma and deviance as synonyms. Falling into the category of stigma (or deviance) are a variety of behavioral norm violations, such as premarital sex where chastity is prized, receiving welfare where self-sufficiency is esteemed, alcohol use where sobriety is a requirement, homosexuality where heterosexuality is considered proper, and smoking where health is stressed. Also included are nonbehavioral norm violations, such as old age in a youth-oriented nation, paraplegia where physical mobility is emphasized, being black where whites are considered superior, poverty where affluence is admired, shortness where tallness is rewarded, left-handedness in a right-handed society, blindness in a sighted world, ugliness where physical attractiveness is wanted, obesity where fitness is valued, holding to egalitarian beliefs where racism prevails or being Jewish when Christianity is preferred.

To be sure, grouping behavioral and nonbehavioral characteristics of persons into a single category creates a serious problem. When this is done, no etiological theory is adequate. To illustrate, because short persons did not choose to become that way, it makes little sense to ask as we might about criminals: Why did they do it? In such cases, we would be more concerned with asking why some characteristics of persons are norm violations and not others (e.g., why shortness and not blond hair?).

The foregoing illustration calls attention to an issue that often is discussed in writings about deviance—the issue of responsibility. Some commentators on the subject consider responsibility central to defining deviance. For example, Cohen (1966) argues that

> whereas deviant roles are socially disvalued roles . . . , not all disvalued roles are deviant. . . . What [deviant roles] have in common is the notion of a person who knows what he is doing . . . and *chooses* to violate some normative rule. (p. 36)

Similarly, McHugh (1970) contends that a deviant act is one that persons deem "'might not have been' or 'might have been otherwise'" (p. 61). Simply put, blameworthiness is viewed as the essence of deviance; if any characteristic is unavoidable (or perceived to be so), then presumably it is not deviant. What this view ignores is that many characteristics that are beyond a person's control (mainly nonbehavioral characteristics) arouse similar feelings to those elicited by more willful ones. Friedson (1965) clearly illustrates the point:

> The simple moral dichotomy of responsibility does not allow for the halo of moral evaluation that in fact surrounds many types of behavior for which, theoretically, people are not held responsible, but which in some way damage their identities. Some diseases, such as syphilis, leprosy, and even tuberculosis, are surrounded with loathing even though they are all "merely" infections. And many forms of organic dysfunction or maldevelopment for which the sufferer is not held responsible occasion responses of fear or disgust—epilepsy, dwarfism, and disfigurement, for example (p. 76).

To resolve the dispute, it is helpful to distinguish attributes of norm violations that are true by definition from those that are contingent—that is, attributes that vary from one norm violation to the next. Norm violations have been described as running the gamut from responsibility to its absence (i.e., nonresponsibility). At the former extreme, one might place crime or premarital sex, and at the latter, mental retardation and stuttering. Rather than enter *responsibility* into the definition of a norm violation, it is preferable to treat it as a contingent attribute to emphasize purely empirical issues. There is, for example, considerable evidence that individuals are evaluated more favorably when they are not held responsible for their stigmas, as when obesity is attributable to a glandular or other physical disorder (Jones *et al.*, 1984, pp. 56–63). Friedson (1965) observes that "when the individual is believed to be responsible . . . , some form of punishment is likely to be involved. . . . When he is believed not to be responsible . . . , permissive treatment . . . is used" (p. 76).

Like responsibility, the "permanence" of a norm violation should be treated as a contingent attribute (Sagarin, 1979). Some norm violations are impermanent, ephemeral. An obese person might lose weight. Someone may have acne that heals and is thus less defacing over time. Or an unemployed person might obtain a job. In contrast, other norm violations are relatively permanent—ugliness, epilepsy, blindness, and being black, to identify just a few. The notion of "permanence" is especially important in considering behavioral characteristics of persons. People can and do change their behavior; hence many, though certainly not all, behavioral norm violations lack continuity or chronicity. Compared with permanent characteristics of persons, they are only temporary phases of being. In some social units, for example, both theft and being black might be stigmas (i.e., characteristics that are inconsistent with what is believed to be an "ideal" person). However, although persons can commit theft, "repent," and change their ways, being black is ineffaceable. What complicates matters is that some behaviors tend to assume a permanent quality even though they may be only one-time events. One can go from being a murderer or rapist to an ex-murderer or ex-rapist, but one can never shed these latter identities. Like being black, the behaviors become inextricably linked with persons. Why is this more the case with some behaviors than others (e.g., why murder and rape more than theft)? Sagarin (1975) argues that there are several key factors, including (a) the seriousness of the behavior; (b) whether the behavior represents a threat to others if repeated; and (c) whether the behavior is seen as involving the entire "moral character" of the person (p. 49).

MEASURING STIGMAS

As with any concept, stigma is an *abstraction;* hence, stigmas cannot be identified systematically without a measurement procedure. Because stigma is defined here in terms of norms, one procedure to identify the stigmas in a social unit is to solicit responses from all members (or a representative sample) to "normative" questions. The immediate problem is to find a way to word normative questions to cover the full range of stigmas. Schur (1979, pp. 269–271) suggests that questions might take the following form: (a) present respondents with a list of characteristics (e.g., armed robbery, political corruption, homosexuality, mental illness) that might be considered disturbing or fearsome, and then (b) ask them to rank the characteristics from most to least disturbing and so on. An alternative that more closely reflects the notion of "identity norms" is to ask respondents to think of the characteristics of an ideal person (or the kinds of characteristics that an ideal person ought to have). They then could be given a list of characteristics of persons and be asked to indicate how much each detracts or deviates from the ideal (e.g., substantially, somewhat, not at all).

Whatever the wording, normative questions should recognize

a distinction between respondents' personal beliefs and their perceptions of the beliefs of others (Gibbs, 1972). Suppose, for the sake of illustration, that all members of a social unit believe that paraplegia detracts substantially from what constitutes an ideal person. By the criterion of *personal normative beliefs*, then, paraplegia would be stigmatizing to the maximum degree. Further, suppose that all members perceive that all others believe that paraplegia detracts substantially from the ideal. Paraplegia would thus be maximally stigmatizing according to *perceived normative beliefs*. The illustration is misleading in that there is no necessary relation between personal and perceived normative beliefs. All members of a social unit might believe that paraplegia does not detract at all from an ideal person but perceive (albeit erroneously) that others believe differently (i.e., perceive that others believe it is a substantial deviation from the ideal). In this case, paraplegia would be a stigma by one criterion (perceived normative beliefs) but not by the other (personal normative beliefs). The distinction is important because persons may orient their behavior around their perceptions of others' beliefs more than their own (e.g., when an individual avoids being seen in public with a disabled friend out of concern for what others will think). The more general point, however, is that there are two distinct criteria for identifying stigma, and a characteristic is stigmatizing to the extent that it is contrary to one or both criteria.

As mentioned earlier, stigmas have a collective quality. That is, in any given social unit, there is likely to be a high degree of consensus about what is considered a stigma. Few Americans are likely to believe that child molesting and robbery are valued characteristics of persons. Even when it comes to seemingly esoteric matters such as physical attractiveness (consider the idea that "beauty is in the eye of the beholder"), there is remarkable consensus (Jones *et al.,* 1984, pp. 47–56; Mazur, Mazur, & Keating, 1984). The consensus is rarely complete, however, and therein lies a crucial question: What percentage of individuals must express the same belief before we can say that there is a norm? The obvious figure is 51% (i.e., a majority), but that or any other figure is arbitrary. In one of the few instances where social scientists have confronted the issue directly, Meier (1981) offers what may be the only defensible solution: "If two or more persons share the same evaluation, it is a norm" (p. 18). As such, there may be no such thing as *the* norm, especially in large, heterogeneous social units. Instead, there may be many norms.

There is an additional issue that is not so easily resolved. First, returning to the paraplegia illustration, suppose that one respondent is a corporate executive and that another is a janitor. Gibbs (1981, p. 13) argues that it would be questionable to assign equal weight to their normative beliefs because corporate executives have more power to impose their beliefs on others. If a corporate executive believes that paraplegia does not detract at all from an ideal person, he or she clearly would have more opportunities to act on that belief (e.g., by hiring the physically disabled). More generally, normative beliefs are likely to vary along ethnic, class, age, gender, geographic, and occupational lines, and it may be that the opinions of some categories of persons ought to be "counted" more than others. At present, there is no defensible procedure for assigning "power weights" to normative questions, but it is unrealistic to ignore differential power in identifying stigmas.

To illustrate still another issue, suppose again that a respondent answers a normative question about paraplegia by saying that it does not detract at all from what constitutes an ideal person. If pressed on the matter, however, the respondent might answer that it detracts somewhat from an ideal spouse but not at all from an ideal employee, neighbor, or friend. Then consider this normative question: Does premarital sex detract from an ideal person? Many Americans might answer in the negative but give a different answer if asked about people below age 14. All such answers suggest that persons assume a variety of roles (i.e., socially sanctioned demands and expectations associated with particular categories of individuals or statuses), and beliefs about what constitutes an "ideal" person may vary from one role to the next (e.g., the "ideal" spouse or the "ideal" young person). Although some characteristics are likely to detract from virtually any role that individuals might assume (a "master status," according to Hughes, 1945), others might have more limited scope.

For example, because physical attractiveness figures mainly in face-to-face interactions, ugliness may have little bearing on normative beliefs about roles involving only minimal social interaction (e.g., a telephone salesperson). A stigma may even be a requirement for some roles—as a case in point, when it is believed that stigmatized persons are best qualified to counsel other, similarly stigmatized persons. We know very little about which roles are relevant in considering different stigmas, but roles are important because the same characteristic may be considered more or less stigmatizing, depending on the role.

SOCIAL CONTROL

Social control involves reactions to stigmas (or deviance [Meier, 1982]). Reactions may occur for various reasons (e.g., fear, vengeance), but an important consequence is often the restriction or termination of social relations. Common examples are the exclusion of a skinny child from a neighborhood game of baseball and avoidance of an ugly person as a dating partner. Other examples abound: (a) persons who have been convicted of committing crimes tend to experience limited employment opportunities (Schwartz & Skolnick, 1962); (b) obesity has reduced young women's chances of admission into socially prestigious New England colleges (Cahnman, 1968); and (c) hospitalized mental patients receive very few visits from relatives and friends, and most visitors do not return (Schwartz, 1956).

Such consequences are not necessarily limited to persons who possess stigmas. People who ordinarily would not be disvalued, if considered alone, can by association acquire some of the disvalued characteristics of a stigmatized person. Goffman (1963) refers to this as a "courtesy stigma" that can "spread from the stigmatized individual to his connections" (p. 30). Like personal stigmas, courtesy stigmas often result in restricted or terminated social relations. The birth of a mentally retarded child, for example, restricts the social activities of a family. Fewer people are invited into the home, and visits to others' homes are curtailed (Birenbaum, 1970; Levinson & Starling, 1981).

In the case of stigmas for which people cannot be held responsible, the restriction or termination of social relations is likely to be an end in itself. Racial discrimination, for example, tends to remove blacks from competition for high-prestige jobs, and institutionalization of the mentally retarded can remove them from the social mainstream altogether. With stigmas over which persons have some control, however, the restriction or termination of social relations may not be the only end. Suppose that religious heretics are banished from a country. Such a reaction has the immediate consequence of ridding the country of persons with deviant religious beliefs. At the same time, it can be a means of discouraging other persons from adopting similar beliefs.

Individuals can intentionally restrict or terminate social relations with stigmatized persons (as when a wife divorces her husband because of his alcoholism), but intention is not a crucial consideration. There are many situations where social relations are restricted or terminated, even though this is not the intended consequence. Kanter (1977) shows, for example, that one of the most effective ways to limit the advancement of women in corporations is largely unintentional. Often, in dealing with customers and managers, women "felt themselves to be treated in more wifelike and datelike ways than a man would be treated by another man, even though the situation was clearly professional" (Kanter, 1977, p. 981). Treated as outsiders, women could not enter the (male) camaraderie of the workplace.

Reactions to stigmas are not always negative—that is, hostile, rejecting, or punishing. Consider a situation where a sighted person helps a blind man negotiate a difficult flight of stairs. Moreover, Hoebel (1954, p. 71) observes that among some Eskimo there are redemptive ceremonies in which members of a crowd react to the public confessions of taboo violators with cries for forgiveness.

There is considerable evidence that reactions to many stigmas are mixed, both positive and negative (for reviews, see Jones et al., 1984; Katz, 1981). For example, Gergen and Jones (1963) describe the mixed reactions to persons with mental illness. On the one hand, avoidance can result from beliefs that the mentally ill are obstructive, sullen, self-centered, and irrational. On the other hand, mental illness is often seen as a tragedy, and the mentally ill are viewed as victims. Consequently, mental illness can arouse nurturant reactions. Similarly, Kleck, Ono, and Hastorf (1966) indicate that subjects talked longer with a male confederate in a wheelchair than they did with an able-bodied confederate when they thought that they were helping him perform his task as an interviewer. However, the subjects talked longer with the nondisabled confederate if they had no reason to believe that continued interaction could help. Kleck *et al.* (1966) reason that people want to treat disabled persons kindly but consider face-to-face interaction aversive. Doob and Ecker (1970) report evidence consistent with this reasoning. Persons were more likely to complete and return a questionnaire for a female door-to-door canvasser who wore an eyepatch than for one who did not. The woman with the eyepatch was not favored, however, if the request was for an interview.

An important feature of reactions to stigmas is that they vary so much from one social unit to the next and over time. In some social units, persons have been branded for committing crimes (Newman, 1978, pp. 118–119). A wife's punishment for adultery could include public gang rape in certain New Guinea tribes (Berndt, 1962). Moreover, deformed infants in preliterate societies were sometimes left exposed to die. As Seneca put it during Christ's time, "Mad dogs we knock on the head, the fierce ox we slay; sickly sheep we put to the knife to keep them from infecting the flock; unnatural progeny we destroy" (p. 145).

Why are such reactions uncommon in the U.S. today? Or, stated more generally, what are the causes of variation in reactions to stigmas? Social scientists have done little to answer such questions. Any existing answers, however, are likely to point to another feature of reactions to stigmas. For any given stigma, there is at least one corresponding *reactive norm;* that is, shared beliefs about how people should react (Clark & Gibbs, 1965). For example, no one is likely to condone whipping stutterers or tarring and feathering paraplegics. In these cases, the reactive norms tend to promote sympathy and the inhibition of aggression. Needless to say, however, reactive norms do not always correspond to actual reactions.

Like reactions, reactors are also normative because beliefs about what should happen in reaction to a stigma include a belief about *who* should react. Americans think that it is appropriate for relatives to react to such stigmas as alcoholism, obesity, mental illness, cancer, and unemployment. This does not mean that members of a social unit will always agree in stipulating appropriate reactors, however. On the contrary, Americans are likely to disagree about who, if anyone, should intervene in issues such as domestic quarrels and homosexuality.

SUMMARY AND CONCLUSIONS

Our proposed definition of stigma emphasizes norms. In contrast to many previous treatments of norms that have been limited to behavior, we argue for a broader treatment that includes both behavioral and nonbehavioral characteristics of persons. Norms are measurable, and this means that stigmas can be studied empirically. More than anything else, stigmas represent disvalued characteristics of persons, departures from what constitutes the "ideal" person. Because stigmatized persons are disvalued, they become objects of social control, which functions to limit their social participation.

In light of the many conceptual issues that we have discussed, one might well ask: If these issues have not been resolved by now, how is it that social scientists have studied stigma for decades? They have done so mainly by leaving conceptual issues implicit. Moreover, they have tended to focus on phenomena that would be highly stigmatizing regardless of the criterion employed (i.e., extreme stigmas such as crime [Toby, 1981]).

Research has been fragmented, however, with studies of one kind of stigma only infrequently informing studies of other stigmas. If the study of stigma is ever to become truly cumulative, researchers must search for commonalities across a wide range of stigmatizing phenomena, and any such search requires a defensible definition of stigma. One might opt for a different definition than the one proposed here. However, the conceptual issues will not go away if ignored.

Perhaps the most important unresolved question has to do with social change: How can particular characteristics of persons be *destigmatized?* How, for example, can the disvaluation of old age be alleviated? Or poverty? Or being female? Or homosexuality? The answer may appear obvious: If stigmas involve norms, then destigmatization would require a major overhaul of our normative system. But how is this to be accomplished? Educational programs aimed at destigmatization (e.g., programs emphasizing the virtues of old age) are likely to be only partially effective. Another strategy would be to integrate the stigmatized with the nonstigmatized. Equal-status contacts between the two groups, especially contacts showing the stigmatized in roles not usually associated with them, could possibly aid in destigmatization. In recent years, destigmatization has been facilitated by stigmatized groups acting on their own behalf to change others' evaluations of them. Organizations such as the Little People of America, the Anti-Defamation League, and the Gay Activist Alliance have sought to solve the many problems deriving from their stigmas. Although destigmatization may be difficult to achieve, there is reason for optimism. Because stigmas do not necessarily inhere in behaviors or types of persons, they can be changed.

PART **II**

THE STIGMATIZING PROCESS

CHAPTER 6

Stigma and the Dynamics of Social Cognition

Jennifer Crocker and Neil Lutsky

INTRODUCTION: COGNITIVE APPROACHES IN THE STUDY OF STIGMA

The study of how and what we think about groups and persons who are stigmatized plays a critical role in a comprehensive analysis of stigma. This is apparent if we assume that behavior in actual or symbolic encounters of the general public with persons who may be stigmatized, such as members of persecuted minorities, can be understood in terms of how and what the participants in the encounter are thinking. This chapter focuses on the study of such thought and considers its character, origins, development, functioning, and consequences from a cognitive social psychological perspective.

The importance of understanding features of social thought about those who are stigmatized is apparent from a multidisciplinary point of view. As other chapters in this volume suggest, stigma can be understood in terms of large-scale cultural, social, and historical forces, but these influences ultimately require the participation of the individual members of a society. How does individual thinking about stigmatized persons reflect these larger trends? How does it mediate the impact of forces of social control on interpersonal behavior and social judgment? How may social thought, in turn, alter the character of the social order that subsequently defines stigma and the social perception of it? These are fundamental questions that link the social psychological study of social cognition in this chapter to the wider study of stigma in this book.

Traditionally, cognitive studies of stigma have sought to document the content and nature of social beliefs about stigmatized persons and groups. This was in keeping with the character of social psychological treatments of social cognition in general. More recently, however, social psychologists' attempts to understand *what* persons think about various social objects have been reformulated in light of theory and research on *how* persons perceive their social worlds. This work on "the processes involved in the representation and utilization of knowledge" (Isen & Hastorf, 1982, p. 4) has significantly redefined social psychological perspectives on social cognition (e.g., Fiske & Taylor, 1984; Hastorf & Isen, 1982). The possibility that this shift may have equivalent effects on cognitive analyses of stigma underlies much of our later discussion as we attempt to identify, develop, and evaluate applications of this more general change. We will begin with an introduction to the more traditional cognitive approach that has been pursued in attitudinal analyses of stigma and then consider how the current process orientation of cognitive social psychology—which we will label "schematic" in this chapter—may recast cognitive approaches to the study of stigma.

ATTITUDINAL ANALYSES OF STIGMA

In everyday usage, to describe an individual as "stigmatized" ("Person X is stigmatized by his or her association with Attribute or Event Y") is to suggest that a primary, discrediting belief dominates perceivers' thoughts about the individual. Similarly, when a category of persons is stigmatized in society, it is likely that an equivalent set of attitudes and beliefs exists to define social reactions to category members and to the category label. In Goffman's terms, a stigma can be seen as a relationship between an "attribute and stereotype" (1963, p. 4), where *attribute* refers to a "mark" that may define membership in a stigmatized category of persons (see Jones, Farina, Hastorf, Markus, Miller, & Scott, 1984, p. 8) and *stereotype* refers to a set of generalized beliefs that are invoked by that category membership. To understand a stigma, then, is to identify relevant stereotypic beliefs that exist in association with a mark.

This describes the general approach that social psychologists have traditionally taken to the topic of stigma—an approach that locates the study of stigma in a more general consideration of attitudes, stereotypes, and prejudice. In particular, stereotyping is thought to be "at the heart of the stigmatizing process" (Jones *et al.*, 1984, p. 155), and identifying the kinds of beliefs that are stereotyped and documenting the contents of those beliefs have been at the heart of social psychological studies of stereotyping (Brigham, 1971; Hamilton, 1981).

Most often, social psychologists have examined beliefs about what stigmatized persons are like, especially in terms of personality traits (Ashmore & Del Boca, 1981) and beliefs about why persons come to have their characteristics or deserve their fates. Thus, research has suggested that—among other stereotypic associations—blacks are seen as lazy (Brigham, 1971), elderly persons are thought to be passive (Lutsky, 1980), and the physically disabled are viewed as inferior (Katz, 1981). Underlying much of this work is a concern about judgments of personal character (see Sabini & Silver, 1982, Chapter 8). As a result, research on beliefs may document the existence of a stigma when it provides evidence that members of a particular social category are associated with a discredited personal character.

In contrast, recent treatments of belief content have emphasized more specific expectations of likely moment in interactions. Jones *et al.* (1984), in particular, have detailed how a perceiver's stereotypic anticipations of a marked person's likely abilities, behaviors, and reactions can influence social interaction involving stigmatized persons and others. In addition, they have discussed how a stigmatized person's expectations about the likely beliefs, reactions, and behaviors of nonstigmatized persons can affect that interaction. Illustrations of this latter dynamic can be found in the autobiographical writings of Ved Mehta (1985). For example, Mehta, who is blind, believed that using a cane was a "blindism" likely to elicit reactions of pity or rejection, and this led him to forego its use.

These attitudinal analyses of stigma account for social behavior by reference to particular contents in a structure of beliefs about the stigmatized. Thus, behavioral reactions to women who have been raped may be seen as consistent with beliefs about rape and rape victims (Feild, 1978; Weidner & Griffitt, 1983). Most often, behavior in the presence of a stigma has a hostile or at least dysfunctional character to it. Outcomes of this kind can then be explained by reference to serious faults in ancillary beliefs about the stigmatized (cf. Brigham, 1971; McCauley, Stitt, & Segal, 1980) or by reference to a fundamental belief in the inherently problematic and usually strongly negative character of members of a stigmatized social category.

Attitudinal analyses share much in common with a sociological account of stigma. Both tend to assume that perceivers hold strong preexisting beliefs about marked groups and individuals, that these beliefs are fairly well articulated and well organized, and that certain, usually obvious and monolithic cues and labels make these beliefs salient. These features suggest that perceivers have internalized explicit systems of social meaning (e.g., Berger & Luckmann, 1966), which may serve to protect social institutions (see Jones et al., 1984, Chapter 3) or represent existing social practices. Thus, the phenomena of stigma may be sustained by individually held social attitudes that are directly reflective of larger social forces.

Toward a Schematic Perspective on Stigma

Recent thinking in social psychology views social cognition as a more open set of operations on past and present information, and this sets at issue a number of the assumptions associated with the attitudinal approach. In particular, the current schematic approach suggests that perceivers may themselves construct the beliefs they hold, that these are less likely to be directly socialized or socially given. What persons think about social objects may also be more open, complex, and fluid than traditional attitudinal analyses recognized. This means that how and when perceivers use both previously held and current information become more prominent concerns in a schematic account of social cognition. In sum, if we are to understand social thought, including thought about stigmatized individuals and groups, the schematic perspective would have us examine those cognitive processes that may be responsible for the construction, application, and revision of social perceptions and evaluations (Fiske & Taylor, 1984; Hamilton, 1981; Isen & Hastorf, 1982).

What is the nature of preexisting beliefs and attitudes toward the stigmatized, in this view? A schematic perspective on stigma would suggest that these are continually constructed and reconstructed as persons select, organize, and evaluate their own social experiences for particular purposes. This constructivist perspective on beliefs toward the stigmatized further suggests that such beliefs may not always be well developed, monolithic, or systematic. It is possible, then, that perceivers hold no specific expectations, a multiplicity of isolated beliefs, or systems of interrelated beliefs about a social category. For example, perceivers may hold a view of what elderly persons are like *in general* as well as other *distinct* views of what specific categories of elderly persons such as "grandmothers" or "elderly statesmen" are like (Brewer, Dull, & Lui, 1981). Perceivers are also likely to have knowledge of others' or conventional societal beliefs about a category of persons, even if they do not personally endorse those beliefs.

Given this abundance of cognitive possibilities, it becomes important to understand when and how perceivers use particular kinds of previously held information in response to some specific stimulus or how they construct appropriate beliefs as required by cognition-demanding circumstances (Taylor & Fiske, 1978). This has sparked an interest in processes associated with the recognition of a stigma, with labeling or categorization, and with the elaboration of meanings associated with a category membership.

As discussed earlier, these processes may be more problematic for perceivers than had been assumed, and they may also have important functional effects on reactions to stigmas and the persons who bear them.

The schematic approach also raises questions about how previously held information is used, how present information is processed, and how these two interact when stigmas are perceived and discussed. Are there ways in which the presence of a stigma alters *how* generalizations influence the perception of particular persons? Is specific information about a person who is marked evaluated differently from information about someone who is not? All of the preceding considerations suggest that behavior in the presence of a stigma may be understood not only in terms of *what* people think but also in terms of *how* people think when they think about stigmatized groups and individuals.

Finally, another important feature of current treatments of social cognition is their renewed interest in the role of affect in social perception and judgment (e.g., Fiske, 1981; Fiske & Taylor, 1984; Isen & Hastorf, 1982; Zajonc, 1980). This is especially relevant to the study of stigma, which must confront the strong emotional components of interpersonal, social, and institutional responses to the stigmatized. As suggested earlier, a certain type of social affect—disgrace—is widely associated with stigma and distinguishes it as a source of social rejection. This affective foundation is likely to have widespread effects on social cognition in the context of stigma, and these will be considered in the discussions that follow.

Is stigma best understood in terms of strong, socially articulated attitudes and beliefs, or via a study of component processes of social cognition (e.g., categorization, attitude construction, information application) that may operate on various past and current sources of information? We have suggested that a shift in emphasis in favor of the latter approach has occurred in social psychological treatments of social cognition. Pursuing the contributions such a strategy might yield for our understanding of the real and important features of stigma constitutes the intellectual experiment that we now begin.

THE ORIGINS OF SOCIAL THOUGHT
ABOUT THE STIGMATIZED

In considering psychological accounts of the origins of social thinking about the stigmatized, we ask the following questions: Why do we think about members of stigmatized groups in the ways that we do? What functions do stigmatization in general and beliefs about the stigmatized in particular have for the individual or for the larger social unit? Traditional attitudinal analyses of these issues typically emphasize either sociocultural processes or motivational processes (Ashmore & Del Boca, 1976, 1981). In addition, we will emphasize a schematic approach that analyzes stigma in terms of cognitive processes. We will consider, in particular, how each of these treats the origins of both our classification of selected groups as "different" and our stereotypic beliefs and attitudes toward members of those groups.

THE SOCIOCULTURAL PERSPECTIVE

Of central importance to the sociocultural perspective is the observation that beliefs and cognitions are influenced by the social context. According to this perspective, stereotypes and other components of social thought about the stigmatized are aspects of the cultural wisdom or folkways of a culture, transmitted from members of one generation to members of the next through the process of socialization. Thus, children learn which groups are stigmatized and stereotypes about these groups from their parents, teachers, television shows, books, and other socializing agents. This perspective suggests that there will be widespread agreement among members of a culture with regard to which groups are stigmatized as well as how those groups are stereotyped. Furthermore, the sociocultural approach suggests that people may develop beliefs about stigmatized groups without ever having met or learned about any individual member of a group.

The functions of stereotypes of the stigmatized are linked to the structure of the society and of intergroup relations within that society. Some theorists argue that stereotypes about the stigmatized are created to preserve the social structure or to permit exploitation of a group or its resources. This argument is frequently advanced to account for racial stereotypes in the United States that developed, it is argued, to justify and maintain slavery (Cox, 1984) and may persist in order to justify the continued economic disadvantages of blacks.

An alternative view of the link between stigmatization and the social structure argues that categorizations and stereotypes develop as a result of the realistic conflicts between groups (Bernard, 1957; Levine & Campbell, 1972; Sherif, Harvey, White, Hood, & Sherif, 1961). Evidence in support of this theory is provided by historical studies showing that intergroup attitudes change following a change in the relations between the groups, and by studies in which the nature of intergroup relations is experimentally manipulated and intergroup attitudes are observed to change (see Ashmore & Del Boca, 1976, for a review and discussion).

THE MOTIVATIONAL PERSPECTIVE

In contrast to sociocultural explanations, motivational explanations emphasize the individual origins of social thought about the stigmatized. A variety of motivational accounts of prejudice toward the stigmatized have been proposed. Each of them suggests that prejudice or certain specific beliefs about a target group protect the individual from particular thoughts or desires that may be threatening or unpleasant.

The theory of the authoritarian personality (Adorno, Frenkel-Brunswick, Levinson, & Sanford, 1950), which draws heavily on Freudian theories of psychosexual development, argues that prejudice results from the use of psychological defense mechanisms that attempt to protect persons from acknowledging their unacceptable sexual and aggressive impulses. Freudian theory states that children who are reared in strict discipline-oriented, authoritarian families are not permitted to express the aggressive and sexual impulses that all children have. To cope with these impulses, the child attributes his or her aggressive and sexual feelings to others, particularly to members of relatively powerless and symbolically prototypic groups. The child eventually grows into an adult who is ethnocentric, authoritarian, and politically and economically conservative. Thus, beliefs about the stigmatized may represent the projections of the unacceptable impulses of the nonstigmatized onto members of relatively powerless groups, and emotional reactions to the stigmatized may reflect personal anxieties about those impulses. However, the original research support for the theory reported in *The Authoritarian Personality* has been widely criticized (see Ashmore & Del Boca, 1976; Brown, 1965; Christie & Johoda, 1954). In particular, the theoretical claim that relates prejudice to needs arising from early childhood experiences in authoritarian families has not been established through subsequent research.

An alternative motivational account posits that people have a need to believe that the world is a safe, predictable, and orderly place in which people get what they deserve (Lerner, 1980; Lerner & Miller, 1978). Thus, people are motivated to believe that others deserve or bring upon themselves the unpleasant events that befall them because the belief that "bad things happen to good people" would lead to unacceptable feelings of vulnerability. According to the just-world theory, then, when people are the victims of undesirable conditions, it is reassuring to believe that they deserved their fates. Attributing a fundamental moral failure to the stigmatized (Goffman, 1963; Jones *et al.*, 1984) may satisfy psychological needs by explaining why the stigmatized deserve a particular lot in life and why one does not deserve such a fate oneself. Empirical support for the belief in a just world is strong (Lerner, 1980; Lerner & Miller, 1978), but research has not directly tested its role in thinking about the stigmatized.

According to self-enhancement theory, people have a need to believe that the self is good and worthwhile. Because evaluations of the self are largely derived by comparing the self to other people (Festinger, 1954; see Gruder, 1977, for a review), it is important to identify others who can be regarded unfavorably to ensure enhanced evaluations of the self (Taylor, 1983; Wills, 1981). Thus, those who feel most unsure of their own worth should be most likely to identify and have negative stereotypes about members of stigmatized groups.

Considerable empirical support exists for the general hypothesis that evaluations of other social groups are related to evaluations of the self, such that low self-esteem individuals are more prejudiced (see Ashmore & Del Boca, 1976; Ehrlich, 1974; Wills, 1981; and Wylie, 1979, for reviews and discussion). However, low self-esteem individuals tend to be more negative in their evaluations of all targets, including the self, the in-group, others in general, and members of out-groups (Crocker & Schwartz, 1985). Thus, the prejudice of low self-esteem individuals appears to stem from a general negativity, rather than from a self-serving hostility against out-groups in particular.

THE COGNITIVE PERSPECTIVE

According to the cognitive view, categorization and stereotyping are normal consequences of the cognitive operations of the human mind (see Ashmore, 1981; Ashmore & Del Boca, 1976; Hamilton, 1976, 1979; Jones, 1982; Rothbart, 1981; and Taylor, 1981, for more extensive discussions). Although perceivers encounter a multitude of people who vary on a virtually infinite number of dimensions, the perceiver's information-processing capacities are limited (Fiske & Taylor, 1984). Consequently, people need to simplify and organize social information. Categorizing people on the basis of similarities and differences and developing generalizations about members of categories provide means of simplifying social information. According to the cognitive approach, the need to organize information in the social world means that if socially given category and belief systems did not exist, people would need to create them.

When category systems are cognitively constructed rather than socially given, what principles govern the development of categories? One such principle for objects in the natural world is that of the most information for the least cognitive effort (Rosch, 1981). Visual cues—such as those associated with skin color, physical disabilities, and group differences in dress and ornamentation—seem to be particularly important category markers. This may be due to their informational properties as salient, novel, and temporally primary stimuli (McArthur, 1982) as well as to their association with other meaningful behavioral, class, or cultural differences.

Once established on any grounds, these categories may influence the way perceivers organize and evaluate subsequent information about category members. For example, differences in physical appearance may give rise to widely held, negative, and extreme stereotypes (McArthur, 1982). Furthermore, mere categorization can result in the magnification of between-group differences and within-group similarities (Hamilton, 1979). Many stigmas, of course, are based on more significant and concrete characteristics. Therefore, it is not surprising that perceivers may overestimate the role of such characteristics in the personal and social lives of persons manifesting them, as a member of the general public might do, for example, in constructing a conception of what a person who is blind or paralyzed is like. In sum, there are a number of cognitive processes that may make use of apparent or real differences between groups as a basis for overgeneralized beliefs about what those differences mean.

IMPLICATIONS

Stigmatization is undoubtedly an overdetermined phenomenon. We have viewed it previously in this chapter as the result of social justifications for relations between groups, individually motivated needs, and natural cognitive tendencies to identify differences and construct generalizations that give order to a complex social world. These cognitive results and processes may influence each other and also interact with larger historical and social forces. For example, people who have a psychological need to stigmatize may be most likely to adopt and reinforce culturally given stereotypes. Waite's (1977) psychohistorical account of the development of Adolf Hitler's anti-Semitism illustrates this quite powerfully. Existing social relations may provide basic data that interact with individual motivational needs or cognitive tendencies. There are also both superficial and deeper attributes (e.g., appearance and physical disabilities, respectively) that perceivers may, on cognitive grounds, reliably elaborate in terms of group differences and stereotypes. It would not be surprising if there were equivalent

historical and cultural tendencies that also operate on these naturally salient attributes.

There are also interesting differences in social thought about
the stigmatized that may be associated with the source of information giving rise to that thought (Crocker, 1983). In other words,
the source of information upon which a stereotype is based may
affect the content and consequences of the stereotype. Cognitively
constructed stereotypes, which are often acquired through contact with individual members of a group, may emphasize characteristics that can be observed or easily inferred from behavior.
These may include appearance, typical behaviors, settings in
which group members are likely to be found, and social roles that
are enacted by group members. Socially given stereotypes, on the
other hand, often emphasize characteristics that cannot be directly observed and so cannot be easily disproven through contact
with group members. These stereotypes may include information
about motivations, intentions, and morality.

Socially given stereotypes may also be tied more directly to the
values and ideology of the culture. For example, the stereotype that
welfare recipients want something for nothing violates the value of
individualism in this country and may, consequently, arouse feelings of moral indignation (Kinder & Sears, 1981, 1985). In addition, stereotypes acquired through the socialization process are
more likely to be shared among the members of a culture. This can
result in a unified public opinion about the group and can influence public policies toward members of the group.

FUNCTIONING AND CONSEQUENCES
OF THE SOCIAL COGNITION OF STIGMA

We have seen that perceivers may bring preexisting social
thoughts about the stigmatized to interpersonal encounters with
and social discourse about them. This leads us to consider how
and when particular beliefs and cognitive processes operate to
influence such interactions. We turn now to survey ideas and
findings that may help to clarify the role of social cognition in
perceivers' responses to stigma. In particular, processes involved

in the cognitive recognition of a stigmatized person or group will be discussed, and social psychological analyses of the major cognitive and behavioral consequences of those processes will be reviewed.

THE COGNITIVE RECOGNITION OF STIGMA

For the social cognition of stigma to be of some consequence, it is necessary for a stigma to be recognized as relevant to an interaction. This involves, most often, the perception of some mark, the association of the person possessing the mark with an appropriate category of persons, and an elaboration of the meaning of that categorization in terms of beliefs, evaluations, and current cognitive operations. If the cues associated with a stigma are obvious, the category structure associated with those cues monolithic, and the beliefs associated with that category label strong and clear, then this recognition sequence may not be problematic for a perceiver. Similarly, if the relevance and nature of a stigma are indicated clearly in the explicit or imputed meanings of social discourse, then the recognition of a stigma is essentially completed by the social environment. If, however, external cues are ambiguous and/or internal meanings are manifold or poorly articulated—conditions thought more likely in the schematic model of social cognition discussed earlier—then the processes through which a stigma is recognized and defined become important objects of study in their own right.

The Perceptual Recognition of Stigma

Typically, the social cognition of stigma begins with the perceptual recognition of a distinctive stimulus. Some apparent stigma is noticed and then, if social norms allow, elicits continued attention (Langer, Taylor, Fiske, & Chanowitz, 1976). In many cases, stigmas are associated with observable signs that are among the most novel social stimuli a perceiver is likely to encounter (see Fiske & Taylor, 1984, and McArthur, 1982, for reviews). Thus, even if all other things (e.g., preexisting social meanings) were equal, individuals bearing the visual marks of various stigmas are more likely to be noticed in social encounters (McArthur, 1982).

Not all signs of stigmatizing conditions are so unambiguously or concretely given to perceivers. Many may be made salient by the situation. Perceivers may associate certain places, roles, or situations with particular stigmatized groups and may be prepared to identify relevant cues in those circumstances. For example, visitors to San Francisco may be more sensitive to supposed signs of homosexuality than they would be elsewhere. Contrasts in a context may also make some attributes more salient to perceivers. For example, a woman's gender is likely to be salient if she is the only woman in a group of males (see McArthur, 1981 and 1982; Taylor & Fiske, 1978, for reviews). Finally, some signs may be ambiguous and may prompt attempts to observe or elicit additional information to evaluate the person further.

The perception of a cue may have significant consequences in its own right. Noticing a cue may disrupt normal social cognition and behavior independently of associated attitudes (see Jones *et al.*, 1984, Chapter 2, for a review) and require careful self-monitoring on the part of the perceiver (Langer *et al.*, 1976). As discussed earlier, focusing on a visibly apparent cue may also influence the impressions formed of a marked person and the general development of a stereotype (McArthur, 1982). Finally, the fact that attention is drawn to a particular person and mark makes further elaborative cognitive activity on the part of the perceiver more likely.

The Categorization of Stigma

Cues, once noticed and observed, may give rise to attempts to label the persons bearing them. There are many circumstances under which this process is problematic. In particular, the criteria for category assignment may be ambiguous or the signs identifying status on critical dimensions nonobvious (Jones *et al.*, 1984). Also, multiple categories or subcategories may potentially apply to a stimulus person. For example, a Vietnam War veteran may be subcategorized as a war hero, regular soldier, traumatized victim, former POW, or mass murderer, and perceivers may feel, under certain circumstances, that it is necessary to use one of the more specific categories to direct their thinking and responses. Under these conditions, it is likely that perceivers seek and use additional stereotypic diagnostic indicators (in the example given, such signs as appearance, comments the veteran may have made about the war, and emotional demeanor) to determine subcategory membership.

Perceivers may also employ assumptions about the prevalence or significance of particular subgroups in a larger category in the absence of more diagnostic information (Ashmore, 1981). For example, a default assumption might be that most veterans of Vietnam were regular soldiers who have readjusted to civilian life. These default values may be in error, and such errors in categorization judgment rather than in belief content per se may be responsible for some stereotypic misconceptions. For example, when thinking about the general stimulus, "elderly persons," perceivers' responses may be based on references to the unrepresentative subcategory "sick old person" (Lutsky, 1983). The absence of specific diagnostic information, as in everyday passing discourse or numerous questionnaire studies, may also encourage perceivers to use a generalized level of categories that differs from the more specific ones elicited by social interaction with specific individuals.

The very fact that categorization occurs is a particularly prominent and important feature of the social cognition of stigma. Allport (1954), Goffman (1963), and Sartre (1948), among others, have all noted that persons who are stigmatized are described as distinct types of persons. Thinking about a person as a type of person using first-order categories of the form "X is a Y" (e.g., "X is a redhead") rather than in terms of particular attributes (e.g., "X has red hair") may have important consequences. Coding a person in this way distances the perceiver from the person perceived, insulating the former from the affective or cognitive implications of the status or state of the marked person. It also emphasizes within-category homogeneity (see Fiske & Taylor, 1984, and McArthur, 1982, for reviews) and the significance of the category-defining attribute over all others (Allport, 1954; Jones et al., 1984; Lutsky, 1983; Sartre, 1948).

Finally, as discussed shortly, a separation and labeling of a set of persons that implicitly conveys the message that "these people are fundamentally different" may be sufficient to elicit responses and invoke interpersonal strategies that alter interaction between stigmatized and nonstigmatized individuals, even in the absence of more specific expectations about the nature and meaning of a concrete difference.

The Cognitive Elaboration of Stigma

In earlier discussion, we raised the possibility that any one perceiver may hold multiple meanings for a specific stigma. How, then, do particular meanings become salient in individual interactions? In part, categorization mediates stereotype elaboration as it activates the beliefs and attitudes a perceiver holds about a specific category or subcategory. A few beliefs, strongly associated with the particular category used, may be highly accessible (Fazio, Powell, & Herr, 1983), but other beliefs may not be immediately activated or may remain undeveloped. What prompts an effort to identify or elaborate nonobvious beliefs and attitudes about the attitude object?

The demands and nature of the encounter may play an important role in the cognitive elaboration of stigma. Both the purposes of the perceiver and the social situation may influence the extent to which particular beliefs or attitudes are reconstructed or made salient (Snyder & Swann, 1976). Information that is needed for appropriate behavior and understanding will be sought from some source. In the absence of relevant, deep personal opinion—an absence that may be common, given the uncommonness of experience with those who are stigmatized—perceivers may be forced to respond in a "top-of-the-head" fashion using available social stereotypes (e.g., Taylor & Fiske, 1978). The information currently presented to a perceiver in an encounter may also stimulate or obviate an elaboration of beliefs about a stigma. Information that may be suggestive of some stereotypic association may interact with the stereotype and make it more salient. On the other hand, clear, concrete, and specific information about the particular

qualities of the individual person or interpersonal tasks encountered may direct a perceiver's attention away from the generalized
assumptions upon which he or she might otherwise rely.

The affective character of responses to stigmatized persons
may also prompt elaborative activity as perceivers attempt to understand and define their arousal in the presence of a stigmatized
individual (Jones *et al.*, 1984). Langer *et al.* (1976) suggest that
persons may sometimes confuse such discomfort with derogation
itself. This affect may arise from socialized associations to stigmatized stimuli. Alternatively, it is possible that a lack of association or elaborated meaning may give rise to such affective responses. Kelly (1955), for example, has argued that anxiety
results when perceivers sense that their cognitive construct systems do not adequately encompass experiences they are having.
In the case of stigma, given that perceivers assume that an individual or group is fundamentally different *in kind* from others in
their normal range of experience, the absence of well-developed
constructs about a stigmatized individual or category of persons
will give rise to the anxieties and consequent avoidant responses
or inappropriate behaviors that often characterize relations with
the stigmatized. For example, Scott (1969) vividly conveys the
uncertainties and anxieties that result from the lack of understanding that both sighted and blind persons have of each other
in interpersonal interaction. In sum, a lack of adequate cognitive
elaboration in the context of strong categorization may be responsible for a number of the most unfortunate consequences of the
social cognition of stigma.

COGNITIVE AND BEHAVIORAL CONSEQUENCES OF STIGMA

If a stereotype has been activated or expectations articulated,
then that cognitive content may have important consequences for
the subsequent processing of information about a stigmatized
individual or group and for related interpersonal behavior (see
Fiske & Taylor, 1984, and Hamilton, 1979, for extensive reviews).
Most social psychological models of these effects suggest that believing that something is true of a stigmatized person makes it

more likely that the perceiver holding the belief will act, have experiences, and think in ways that support that belief.

Cognitive Consequences of Stereotypes

Stereotypes can affect the processing of information about stigmatized individuals in several ways. They may influence what we notice in an encounter, how we evaluate ambiguous information, and how we remember an event or person. The evidence for these effects is reviewed extensively elsewhere (Jones, 1982). We will merely summarize the major findings of this literature.

Perceivers must attend selectively to complex social stimuli in their environments. Stereotypes guide this process by directing attention to information that is relevant to the stereotype. The information that is attended to must be interpreted or encoded, and stereotypes may be used to resolve the common inconsistencies or uncertainties of everyday social experience (e.g., Sagar & Schoenfeld, 1980). In general, perceivers tend to attribute behavior that is consistent with a stereotype to the underlying characteristics of the person behaving, whereas behavior that is inconsistent with an expectation is seen as caused by situational or temporary factors. This has been illustrated in research on perceivers' causal interpretations of male versus female success on stereotypically male tasks (e.g., Deaux & Emswiller, 1974). The same behavior performed by two persons may be evaluated quite distinctly when that behavior is associated with a particular category label (e.g., Langer & Abelson, 1974).

Encoded information is then stored in memory. Evidence suggests that stereotypic members of the category are linked in memory with the category label, whereas unstereotypic members may be linked to different categories (Rothbart & John, 1985). For example, a black doctor may be stored as an instance of a doctor rather than as an instance of a black. The information that has been encoded and stored in memory may subsequently be retrieved from memory. Information that is consistent with the stereotype is more likely to be recalled than inconsistent or irrelevant information (Stern et al., 1984). When information has been forgotten, the stereotype may also provide a cue for retrieving or guessing information that is consistent with the stereotype.

Behavioral Consequences of Stereotypes

How persons act in a situation is determined, in part, by their expectations concerning the consequences of potential courses of action (e.g., Fishbein & Ajzen, 1975). These, in turn, can be linked to stereotypes that persons hold about stigmatized persons and the responses those stigmatized persons are believed likely to make to the actor, and to beliefs about the likely evaluations of significant others concerning the actions contemplated. Reviews of the behavioral consequences of stereotypes in general (e.g., Fiske & Taylor, 1984; Hamilton, 1979) and of stereotypes about the stigmatized in particular (e.g., Jones *et al.*, 1984) develop this view in great detail. Again, we will only discuss it briefly here.

Given either of two conditions in the social cognition of stigma described in this chapter—the existence of strong negative evaluations of stigmatized persons and knowledge of general social rejection of them or the existence of a strong belief in the fundamental difference of a social group coupled with a lack of specific expectations about the group—it is likely that persons will avoid contact with stigmatized persons insofar as that is possible. (Of course, both conditions may be true; there may be individual perceiver or target-group differences in the character of social cognition.) Under the first set of assumptions, interaction with the stigmatized would be avoided due to anticipated interpersonal and normative consequences of such contact. Under the second condition, such interaction would be avoided due to the difficulties and anxieties associated with inadequate experiential grounds for understanding and smooth behavior.

When interaction with stigmatized persons does occur, for these and other reasons, the encounters are often likely to be difficult ones (see Jones *et al.*, 1984, for a review). Moreover, stereotypes may result in outcomes that fulfill the expectations of the stereotype. These "expectancy confirmation processes" have been analyzed in some detail (e.g., Darley & Fazio, 1980) and take a variety of forms. Perceivers holding the hypothesis that members of a stigmatized group are likely to have a certain disposition (e.g., some poor level of ability or tendency to respond antagonistically) may act in a manner that anticipates and elicits evidence of the expected disposition (e.g., by condescending to the stigmatized person or acting aggressively, respectively). That hypothesis might further affect the interpretations that both the actor and target place on each other's behavior, again in a manner that sustains initial expectations. For example, perceivers who believe that targets are striving to repudiate popular expectancies may be likely to attribute resulting behaviors to the target's special efforts rather than to his or her natural tendencies (Hilton & Darley, 1984).

Although many of the cognitive and behavioral consequences of stereotypes may result in confirmation of these stereotypes, the targets of such expectations will sometimes disconfirm the stereotype that others have of them (e.g., Swann & Ely, 1984). Thus, stereotypes about the stigmatized are not immutable, although they often resist change. In the next section, we consider how social thought about the stigmatized changes and identify some of the circumstances that are likely to bring about these changes.

CHANGING THE COGNITION OF STIGMA

The way perceivers think about stigma may have negative consequences for the stigmatized, and therefore it is important to understand how elements of that thinking can be changed. In an earlier section, we identified three psychological perspectives on the origins of social thought about the stigmatized: the sociocultural approach, the motivational approach, and the cognitive approach. Each of these perspectives offers some insights into how the cognition of stigma might be changed. We will consider each of them in turn, paying particular attention to new developments in the cognitive approach.

Sociocultural Analyses of Change

According to the sociocultural approach, what perceivers think about the stigmatized is acquired through the socialization process and is inextricably linked to the nature of intergroup relations. Therefore, either intervening in the socialization process or altering intergroup relations should produce cognitive change. Efforts to intervene in socialization processes have typically centered on removing blatantly stereotypic material from the books that children read and the television shows they watch. Of course, this requires the consent and cooperation of the creators of these materials and, therefore, may more often follow from changes in cultural stereotypes than precede such changes. Changing the ways that parents and other adults socialize children requires altering those adults' beliefs about the stigmatized. But how are the stereotypes of parents and other socializing agents to be changed?

It may be unreasonable to suppose that one can effectively change the stereotypes that are communicated through the socialization process without also changing the nature of relations between the stigmatized and the nonstigmatized on which cultural wisdom is based. In experimental and field studies, it has been shown that manipulating the nature of intergroup relations can have a major impact on the attitudes that group members have toward each other (Sherif et al., 1961). For example, racial stereotypes have been reduced in "jigsaw" classrooms, where schoolchildren work together toward common goals rather than competing with each other for grades and the attention of the teacher (Aronson & Bridgeman, 1979).

Motivational Analyses of Change

The need to protect the ego against unacceptable sexual and aggressive impulses, the need to believe in a just and predictable world, and the need for self-enhancement each serve as a motivational impetus to derogate the stigmatized. The motivational approach suggests that changing the social cognition of stigma requires either changing the motivations of individuals or changing how those motivations are satisfied. Unfortunately, the types of deep-seated and generalized motivations that have been posited to lead to prejudice are extraordinarily difficult to change.

Each of these motivational approaches suggests that people satisfy their psychological needs by derogating members of outgroups who are dissimilar to themselves. Changing the way the stigmatized are perceived—specifically, by redefining group boundaries such that the stigmatized are identified as part of the in-group rather than as an out-group—might, then, produce changes in how the stigmatized are stereotyped. For example, research on the belief in a just world has shown that victims are less likely to be derogated if the perceiver expects to be in the victim's position at a later time or if the perceiver expects to interact with the victim in an intimate or sharing way (see Lerner, 1980, for a review).

COGNITIVE ANALYSES OF CHANGE

The cognitive analysis suggests that cognitive change occurs by changing the content of stereotypes, by changing the way that stereotypes are used in processing information about members of a category, or by changing the categorization process itself. Evidence that a stereotype is wrong should eventually lead to adjustment of stereotypic generalizations. This suggests that exposing people to information about members of stigmatized groups who do not fit the perceiver's stereotype about those groups should lead to stereotype change. Unfortunately, however, exposure to information about individual members of a group who violate a stereotype does not always lead to changes in generalizations about the category as a whole (Cook, 1984; Rothbart & John, 1985).

In order to understand the effects of disconfirming information, we need a more detailed analysis of the cognitive processes involved in belief change. Recall that the schematic approach suggests that social categories (and their associated stereotypes) are structured in memory, so that relatively specific, subordinate categories are subsumed by more general superordinate categories. Thus, evidence about unstereotypic group members can be accommodated by the creation of more specific, differentiated category structures to account for both the individuals who fit the stereotype and those who do not fit the stereotype (the exceptions to the rule). For example, the stereotype that women are emotional may accommodate information about a few very unemotional women through the development of a subcategory of "cold women" that accounts for some subset of the superordinate category of women (Ashmore & Del Boca, 1981; Deaux, Winton, Crowley, & Lewis, 1985; Taylor, 1981). This development of subcategories may "insulate" or protect the superordinate stereotype from change because disconfirming individuals who are identified as exceptions to the rule will have less impact on impressions of the group as a whole.

When will disconfirming information lead to a change in the "default value" or typical attributes of the group as a whole, and when will it lead to the development of a more differentiated category structure? One factor that appears to be important is whether a fixed amount of disconfirming information is concentrated within a very few group members or dispersed across more members of the group. A few group members who dramatically disconfirm the stereotype of their group may draw attention, but they are more likely to be subtyped as exceptions than are a larger number of individuals who, in many ways, are typical group members but who each show one or two stereotype-inconsistent attributes (Weber & Crocker, 1983).

A second factor that may influence whether exposure to individuals who violate the stereotype will result in stereotype change is the content of the stereotype—specifically, whether the stereotypic attributes are disconfirmable. Some stereotypes may be quite difficult to disprove because they lack either logical disconfirmability or practical disconfirmability (Crocker, Fiske, & Taylor, 1984; Jones et al., 1984; Rothbart & Park, 1985). A logically disconfirmable stereotype specifies what attributes or behaviors would contradict the stereotype and would prove it incorrect. A logically undisconfirmable stereotype is vague about what behavior would contradict the stereotype.

This notion of logical disconfirmability may explain why imputations of immorality to the stigmatized are so persistent (Goffman, 1963). Occasional lapses into immoral behavior are sufficient to define a person as immoral (Reeder & Brewer, 1979). Thus, stereotypes that the stigmatized are morally inferior lack logical disconfirmability because no amount of moral behavior can prove that a person who is stereotyped as immoral is actually moral.

The second kind of disconfirmability is practical disconfirmability. Given that there are behaviors that could prove the stereotype wrong, how likely is it that the perceiver will have the opportunity to observe such behaviors? If the perceiver never has contact with members of the stigmatized group, then he or she will have no opportunity to observe that the stereotype is incorrect. Even with contact, if the behavior is something that occurs very rarely (e.g., heroic acts that would contradict an imputation of cowardice) or occurs in private, then the perceiver will likely hold fast to an erroneous stereotype.

Given the difficulties with directly changing the content of at least some stereotypes about the stigmatized, it might be more productive to concentrate on changing whether and how stereotypes are used in processing information about specific members of stigmatized groups. Unfortunately, this topic has received little attention from researchers. Nonetheless, based on the available evidence, there appear to be some conditions that might alter or minimize the impact of stereotypes on processing information about individual members of stigmatized groups.

The goals of the perceiver may affect the extent to which stereotypes are used. When perceivers are motivated to be accurate in their judgments of another, such as when their outcomes are dependent on the other, then perceivers will attend more to information that is inconsistent with their initial impressions (Erber & Fiske, 1984). Thus, stereotyping may be reduced when the outcomes of the nonstigmatized depend on the behavior of the stigmatized.

Both the perceiver's goals in a particular situation and the kinds of information available to the perceiver have been shown to influence the effects of stereotypes on judgments about individuals. When the perceiver's task is to predict the future behavior of a member of a stereotyped group in some domain (e.g., assertive behavior) and the perceiver has available individuating information about that specific group member's past behavior in that domain, judgments about the individual group member seem to be more influenced by the individuating information than by the group stereotype (Locksley, Borgida, Brekke, & Hepburn, 1980; Locksley, Hepburn, & Ortiz, 1982; Rasinski, Crocker, & Hastie, 1985). Thus, providing perceivers with relevant individuating information about specific members of stigmatized groups may lessen their use of stereotypes in making judgments about those individuals.

Yet a third way to change stereotyping that is suggested by a cognitive analysis is changing the assignment of individuals to categories, such that perceivers organize the social world in ways that are not based on stigmatizing attributes. To satisfy the perceiver's need for cognitive efficiency, the new category system must facilitate information processing as well as the old system. Using more valid but less visually accessible bases for categorization may, however, require more cognitive effort and conflict with the perceiver's need to simplify the information-processing task.

Alternatively, the boundaries of existing categories might be changed. By changing the boundaries of in-group membership so that stigmatized individuals are regarded as "one of us," the detrimental effects for the stigmatized of in-group favoritism and derogation of out-groups may be reduced. For example, recent research reported in Brewer and Miller (1984) indicates that cooperative interaction between in-group and out-group members modifies intergroup perception only when the setting deemphasizes the in-group/out-group categories, either by emphasizing individual differences orthogonal to those categories or by introducing goals irrelevant to the intergroup divisions.

What do these approaches suggest about the conditions that facilitate change in the social cognition of stigma? A common thread through these analyses is that when the stigmatized and nonstigmatized interact in situations of cooperative interdependence, stereotype change may follow. Cooperative interdependence has multiple effects. First, according to the sociocultural approach, it changes the exploitive relationship between the stigmatized and the nonstigmatized and therefore eliminates the sociocultural motivation for stereotyping. Second, it may increase the perceived similarity between the stigmatized and the nonstigmatized because the two groups share common goals. Thus, the stigmatized become one of "us" rather than "them," and consequently the perceivers' psychological needs are no longer satisfied by derogating the stigmatized. Third, cooperative interdependence should not only change the kinds of information that perceivers learn about the stigmatized, it may also change the way that perceivers categorize the stigmatized and process information about them.

CONCLUSIONS: COGNITIVE APPROACHES IN THE STUDY OF STIGMA

The questions we have considered in this chapter have been fundamental ones. How and what do people think when they respond to stigmas? What are the social psychological sources of this thought? What are its consequences for social behavior? How can this thought be changed? We have suggested that in many cases the social cognition of stigmas may be channeled by the biases of well-developed systems of stereotypes, but that in others a simple and strong perception of difference "in kind," in the kind of being or category of person another is thought to represent, may evoke the cognitive and behavioral responses associated with stigmas. We have also attempted to advance a cognitive analysis of stigma that integrates the study of attitudes about stigmatized groups with the study of cognitive processes or how those attitudes may be used or evoked under particular conditions. We have suggested that understanding how previously held information and currently received information influence each other may illuminate some of the more pernicious and intractable characteristics of stigmas. In particular, we have seen that a number of psychological tendencies operate to reinforce or reestablish the general phenomenon of stigma as well as its current manifestations in specific social practices and beliefs. Obviously, however, what we have presented is a general sketch of an approach to stigma illustrated with specific examples. We cannot now make strong claims about the cognitive character of responses to stigma.

Our arguments have also emphasized distinctly psychological factors in social cognition that may influence the development and functioning of the social response labeled "stigma." This suggests that specific features of stigma may be constrained or facilitated by psychological dynamics and that those features may be misinterpreted, at least in part, as outcomes of cultural or economic forces alone. Stigmas may be sustained by natural cognitive biases; they may serve important personal functions; they may be reinforced for reasons other than or in addition to social and historical ones. At the same time, these psychological effects interact with larger forces as persons encounter a given social and existential world. It is this multidimensionality of the phenomenon that makes it so challenging to understand and so refractory to reform.

CHAPTER 7

Stigma and Interpersonal Relationships

Frederick X. Gibbons

Stigma has been and continues to be a topic of interest to people from a wide variety of disciplines with many different perspectives. If there is one point upon which scholars from diverse backgrounds can agree, however, it is that there is no single common experience associated with the process of stigmatization. There is likely to be nearly as much variability among a group of people with a particular stigma, phenomenologically, as there is across groups of people with different types of stigmas. Some people acquire stigmas, for example, whereas for others a stigmatizing condition may be present from birth. For some people, a stigma can be permanently disruptive, whereas others seem to adjust quite quickly. In each case, the social psychological impact of the stigma is likely to be somewhat different.

More than anything else, stigmatization is a social phenomenon. As stigmas are created, develop, and affect those who have them, each stage involves relationships among people. In this respect, the topic of stigma lends itself readily to a social psychological analysis. In this chapter, I will examine certain key psychological factors associated with stigmatization that have an effect on the social lives and social relationships of people with different types of stigmas. The primary emphasis will be on intimate relationships, or couples, of which two different types will be considered: those involving a stigmatized and a nonstigmatized person ("mixed" relationships), and those consisting of two stigmatized people.

Most of the examples presented here reflect research in the areas of mental retardation and physical disabilities. This research also serves as a basis for the discussion of other types of stigma. Although generalizing from one stigmatized group to another is at best a risky proposition, there are certain social experiences and psychological factors that form a basic part of the stigmatization process, and are, therefore, common to many different types of stigma. These will be pointed out wherever they are thought to exist. In addition, I will discuss how other factors (e.g. gender, social norms, legal trends) interact with stigmas to inhibit or promote interpersonal relations.

Before beginning, it would be worthwhile to put the discussion into some historical perspective. The vast majority of the research and theory presented here has appeared only within the last 20 years. In addition, so many important social and legal changes have taken place in recent years that it would be safe to say that a chapter such as this one could not have been written as recently as 25 years ago. Prior to the implementation of these changes, restrictions on the social behavior of most stigmatized persons were so severe that few of them were capable of becoming involved in social relationships. The relationships that did develop bore little resemblance to those of nonstigmatized persons and therefore received little attention from social scientists. All of that has changed. It is worth noting, however, that much of what will be discussed reflects the social and psychological *effects* of modern laws and social movements, rather than the historical and cultural *antecedents* that led up to them.

STIGMA AND MORALITY

According to Goffman (1963), the process of stigmatization is inextricably bound up with the concept of morality. The primary issue in the eyes of nonstigmatized persons, Goffman believes, is one of responsibility: What or who caused the stigma to develop in the first place? More often than not, the blame for the stigma's existence is attributed, at least in part, to the personality of the stigmatized person himself or herself. It is assumed that the person has committed some immoral act and that the stigma is punishment for this moral transgression. By implication, those who remain morally pure will avoid the punishment of stigmatization.

Attributing responsibility to stigmatized persons for their condition helps to distance an observer from those persons and from the stigma itself. It also helps to reduce the threat associated with the stigma—that being the possibility that it could happen to anyone (cf. Vann, 1970). This is the reasoning behind Melvin Lerner's just-world theory (1980). According to the theory, most people believe that the world is a just place, in which people generally receive what they deserve. It is assumed, for example, that people who are rich and successful must have earned their wealth, and, by the same token, those who are poor or unsuccessful, or those who have lost what they once had, must have done something to deserve their misfortune. Again, there is a definite overtone of morality here. For some stigmatized persons (e.g., ex-convicts), the crime and the punishment are obvious, but for many others, such as accident victims or people with mental retardation, culpability must be created in the mind of the observer. Whether guilty of real or imagined crimes, however, the stigmatized person must often bear the burden of moral responsibility for the "mark" (Jones, Farina, Hastorf, Markus, Miller, & Scott, 1984), and this label may very well be more difficult to cope with than the stigma itself.

The social consequences of the morality stereotype are evident historically in the way stigmatized people have been treated by others in their communities. Due to the moral "taint," and perhaps out of a fear of contamination, stigmatized people have traditionally been isolated from the community, and segregation—either de facto or de jure—has been the norm for ages (Goffman, 1963). Moreover, even though progressive social developments of the last two decades (e.g., the "deinstitutionalization" of disabled persons mandated by Public Law 94-142) have significantly increased contact between stigmatized and nonstigmatized persons, this contact is still mostly of a functional or business nature rather than social, and it seldom occurs on an equal-status level.

In mainstreamed classes, for example, disabled children are often socially isolated, having contact primarily with other disabled children. (See Sigelman & Singleton in this volume for a review of the literature.) Several theorists have suggested that this occurs because stigmatization has a "negative halo effect," which means that being associated with a stigmatized person can in itself be stigmatizing (Goffman, 1963; Wright, 1983). Naturally, most ablebodied children are not willing to take this risk, especially if they believe that their own status in the group is tenuous (Richardson, 1983).

If nonstigmatized people do have occasion to interact with stigmatized others, the communication is frequently distorted and negative (Edelsky & Rosegrant, 1981; Jones *et al.*, 1984). Certain topics, such as current events, or jobs, or families, are seldom discussed in the presence of stigmatized people; instead, the discourse is usually restricted to task-oriented issues or such topics as the weather (Coleman, 1983). Interactions involving physically disabled children are terminated sooner and more abruptly than interactions with other children, and in most cases disabled children are not permitted to function as "normal" or active participants in the conversation. This type of experience is not likely to leave disabled children with positive feelings about interpersonal relations with others who are not disabled.

This pattern of behavior is not likely to change much as children grow up, either. Like children, most nonstigmatized adults do not seek out relationships with stigmatized persons. Again, a primary reason for this is that adults have many opportunities to pursue relationships with people who are similar to themselves and are not stigmatized, so there is little incentive to engage in social interaction with a stigmatized person. The risks—ranging from guilt by association to actual fear of contamination—are too great. As Dunkel-Schetter and Wortman (1982) have pointed out, cancer victims often find themselves shunned by others who, at some level, fear contagion even though they probably realize the impossibility of disease transmission. The same kind of experience has been reported by persons with stigmas of character, such as prostitutes, divorcees, or unwed mothers, who believe they are avoided out of a similar fear—that of moral contamination.

Perhaps the clearest evidence of the morality factor can be seen in the way that different cultures have dealt with the issue of sexuality among stigmatized persons. The concepts of stigma and sexuality have, almost universally, been thought to be mutually exclusive (Wright, 1983). Physically disabled people, in particular, often complain that others do not or cannot allow them the usual freedoms of sexual expression. Traditionally, they have been seen as nonsexual beings, apparently because it is thought either that they cannot perform sexually, or that they should not, lest they produce more disabled persons. In general, a fear of sexual activity among stigmatized persons—either with each other or, worse yet, with nonstigmatized persons—has historically been a primary reason why they have been isolated from society and segregated, by sex, from each other.

A Theory of Ambivalence

In spite of the way that stigmatized persons have been treated historically, it would be inaccurate to simply conclude that they are universally despised by those who are not stigmatized. In fact, recent theoretical and empirical evidence suggests that attitudes toward stigmatized persons may not be nearly as negative as their treatment might indicate (cf. Katz, 1981). In this regard, a number of theorists have suggested that the main reason why nonstigmatized people avoid those who are stigmatized is not because of a strong distaste but instead because they are confused about the nature of their own feelings. The confusion stems from the fact that nonstigmatized people maintain both negative *and* positive feelings toward those who are stigmatized.

One of the leading proponents of this "ambivalence" notion is Irwin Katz (1981). Katz believes that members of the majority are likely to feel sympathy for an individual minority group member or disabled person, as well as some admiration for the courage the person has displayed in coping with her or his problems. At the same time, however, they experience some aversion toward the stigma itself as well as feelings of differentness. Due to this inner conflict, outward behavior toward stigmatized individuals can vary considerably, apparently as a function of the particular situation. If the context should happen to present the disabled individual in a positive light, then the person is likely to receive favorable reactions from others—more favorable than would be the case if she or he were not stigmatized. Just the opposite may occur, however, if the situation should present the person negatively (cf. Gibbons, Stephan, Stephenson & Petty, 1980). Understandably, the inconsistent behavior associated with the ambivalent attitude can be confusing for both the disabled and the nondisabled person. Thus, interactions between stigmatized persons and nonstigmatized persons have been characterized as uncomfortable or, at worst, aversive (cf. Wright, 1983), and this seems to be the case for both parties (Comer & Piliavin, 1972). It is not surprising, then, that in the past the two groups have simply chosen to avoid one another.

A Legal Mandate

So thorough has been the exclusion of stigmatized people from the mainstream of society that until fairly recently the possibility of social interaction with other members of society would have been unthinkable. Only within the last 30 years has the humane treatment of mentally retarded and mentally ill persons been an active social issue, and the notion of creating therapeutic (rather than just custodial) environments in facilities for disabled persons is an even newer concept. In fact, the current movement toward integration of disabled people into the community and, in general, toward "normalization" of life-styles for developmentally disabled people received most of its impetus from Public Law (PL) 94-142, which was passed only 10 years ago. This legislation, often referred to as the "mainstreaming law," mandated that all disabled persons have a right to receive services (e.g., an education) in an environment that could be considered "least restrictive." The enactment of this legislation (and also the Rehabilitation Act of 1973, PL 93–112) has had a tremendous impact on the social lives of stigmatized persons and on the social attitudes of nonstigmatized people as well.

One reason that the law has made such a difference is that it specifically prohibits any form of environmental constraint that could unnecessarily restrict normal social development. Thus, artificial segregation by gender and prevention of normal social interactions between men and women are forbidden. Moreover, because the state hospitals for the disabled are themselves seen as a "restrictive" environment, many people have been taken out of them and placed in the community. Of course, the more time that stigmatized persons spend outside the institution, the more opportunities they have for social contact with nonstigmatized persons. Consequently, along with the increased visibility of disabled persons in the community, there has also been a tremendous increase in the number and types of relationships that have developed between disabled and ablebodied individuals. These relationships are more likely to involve equal-status participants and in general are of a very different nature than was the case 25 years ago.

RELATIONSHIPS BETWEEN DISABLED
PERSONS AND OTHERS

In examining the nature of relationships between disabled persons and those who are not disabled, three factors seem to be of primary importance. The first factor is whether it is the male or the female who is stigmatized. "Mixed" marriages in which the female is disabled are more common, presumably because they do not challenge traditional sex roles for men and women. The older, more capable male can watch over the younger, more dependent female, often in a benefactor–protégée type of relationship (Goffman, 1963). In contrast, when it is the male who is stigmatized, the disability may interfere with his capacity to maintain economic independence and, in particular, to provide for his family. Consequently, relationships of this kind are likely to experience more stress and face more difficulties.

The second important factor to be considered is when the stigma was acquired. If the onset of the stigma preceded the development of the relationship, the chances again are greater that the stigmatized person will be female. Such relationships seem to be more acceptable to others and to the couple as well, and therefore are more likely to develop. If the stigmatizing condition is a physical disability, for example, this type of stigma interferes more (psychologically) with the male sex role than with the female (Wright, 1983).

The third major factor affecting the relationships of stigmatized persons is how the stigma itself is viewed by the stigmatized person and his or her partner. In other words, do the two people maintain the same ambivalence toward the stigma that characterizes others' attitudes? The importance of this factor, especially for the stigmatized partner, is illustrated in Robert Edgerton's (1967) discussion of the social lives of formerly institutionalized mentally retarded persons. Edgerton was interested in the way these mentally disabled people were attempting to integrate or reintegrate into the community after their discharge from the institution. The thing that impressed him most was their desire (almost an obsession) to avoid being identified as mentally retarded and to "pass" as nonretarded. Recognizing the disgrace associated with their particular stigma, these retarded persons invested considerable energy in hiding their retarded identity from those in the community. As a way to cope with their stigmatizing condition, they simply denied its existence.

This desire to pass was especially clear among the formerly institutionalized women. For them, association with the institution and the mental retardation label was something to be avoided at all costs. This also meant avoidance, where possible, of other retarded persons, or anyone who might somehow link them with the institution. At the same time, the women sought associations with nonretarded persons, at least in part because they believed this would facilitate passing. Retarded women were much more successful at finding nonretarded persons, as companions as well as guardians or benefactors, than were the men. In fact, many of the marriages that these women entered into evolved out of a kind of benefactor–protégée type of relationship. In contrast, the men were much less likely to have nonretarded persons as benefactors or as spouses than were the women.

The desire among some stigmatized persons to "pass" as normal, or to "cover" (i.e., disguise) their stigma (Goffman, 1963) is likely to have a profound effect on the types of social relationships in which they choose to become involved. Passing and covering allow disabled persons to enter into the mainstream of community life. At the same time, however, they require that associations with other similarly disabled persons, or anyone who can link them with the stigma, be avoided. In making choices of this nature, the person is saying something about his or her perception of his or her own disability—he or she is rejecting it and devaluing it in much the same way that nonstigmatized persons may do (Lewin, 1948). In so doing, he or she is denying himself or herself many of the benefits—the social support, social services, social relationships, and the like—that come with an acceptance of the condition itself and, more importantly, others who have it. In the long run, that may be the most significant cost associated with the process of passing. As Goffman (1963) has suggested, stigmatized people experience some of the same ambivalent feelings toward others like themselves, as do nonstigmatized persons. How that ambivalence is resolved will determine, to a large extent, the nature of their relationships with their peers.

In summary, there are a number of factors that historically have worked against the development of normal relationships between stigmatized and nonstigmatized persons. Traditionally, stigmatized persons have been socially and physically segregated from childhood, and the interactions they have with nonstigmatized persons tend to be stilted and often take place under circumstances that highlight rather than downplay the salience of the stigma (e.g., in special classrooms, in or near hospitals or institutions). Such situations make interactions difficult and are not likely to promote long-term involvement. Nonetheless, relationships between stigmatized and nonstigmatized persons do develop, a common example being that involving a benefactor and a stigmatized protégée. Romantic or intimate relationships of this nature are relatively rare, but those that have developed appear to be healthy and capable of withstanding the problems that the stigma creates (cf. Brighouse, 1946). Finally, and perhaps what is most important, federal legislation of the past 20 years has resulted in a tremendous increase in the amount of contact that disabled persons have with others in the community, and consequently in the number and variety of relationships that they can become involved in with others who are not disabled. Moreover, there is every indication that this trend will continue during the next 20 years.

RELATIONSHIPS AMONG STIGMATIZED PERSONS

Increased contact between stigmatized and nonstigmatized persons has not been the only consequence of the various disability social movements of the last 20 years. By reducing the number of social restrictions that traditionally have been placed on stigmatized persons, these laws have also resulted in a significant increase in the amount of social contact that stigmatized people have with each other. And that contact is now occurring in much more socially liberal environments. It is surprising, however, that this increase in social contact has not been accompanied by a corresponding increase in relevant psychological research. Nonetheless, the topic of how stigmatized persons relate to one another is certainly one that has considerable relevance to a general discussion of the stigmatization process. In order to examine this issue, I shall begin with an examination of how stigmatized persons view themselves and others who share their stigma.

SELF-ESTEEM

After observing and interviewing mentally retarded persons about their interactions with others in the community, Edgerton (1967) had little difficulty in understanding why they were so intent upon avoiding their label and on passing as nonretarded. In his opinion, the stigma associated with mental retardation is very severe. He states:

> The label of mental retardation not only serves as a humiliating, frustrating, and discrediting stigma in the conduct of one's life in the community, but it also serves to lower one's self-esteem to such a nadir of worthlessness that the life of a person so labeled is scarcely worth living. (p. 145)

The zeal with which the retarded persons in the Edgerton survey pursued their goal of passing suggested that they were aware of the stigma associated with their label. Subsequent research has provided further evidence of this awareness among mentally retarded persons (Budoff & Siperstein, 1980; Gibbons, 1981). Similar surveys with blind persons led Scott (1969) to conclude that they, too, have a strong idea of how others perceive them. Blind people clearly sense that they are evaluated negatively—more negatively, in fact, than may actually be the case (Scott, 1969). In general, however, the perception that stigmatized people have about others' attitudes toward them is fairly accurate and that means they recognize that others view them in a negative light. This being the case, one might expect that the low status that stigmatized people typically maintain in society would be reflected in equally low or negative self-concepts, much as Edgerton has suggested.

It is surprising that the existing research indicates that the self-esteem of stigmatized persons, including those with mental retardation, may not be as low as Edgerton (1967) thought. Although some studies have found evidence of negative self-concepts among different stigmatized groups, the majority have found little or no difference from the general population, and there are even a few studies indicating a positive effect. Several studies of retarded children, for example, have found no difference between them and their nonretarded counterparts with respect to self-concept. In a few cases (e.g., Fine & Caldwell, 1967; Willy & McCandless, 1973), positive discrepancies have been found. These rather puzzling results led the authors (Willy & McCandless, 1973) to conclude that retarded children's self-concepts were "inaccurate, inflated, and unrealistic." Similar and also counterintuitive results have been found among children with physical disabilities (Coleman, 1973), epilepsy (Arluck, 1941), and blindness (Williams, 1972).

How is it possible that stigmatized persons can maintain some semblance of positive self-regard when the behavior of most people toward them is so decidedly negative? Obviously, this is a complex issue, and there are a number of factors involved, including the nature of the stigma, its visibility, and how debilitating it is. Some types of stigma are simply less stigmatizing than others, and it is easy to understand why they might not have much psychological effect on people who have them. Other types of stigma are potentially very debilitating socially, however, and it would be enlightening to learn how people with severe stigmas are able to maintain a relatively favorable self-concept under these circumstances. To investigate this process more closely, I will again focus on interpersonal behavior, specifically the social comparison behaviors that stigmatized persons engage in. I will examine two types of social comparisons that seem to have a similar, positive effect on self-esteem but that involve very different processes.

SOCIAL COMPARISON

In his original statement of social comparison theory, Festinger (1954) suggested that people engage in social comparison with others in order to find out more about themselves. Information can be obtained about almost any aspect of the self, and the comparison can produce almost any type of outcome, favorable or unfavorable, depending on who is chosen as a target for comparison. Usually people choose others who are like themselves, primarily because similar others are most likely to provide useful comparative information. Presumably the same tendencies hold true for people who are stigmatized. Thus, we would expect physically disabled persons, for example, to seek out others who are similarly disabled for purposes of comparison, especially when the comparison involves physical abilities or behaviors that are directly related to the stigma. Comparing with ablebodied persons on these dimensions would, for the most part, be pointless and perhaps upsetting. In this regard, a study by Strang, Smith, and Rogers (1978) illustrates the importance of social comparison among disabled children.

Strang *et al.* examined the self-concept of mentally disabled children who had been placed in one of three academic groups: segregated with other disabled children, mainstreamed with disabled children, or integrated part time with both groups. Results indicated that the third group, as a whole, had the most favorable self-concepts. The main reason, according to the authors, was that in terms of social comparison possibilities, these students experienced the best of both worlds. They could compare themselves (favorably) with their disabled peers on academic matters but also feel as if they belonged socially with the nondisabled majority.

This process, which is referred to as "selective comparison" (Taylor, Wood, & Lichtman, 1983), can occur essentially in one of two ways. One way is for an individual to identify what she or he thinks is a particularly positive trait or ability in herself or himself and use that as the primary focus of comparison with others in the reference group. The other method is to seek out people who appear to have less of the trait or to be doing worse at the behavior and choose them as the primary reference group. This latter technique, which has been called "downward social comparison" (or just "downward comparison," cf. Wills, 1981), seems to be prevalent among some stigmatized persons (Taylor *et al.*, 1983). It also appears to have a significant impact on the self-esteem as well as the social relationships of many stigmatized persons.

Downward Comparison

In a recent theoretical discussion of the downward comparison process, Wills (1981) suggested that one of the primary motives behind this type of social comparison is the desire to boost threatened self-esteem (cf. Brickman & Bulman, 1977). It is not surprising, then, that stigmatized persons, whose self-esteem is continually threatened, would be particularly inclined to indulge in this process (Goffman, 1963, p. 107). For example, Edgerton (1967) has suggested that some institutionalized mentally retarded persons engage in a form of downward comparison. It is his belief that the institution provides higher level retarded persons with the opportunity for self-aggrandizement through comparison with others who appear to be more severely retarded—a behavior similar to that of some of the mentally disabled children in the Strang *et al.* (1978) study. More recent research indicates that downward comparison is also prevalent among persons who have been stigmatized by some kind of injury or misfortune (e.g., accident or cancer victims; see Taylor *et al.*, 1983). In an attempt to cope with their problems, these people look for others—or, if others are unavailable, imaginary persons—who appear to be more severely stigmatized, for purposes of comparison.

If this pattern holds true, then we might expect such comparisons to occur within a variety of stigmatized groups: mildly retarded with profoundly retarded, octogenarians with nonagenarians, outpatients with inpatients, and the like. No matter what stigma a person may have, there will always be someone else who has it worse, and that can be reassuring.

Downward Comparison: An Empirical Example. In a recent study of the downward comparison process, Gibbons (1985) presented retarded persons, who lived either in an institution or a community group home, with pictures of different people. Half of the people were said to be retarded, half not. The subjects were then asked to evaluate the people in the pictures in terms of how physically attractive, socially appealing (i.e., as a dating or marriage partner), and socially successful they seemed. In a subsequent interview, the retarded persons were asked to evaluate themselves on the same dimensions. As in previous research (cf. Gibbons, 1981), subjects showed a clear preference for the nonretarded targets and evaluated them more favorably in almost all of the social behavior categories. Another pattern of results emerged in the self-evaluations. On many items, such as intelligence and friendliness, subjects rated themselves as favorably as the nonretarded targets and more favorably than the similar (or retarded) persons—evidence, then, of downward comparison. Their self *social* behavior items (e.g., dating success or marriage likelihood) differed considerably, however, as these ratings were just as negative as those given to the retarded targets. In short, these stigmatized subjects were very pessimistic about both their own and other retarded persons' chances for a normal social life.

One other finding in this research is worth noting. The tendency to derogate the retarded person was by far the most pronounced among the women living in the community, but only when the target was a male. This finding is consistent with Edgerton's (1967) observations that the formerly institutionalized women in his study were the most interested in passing and in avoiding other retarded persons. Retarded women living in the community are more likely than those in institutional settings to be socially active (cf. Kleinberg & Galligan, 1983) and to have contact with nonretarded men. This contact can make their own stigmatized

status (and their ambivalence) as well as the status of their retarded male peers more salient to them, thereby increasing their
desire to pass and to avoid retarded men.

These data are interesting primarily because they illustrate
some of the advantages as well as the disadvantages associated
with the downward comparison process. On the one hand, it appears that comparison with others who are more severely stigmatized can help to maintain or even to boost self-esteem; there is
no clear evidence in this or other studies that retarded persons
have chronic self-esteem problems. Unfortunately, however, the
process often occurs at the expense of their (opinions of their)
peers and eventually their own social behavior. The fact that they
were so pessimistic about their own chances for social success is
actually a consequence of the comparison process. That is, if their
opinions of their retarded peers—the people with whom they are
most likely to socialize, date, and marry—are very negative, then
it stands to reason that they are not going to be very optimistic
about their own social prospects. In effect, for this particular type
of stigma, those who have the stigma may feel just as negatively
about others who have it as do nonstigmatized persons (Lewin
[1948] calls this negative group concept "negative chauvinism").

In sum, downward comparison appears to be an effective
strategy that is often employed by people with certain types of
stigmas as a means of coping with their stigmatizing condition. It
is also the case, however, that the motivation to engage in this
process is based to a large extent on the recognition of the devalued status of the stigma. By derogating others like themselves,
stigmatized people are derogating the stigma and, to some extent,
accepting the societal perception of it. In this sense, the motivation behind downward comparison is very similar to that which
causes some persons to want to pass as nonstigmatized. In the
long run, this motivation is likely to interfere with the interpersonal relationships of group members and with the social behavior of the group as a whole.

Before concluding that social comparison is causing psychological problems for stigmatized people in general, however, it is
important to keep in mind that the example here has been limited
primarily to that of mental retardation. and mental retardation is

perhaps the most severe form of social stigma (Shears & Jensema, 1969). In fact, a survey of the literature suggests that, although downward comparison is prevalent among persons whose stigma is quite severe, it is certainly not characteristic of all stigmatized persons.

AVOIDANCE

Research with persons who are hard of hearing (Higgins, 1980) has indicated that they choose to *avoid* others who are actually deaf (cf. also Warfield, 1948). Similarly, Wright (1983) has observed that people who have been recently disabled will often stay away from others who are more severely disabled, whereas people with visual impairment try to avoid those who are blind (Criddle, 1953). None of these groups, then, seems to be particularly interested in seeking out similar others for purposes of downward comparison. Instead, they choose to avoid those who are more severely stigmatized, apparently because associating with them is likely to interfere with their efforts to pass as normal (cf. Goffman, 1963). For people who are less severely stigmatized, passing is easier when they are alone or with others who are not stigmatized. Thus, many mildly stigmatized persons (e.g., obese children, Richardson, 1983, mildly retarded adults, Gibbons, 1981, and persons with impaired vision, Criddle, 1953) report the same or very similar sociometric preferences to those of nonstigmatized persons. That is, they tend to prefer the company of others who are not stigmatized and to avoid anyone who can link them with the label they would like to shed.

Lateral Comparison

In contrast, there is considerable evidence that people with more highly visible stigmas tend to prefer the company of others who are similarly stigmatized (Wright, 1983), and this applies to a significant percentage of the disabled population. Persons in wheelchairs, for example, report that interactions with groups of ablebodied persons are uncomfortable (Higgins, 1980), and they tend to shy away from such interactions, especially in public places. This is consistent with Festinger's (1954) belief that most social comparisons are of a lateral nature and occur with others who are thought to be similar. Such comparisons are most likely to provide useful information that is not damaging to the ego, and this is just as true for stigmatized persons as it is for others.

Paradoxically, the desire that motivates some stigmatized persons to avoid others like themselves, and some to seek out similar others, appears to be the same—a desire for social comparison. Moreover, the social comparison process can interfere with in-group socialization when it occurs as downward comparison, and, at the same time, it can promote the development of social relationships when it occurs as lateral comparison. In either case, most stigmatized persons seem to realize some benefit from social comparison with peers, in much the same way that nonstigmatized persons do—that is, through validation, acquisition of useful information, companionship, self-aggrandizement, and the like. Undoubtedly, this is one of the main reasons why peer support groups are flourishing (see below).

Social Comparison: A Summary

Although it appears that downward comparison is common among stigmatized people, it is much more prevalent among some groups than others. In particular, those with more severe types of stigma—such as persons with mental illness or retardation, or people who have been capriciously victimized—are more apt to engage in comparison with others who are worse off, as a means of coping with their stigma. People who are not visibly stigmatized, such as those with moral or behavioral "blemishes," are likely to avoid others who are severely stigmatized in an effort to avoid recognition and consequent guilt by association. In both instances, relationships among group members are likely to be inhibited by general negative group concept. However, persons whose stigma is more obvious (and less degrading) do tend to seek out each other's companionship, and successful relationships among these people are not at all uncommon.

PEER SUPPORT GROUPS

The appeal of similarity among stigmatized persons is evident in the recent increase in popularity of self-advocacy agencies and the proliferation of peer support and political groups. Support groups require disabled persons to come into close contact with one another, thereby opening the way for both enhanced stigmatization through association and also self-aggrandizement through downward and lateral social comparison. In examinations of support groups of this nature, researchers have claimed that some downward comparison does take place (e.g., Coats & Winston, 1983), which undoubtedly causes problem of socialization. Nonetheless, there are a number of clear and significant benefits associated with being among others who share similar types of stigma (Jones *et al.*, 1984).

One such benefit is that the salience of the stigma itself is greatly reduced within the group. Because everyone is stigmatized in one way or another, a particular characteristic, which is salient outside the group, is hardly noticeable inside of it. A prime example would be physical stature in a group of dwarfs (Ablon, 1981a) or wrinkles and gray hair in a nursing home bridge club. Although the stigma may be responsible for bringing the group together—and cannot be forgotten—it is likely to be a much less salient factor in interactions that take place among group members. This contrasts with the interactions that these persons typically experience outside of the group, in which the "mark" is likely to be a predominant and determining factor (Davis, 1961). It also means that the persons interacting are much more likely to recognize and focus upon other characteristics in one another—characteristics such as the warmth, understanding, and compassion that form the basis of lasting and intimate relationships.

Nonstigmatized persons often do not recognize these characteristics because they are unwilling or unable to see beyond the person's "mark" (Davis, 1961; Jones *et al.*, 1984). In this regard, in Taylor *et al.*'s (1983) survey of couples that included a stigmatized partner, a number of couples reported that the onset of the stigma helped them (or, in some cases, forced them) to pay attention to these fundamental traits in one another. In some cases, this served to deepen the couple's relationship considerably.

Another aspect that distinguishes interactions among stigmatized persons from those with others who are not stigmatized is that the factor of morality is deemphasized, if not totally absent. Imputation of immorality to stigmatized persons is a reaction to the threat posed by the stigma (cf. Lerner, 1970). Having been afflicted himself or herself, however, another stigmatized person is less likely to feel threatened and will experience less of a need to attribute the stigma to some moral offense. Many accident victims report that the accident itself made them suddenly aware that "these things" can, in fact, happen to anyone (Taylor et al., 1983). This awareness is likely to translate into less derogation of the stigma, less avoidance, and, in general, into fewer of the barriers to normal social interactions that plague disabled persons' encounters with others.

For the most part, perceived similarity is associated with liking (Byrne, 1971) and with the development of interpersonal relationships. The evidence suggests this is the case among most stigmatized persons, as well (Wright, 1983). Especially for those with severe, debilitating stigmas, interactions with similar others are likely to be less strained, more rewarding, and more intimate than relationships with nonstigmatized persons. In fact, it is not at all uncommon for romantic involvements to develop out of participation in peer support groups, as many disabled persons eventually marry similar others whom they have met at support group functions (Ablon, 1981a; Becker, 1980; Sussman, 1977).

Besides promoting social relationships, one of the most important functions of support groups is to provide members with information that can help them to cope with the stigma and its effects. To begin with, the atmosphere or attitude of these groups can be characterized as one of "shared stress" (Schachter, 1959), leading to enhanced cohesion and liking among group members. This in turn facilitates transference of information. Evidence of effective coping strategies and successful copers abounds, and one cannot help but learn from simply being in the group (Gartner & Riessman, 1977). Of course, the other side of the coin is that such successful models may be seen by some as creating undue pressure to perform, perhaps establishing a standard of comparison that is thought to be unreasonable. (For example, the "supercrip" image [Wright, 1983] is resented by many physically disabled persons who believe that greater relative accomplishments are expected from them simply because they are disabled.) Leaders of the group are likely to be aware of this problem, however, and they will try to avoid it. The result is that most participants find group sessions to be very informative and helpful.

Another benefit associated with support groups is that they can serve as a respite for stigmatized persons from the role pressures that they must face in society. More so than others, people who are stigmatized are expected to put on a certain "face" in public, to play a role that is consistent with others' expectations of their disability (Goffman, 1963; Wright, 1983). This behavior, which is intended to ease the tension surrounding the stigma during "mixed" interactions, serves no purpose in a group where everyone is stigmatized. Such role playing only interferes with social behavior, and its relative absence in support groups is associated with a quicker and more satisfactory acquaintance process. In short, it is much easier for stigmatized persons to be themselves in the midst of their peers and to adopt a more natural "face"—and that, of course, will promote the development of more significant personal relationships.

It is difficult, however, and can be misleading, to apply observations about support group interactions to interactions among stigmatized persons in general. For one thing, the interactions that occur in the group are intended for a common goal, namely coping with daily problems. Moreover, the people who are in the group have voluntarily chosen to join it and are actively seeking what the group has to offer. Still another distinguishing characteristic of support groups is that they are likely to be most widespread among persons whose stigma is either more acceptable to society or more visible (Alcoholics Anonymous being an obvious exception). It is still the case that many stigmatized persons actively avoid such groups, for reasons discussed earlier. Nonetheless, the increase in popularity of these groups is encouraging and suggests that the legislation and social movements of the last 20 years may be changing the attitudes of stigmatized persons themselves as well as those of the members of the community at large.

CONCLUSION

The range of experience associated with the stigmatization process is so diverse in terms of social and psychological impact as to make definitive conclusions on the topic nearly impossible. It is clear, however, that stigmas have a profound effect on the social relationships of people who have them, and the bulk of the evidence suggests that that effect is negative. Stigmas interfere with the development of social relationships—to some extent with others who are stigmatized, and to a greater extent with those who are not. And they can and do cause problems in relationships that already exist. The heart of the problem, as seen here, lies in the attitudes and behavior of the nonstigmatized majority. In this respect, three factors have been identified, common to the general experience of stigmatization, that can be expected to have an influence on social relationships.

One such factor is that of *morality.* In the eyes of others, stigmatized persons are often held morally accountable for their stigmatized condition, regardless of how it occurred. A related factor is that of *isolation.* Stigmatized persons have traditionally been segregated from the rest of society and from each other, making interactions inside and outside the group difficult. A third factor is that of *ambivalence,* which characterizes the attitudes of many nonstigmatized people toward those who are stigmatized. It also characterizes the attitudes of some stigmatized persons who have internalized societal opinion of their own stigma and others who have it. This attitude has the effect of inhibiting "mixed" relationships and of making those that do occur more problematic.

In spite of these obstacles, however, the fact is that stigmatized people do become involved in relationships, with each other as well as with nonstigmatized persons, and their relationships often work quite well. Pessimism, in fact, is more appropriate here in a historical perspective than a contemporary one. More changes have occurred in the last two decades than in the previous half century and there is every reason to assume that this trend will continue. As stigmatized persons become blended into the community, they will have more contact with others and will become more active socially and more independent economically and physically. By the same token, as stigmatized persons become more visible in the community, traditional notions of what is and what is not stigmatizing are bound to change. Attitudes tend to follow behavior (Bem, 1972); thus, as more nonstigmatized persons find themselves voluntarily interacting with stigmatized persons in normal environments, ambivalence and prejudice are likely to decline. The success of the civil rights and women's movements of the last 20 years offer convincing evidence of this.

Of course, the attitudes of others are not likely to be favorable if stigmatized persons themselves hold negative opinions of one another, and this suggests that the group concept (or "negative chauvinism") problem may be particularly harmful. This is a concern that deserves more attention, and a logical place to turn is to the peer support or self-help groups that have become increasingly popular of late among stigmatized persons. More support for these groups is needed from both stigmatized and nonstigmatized persons. Such groups are difficult to organize and maintain, and they can be risky both socially and psychologically. The social comparisons that will inevitably occur in these groups are likely to provide some persons with information about themselves that they do not want to confront or put pressures on them that they feel they cannot meet. Nonetheless, this risk appears to be one that is definitely worth taking. In the long run, the more efforts that stigmatized persons themselves invest in dealing with their social problems, the sooner those problems can be overcome.

CHAPTER **8**

Stigma
A SOCIAL LEARNING PERSPECTIVE

Larry G. Martin

INTRODUCTION

People categorize others and the types of attributes that they possess through the routines of social intercourse in established settings (Goffman, 1963). Through these routines, we quickly ascertain the "social identity" of people we meet. In the process of categorizing others, some people are found to possess attributes that make them different and that are thought to be of a less desirable kind. This raises the issue of stigma. As Goffman (1963, p. 3) notes,

> In the extreme, [the individual is] a person who is quite thoroughly bad, or dangerous, or weak. He is thus reduced in our minds from a whole and usual person to a tainted, discounted one. Such an attribute is a stigma, especially when its discrediting effect is very extensive.

Although people are certainly susceptible to the categorizations that others have of them, it is possible for a stigmatized individual to be insulated from the expectations and beliefs of others, retaining an identity and beliefs of his or her own (Goffman,

1963). The process through which stigmatized individuals and others come to possess certain belief structures, attitudes, values, and identities has been studied by a growing number of social scientists such as Becker (1980) and others. Nevertheless, it is clear that questions remain about how individuals come to know stigma (as an attribute of others or an attribute of oneself).

This past century has seen a massive effort by those stigmatized members of American society—such as mentally retarded and physically disabled individuals, ethnic group members, and women mount various campaigns in attempts to mitigate the effects of stigma and to control the process whereby stigma is perpetuated in society. Current efforts to protect stigmatized individuals include legal measures against unwarranted acts of discrimination and governmental legislation designed to provide for such individuals access to education and employment opportunities. These efforts were made possible because of the various individual and group freedoms guaranteed by the U.S. Constitution. It is likely that such efforts will continue to aid the people who are stigmatized.

As solutions are implemented to ease the burden on one group of individuals (e.g., blacks, women), however, the social, political, and economic dynamics shift and refocus on another stigmatized group. As the economy of the United States changes, for example, from one based on manufacturing to one based on information processing, job and literacy requirements are continuously being redefined so that individuals who failed to complete high school or college are finding it difficult, if not impossible, to find and to maintain employment. These individuals comprise yet another category of stigma that has been labeled by some social scientists as the "permanently unemployed" or the "underclass."

This chapter analyzes the relationship between social learning and stigma and how the nature of the relationship changes over the life course. I specifically focus on the characteristics and factors associated with the social learning of stigma; the social learning of stigma across the life course; the relationship of social learning to the development of beliefs, attitudes, values; and the manner in which individuals assess other people. The chapter concludes with a discussion of the difficulties we face in combatting the perpetuation of stigma in American society.

THE SOCIAL LEARNING OF STIGMA

Stigmas are discrediting marks that are understood by others in social encounters and involve affective responses, such as avoidance, disgust, disgrace, shame, or fear. Stigmas are intricately tied to the learning process. They are products of learning, and in social interactions they often stimulate or initiate the learning process. The task of controlling the amount and perpetuation of stigma in society is complex because the expectations and behaviors that result in stigma are learned, and much of what is learned is determined by experiences society provides.

People have an innate need to share a sense of belonging with their social group and to feel that their lives have worth. It is through individual interpretation of a system of cultural beliefs and values that each person develops a perception of self. The social environment in which one is born and reared exerts a tremendous influence on social reality through social learning; a social reality that an individual may eventually come to accept as "good" or "true." The process of social learning and the effect it has on the willingness of one person to stigmatize another person or to be stigmatized interacts with the maturing physical and mental abilities of each individual and the different social environments to which the individual is exposed.

The socializing process that societies employ to exert control over the lives of their members is a subliminal one (Becker, 1973). Becker argued that

> a person is said to be "socialized" precisely when he accepts to "sublimate" the body-sexual character of his oedipal project. . . . He accepts to work on becoming the father of himself by abandoning his own project and by giving it over to "The Fathers." The castration complex has done its work, and one submits to "social reality"; he can now deflate his own desires and claims and can play it safe in the world of the powerful elders. (p. 46)

Learning is an idiosyncratic social process of appropriating information from the personal environment; it can be either self-motivated or other-directed, intuitive/developmental or purposeful, and pursued consciously or subconsciously. Basic aspects of the learning process must be understood in order to address issues of stigma and social learning. Wedemeyer (1981) suggested that all learning that results in relatively permanent changes in behavior is accomplished in three stages: (a) acquisition, in which the individual acquires information from the immediate environment; (b) transmutation, in which the learner internalizes new information and guided by values and self-perceptions links it to previous experience, and (c) evaluation and application, in which the learner considers new information, tests it, and uses it as a resource.

The Characteristics of Social Learning

Social learning is a form of learning that occurs in the context of a social environment, such as home and family settings, peer groups, school, and employment and recreational settings, with the goal of personal and social adaptation. In contrast to learning that occurs in educational institutions, social learning occurs in the context of real life. The information is often processed through all three stages of learning as opposed to being acquired and transmuted.

Social learning and socialization closely resemble each other. That is, both are instrumental in the acquisition, modification, generalization, and extinction of social behavior. Goldstein (1981) asserted that

> socialization may be considered as social learning insofar as it is aimed at the acquisition of behaviors and attitudes that conform to existing social norms and expectations. But social learning can also have rather contrary purposes when the experience is largely individualistic and the person's pursuits may have little to do with or conflict with established standards. (p. 237)

As a process, social learning molds the individual's perceptions of social reality. In this process, the learner is often autonomous, reacting, and adapting, trying over and over again to fit into the social environment, grounded to some extent by social interactions with others.

The learner interprets experience by comparing and contrasting the various activities and consequences experienced in these social situations. Through this process of synthesis the learner develops fairly stable patterns of behavior and derives a measure of personal control.

Nondeliberate discoveries also frequently serve to initiate the

acquisition of important social learning outcomes. These outcomes also occur as a result of the learner's incidental involvement in chance situations or events; for example, being born into
a particular family, suffering a period of sickness, or having an
accident.

Over time, social learning, whether intentional or unintentional, conscious or unconscious, tends to contribute substantially to the individual's personal view of social reality, shapes his
or her values, and determines the extent to which he or she will
successfully manage encounters with others in the social environment.

Social learning is a powerful mechanism for both the acquisition and maintenance of behaviors that stigmatize others. (Yet,
because of its autonomous and incidental nature, social learning
often contributes to the extinction of such behaviors.) For example, in employment settings social learning can contribute to stigma when groups of workers discuss informally the incompetence
of other workers. In such instances, the observations of incompetence, whether accurate or inaccurate, could contribute to the
proliferation of stigma because of the way each group member
interprets the events. If the target individual belongs to a particular gender or racial group, or is noticeably disabled, and the group
members have had few previous encounters with individuals
from this category, then the group's judgment of incompetence
would probably weigh quite heavily on the expectations or stereotypes the individual group members hold. Katz (1981) explained this process when he argued that in-group schemas are
more complex and differentiated than out-group schemas. The
perceiver is exposed to a larger collection of diverse experiences
with in-group members—generating a larger number of dimensions along which individual members may be evaluated. Because
out-group schemas are characterized by fewer dimensions and
fewer assumptions, new information is greater in proportion to
that already known and is therefore weighted more heavily than
in the in-group case.

Social learning is a pervasive force within the context of life
course development. It is not only an effective mechanism for
individuals to learn the conventional normative behaviors expected of them, it is also the mechanism through which people

learn about and come to expect certain behaviors from stigmatized persons. What is more, it predicates how stigmatized
persons come to expect certain modes of treatment from others,
both those who are stigmatized and those who are not.

> Persons who have a particular stigma tend to have similar learning
> experiences regarding their plight, and similar changes in conception
> of self—a similar "moral career" that is both cause and effect of com-
> mitment to a similar sequence of personal adjustments. (Goffman,
> 1963, p. 32)

THE SOCIAL LEARNING OF STIGMA
ACROSS THE LIFE CYCLE

Goffman identified four "moral career" patterns of stigmatized individuals that span the life course: those stigmatized
by a congenital anomaly; those who are stigmatized but are protected by way of information control; those who become stigmatized as adults; and those who are initially socialized in an
alien community. In the next pages, I will further discuss these
patterns in the context of the broader patterns of social learning
experienced by most people as they cope with their changing social environments while maturing into productive adults. The
broader phases of social learning over the life course are presented here in three parts: survival learning, surrogate learning, and
independent learning (see Wedemeyer, 1981).

SOCIAL-SURVIVAL LEARNING OF STIGMA

Social-survival learning occurs primarily during early childhood (the preschool years). During this life stage, children perceive a need and act directly to satisfy it. Through learning they
thus gain both satisfaction and survival.

Children start by appropriating information from their personal environment through imitation and then begin to develop
their own beliefs, attitudes, and values. With advancing intellectual and perceptual processes, children observe in order to learn
from and about their love objects. They develop their identities

through the process of introjection (Boyd, 1966), absorbing into the ego the personal characteristics of the persons with whom they have strong emotional ties and from whom their ethical standards and values are appropriated.

This period of human development is important for persons stigmatized by innate characteristics such as ethnic background because they are socialized to their condition at this time while simultaneously learning and incorporating the standards against which they fall short. (e.g., the minority child who grows up in a ghetto is often aware that other children do not live in ghettos.)

Nurturing parents who are responsive to the stigmatized child's social-identity needs can make a significant difference in the self-perception the child eventually develops. During this period the child's family, and to a larger extent a local community, can establish a protective capsule within which the stigmatized child is carefully sustained by means of information control. "Self-belittling definitions of him are prevented from entering the charmed circle, while broad access is given to other conceptions held in the wider society" (Goffman, 1963, p. 32). This approach helps stigmatized children to establish an initial identity structure in which they see themselves as ordinary human beings.

Social-Surrogate Learning of Stigma

The second kind of social learning occurs during a child's elementary and secondary school years. During this period, the child's psychosocial identity formation continues. As the young person's independence grows, identification moves from the immediate adult to the image phase of an admired and loved individual, an ego ideal, who sets achievement standards (e.g., parents to teacher). It is during this stage that the individual's identity structure is framed. The development of the ego ideal and the use of models is the last stage of identification (Boyd, 1966).

Much social learning of stigma occurs during this period when children observe who is treated best by teachers in the classroom, who is not liked in their small reference groups, and against whom the rules of social conduct seem to work. For stigmatized children leaving the protected and familiar atmosphere of the home, school often presents a hostile environment. Goffman (1963) suggested that public school entrance is often reported as an occasion of stigma learning, resulting in taunts, teasing, ostracism, and fights.

If stigmatized individuals should escape the early years of school with some images of themselves as normal human beings, they encounter new obstacles during adolescent dating and the search for employment. It is during this same period that a role model, such as an adult who manages a similar stigma well, is important to stigmatized persons, to provide a balance for the developing identity structure as the individual reaches adulthood.

SOCIAL-INDEPENDENT LEARNING OF STIGMA

This type of learning occurs when individuals leave school. They are presumably ready to take charge of their affairs, cope with problems, perform occupational skills with some degree of competence, continue learning in a changing society, and grow in maturity, wisdom, and self-identity (Wedemeyer, 1981). In this final stage of identity development, the psychosocial role model must be given up, although individuals may seek guidance from other respected adults or mentors. For the young adult, the mentor is a transitional figure. "The mentor represents a mixture of parent and peer; he must be both and not purely either one" (Levinson, Darrow, Klein, Levinson, & Braxton, 1978, p. 99).

It is during the period of adulthood that the socialization process of two categories of stigmatized persons takes place: (a) those who become stigmatized in adulthood and; (b) those who are initially socialized as stigmatized. Those persons who become stigmatized as adults do not usually require a radical reorganization of their view of the past; however, those individuals who learn as adults that they have always been discreditable often must reorganize their view of the world. Such individuals would have thoroughly learned the concepts of "normal" and "stigmatized" long before they came to view themselves as deficient. After becoming stigmatized, however, they must rethink who they are. Significant change in identity usually occurs at this time, accompanied by a reduction in self-esteem. Part of the process of developing a new identity structure is brought about through independent social-learning; for example, from encounters with mentors and others who possess a similar stigma, and from social interaction.

Those persons who are initially socialized in an alien community often must later learn new social rules of behavior. These individuals, too, must undergo an identity transformation that is similar to those experienced by other recently stigmatized adults. For these individuals, the independent social learning that occurs in groups, among peers and friends, with mentors, and in the social environment may ease the transition.

THE DEVELOPMENT OF BELIEFS, ATTITUDES, AND VALUES

A central element in determining what an individual will ultimately learn depends on the individual's emerging structure of beliefs, attitudes, and values. The cultural context in which the individual develops will influence how information will be received, categorized, valued, and understood as the individual constructs a social reality. As information is received and interrelated with the various elements of the individual's belief system over time, a perceptual base is created from which the individual not only perceives the environment but also categorizes and interprets experience.

Beliefs about stigmas can thus become central to the belief structures of both stigmatized and nonstigmatized individuals. For example, bigots who have founded their racial views on beliefs that constitute central elements of their belief structures would not be easily convinced to alter them. To do so would require bigots to dismantle the mental and emotional structures that cradle their concepts of self.

> To profess something that violates the self-concept may be worse than admitting error; it is the destruction of the old self in whom that which is now called error was truth. This is not a rational process; it is a deeply disturbing self-induced aggression against the old self and what it stood for. Yet some people undergo this process and are not destroyed. (Wedemeyer, 1981, p. 195)

Development of Beliefs

When an individual sees a relationship between two things and draws a conclusion from it, he or she forms a belief. For example, a person who perceives a relationship between success and being white may come to believe that only whites are successful. Beliefs are central to people's understanding of themselves and their environment. They derive their beliefs from two basic sources: through direct experience and through some external authority. Bem (1970) argues that every belief can be traced back until it is seen to rest ultimately upon a basic belief in the credibility of one's own sensory experience or upon a basic belief in the credibility of some external authority. He suggests that these are "primitive beliefs" that often provide a foundation for other beliefs.

Types of Primitive Beliefs

During the early stages of life, the belief systems of human beings are immensely underdeveloped and malleable. Therefore, the belief system that people eventually come to accept depends to a great extent on the cultural context into which they are born and reared. "Our whole world of right and wrong, good and bad, our name, precisely who we are, is grafted into us; and we never feel we have authority to offer things on our own" (Becker, 1973, p. 45).

Bem discusses how the development of beliefs, attitudes, and values sets the foundation for the way in which people eventually come to interpret their reality and to process other people. During the early stages of life the development of zero-order and first-order beliefs, attitudes, and values forms the reality framework through which all future learning experiences will be interpreted.

Zero-Order Beliefs. These beliefs compose the "nonconscious" axioms upon which our other beliefs are built. Zero-order beliefs are among the first beliefs children learn as they interact in the environment and tend to be continuously validated by experience. People are, therefore, usually unaware of the possibility that alternatives to these beliefs could exist, and for this reason they remain unaware of the beliefs themselves. For example, we seldom question our faith in the validity of our sensory experience.

First-Order Beliefs. These beliefs derive directly from zero-order beliefs. People are usually aware of first-order beliefs because they can readily imagine alternatives to them (e.g., blacks can be successful), but they are usually not aware of any inferential beliefs. As primitive beliefs, first-order beliefs demand no independent formal or empirical confirmation and require no justification beyond a brief citation of direct experience (Bem, 1970).

Not all first-order beliefs are the products of direct experience. People learn about their existence from credible authorities. It is through primitive beliefs based on external authorities that notions about such intangibles as God, religious dogma, and family history first enter a child's system of beliefs. Children often learn primitive beliefs about stigmatized people early in life: for example, that mentally ill or mentally retarded people will harm them. To children, beliefs about stigmatized people are functionally no different from first-order beliefs because they are based upon an axiomatic belief in the credibility of their senses. As sources of information, their parents and their senses are equally reliable.

Generalization and Stereotypes

Very few primitive beliefs are founded upon a single experience. The great majority of them are generalizations of several experiences over time. Each generalized idea arises out of several separate situations but because the person still relates such beliefs to direct experience, they are properly classified as primitive beliefs. (For example, a child who has seen only male doctors may develop the belief that only men can become doctors.)

Generalizations are not true for all instances beyond the set of experiences upon which they are based. When individuals treat such generalizations as if they were universally true, they are "stereotypes," and like other first-order beliefs they demand no justification beyond a citation either of direct experience or of some external authority. Stereotypes are not in themselves evil or pathological but are necessary thinking devices that enable people to avoid conceptual chaos by packaging the world into a manageable number of categories. Stereotypes are often used, however, by people who have ulterior motives, to justify the inequitable treatment of individuals on the basis of assumed group characteristics that neither they nor the group in fact possess. For example, a person might believe that all physically disabled people are also of low intelligence.

HIGHER-ORDER BELIEFS

Bem (1970) argues that beliefs differ from one another in the degree to which they are of differentiated "vertical structure," are of broadly based "horizontal structure," and have an underlying importance to other beliefs' "centrality." These are some of the major factors that contribute to the complexity and richness of our cognitive belief systems.

VERTICAL STRUCTURES

As people mature, they tend to regard their sensory experiences as potentially fallible and similarly learn to be more cautious in believing external authorities. They begin to insert an explicit and conscious premise about the authority's credibility between the belief held and the authority's word. People also learn to derive higher-order beliefs by reasoning inductively from their previous experiences and to derive even higher-order beliefs by building upon premises that are themselves conclusions of prior syllogisms. For example, a white person who observes that nonwhites earn less than whites can conclude that all nonwhites are inferior:

> *1st premise:* The census shows nonwhites earn less than whites.
> *2nd premise:* Only inferior people have fewer earnings.
> *Conclusion:* Therefore, nonwhites are inferior.

Higher-order beliefs have a "vertical structure" of beliefs underlying them, which generate them as the products of quasi-logical inferences. Highly elaborated or differentiated beliefs have a deep vertical structure, whereas unelaborated or undifferentiated beliefs, such as primitive beliefs, have little or no syllogistic reasoning underlying them.

Horizontal Structures

Most higher-order beliefs are bolstered by "horizontal" structures in addition to their vertical structures. These additional structures account for the fact that higher-order beliefs are not vulnerable to disconfirmation when any one of their underlying vertical premises is destroyed. A particular higher-order belief is often the conclusion to more than one syllogistic chain of reasoning and rests upon many syllogistic pillars. It has broad horizontal as well as deep vertical structures. For example, a working or middle-class person may use several lines of reasoning to conclude that rich people are immoral:

> *1st argument:* People become rich by exploiting other people; people have a moral obligation to treat each other fairly; therefore rich people are immoral. *2nd argument:* Rich people buy expensive luxury items; people have a moral obligation to use their money wisely; therefore rich people are immoral. *3rd argument:* Rich people do not work for a living; people have a moral obligation to perform useful work; therefore rich people are immoral.

Over time, the vertical and horizontal structures of a higher-order belief can change without disturbing the belief itself, but the reasons for believing will have to be altered. Also, additional support may be obtained for beliefs that were once primitive beliefs or otherwise lacked reasoned justification.

Centrality of Beliefs

Although beliefs may have both broad horizontal and deep vertical structures, they are still not necessarily important to or central to an individual's belief system (Bem, 1970). Conversely, a belief that is central may have little or no structural support. For example, the zero-order belief in the general credibility of our senses is one of our most central beliefs; nearly all of our other beliefs rest upon it, and to lose our faith in it is to lose our sanity.

The Logic of Beliefs

People do not merely subscribe to random collections of beliefs but attempt to maintain coherent systems of beliefs that are internally consistent. However, for several reasons, beliefs that are consistent are not necessarily logical or rational: (a) an inductive generalization based upon experience is often faulty (not only whites can be rich); (b) even when the logic itself is impeccably deductive, the conclusions to syllogisms can be wrong if any one of the underlying premises is false (not all rich people make money by exploiting others); (c) there are often inconsistencies between different higher-order beliefs even though the internal reasoning behind each separate belief is consistent within its own vertical structure, that is, one line of reasoning leads to one conclusion, whereas a second line leads to a contradictory conclusion; and (d) one's attitudes and "ulterior motives" can distort the reasoning process so that the logic itself is subtly illogical (e.g., a bigot can consciously or unconsciously use "selective" perception to take in only those aspects of reality that support currently held beliefs).

ATTITUDES AND VALUES

Attitudes are our likes and dislikes for situations, objects, persons, groups, and any other identifiable aspects of our environment. Our attitudes have their roots in our emotions, behavior, and in the social influences upon us. Contrary to popular belief, Bem (1970) argues that attitudes are more likely to result from the behavior pattern of the individual than to serve as a predisposition to behavior. The person who is conditioned to treat stigmatized individuals as if they were not human, for example, would likely hold the attitude, which would be consistent with those behaviors, that such people deserve to be treated as subhuman.

The "cognitive component" of attitudes are considered evaluative beliefs in that they can serve as a partial basis for likes and dislikes. Not only is it possible to like something that has been evaluated negatively (e.g., we may like individual minority members, yet have a low opinion of their race), but we may also dislike some things that we evaluate positively: "Many physically disabled people are strong and courageous, but I just don't like being around them."

A value is a primitive preference for, or a positive attitude toward, certain end states of existence, such as equality, self-fulfillment, and freedom, or for certain broad modes of conduct, such as kindness and honesty. Values are ends, and their desirability is either nonconsciously taken for granted (a zero-order belief) or seen as a direct derivation from one's experience or from some external authority (a first-order belief). Values are important because of their centrality to other beliefs and attitudes. To know whether a positive attitude (or an evaluative belief) is also a value for a particular individual, one must know the functional role it plays in the person's total belief system. One person's higher-order attitude can be another person's value. Racial prejudice, for example, can be a means to other values for the politician to exploit in a political campaign but can be an end in itself for the bigot whose central belief structure relies on it.

SOCIAL LEARNING AND STIGMA: A MULTIDISCIPLINARY PERSPECTIVE

From initial perceptions formulated in early childhood to the beliefs, attitudes, and values held by mature adults, social learning has proven to be a powerful mechanism for not only acquiring new information on the conduct of interpersonal relationships but also for influencing the way new information is mentally processed and stored. Social learning influences and is influenced by multiple factors that interact over time in people's minds and become elements of their personal identity structures and the beliefs of the groups in which they hold membership.

This chapter illustrates the degree to which the analysis of social learning factors provides insight into how and why people come to identify and react to stigmas. Nevertheless, many questions remain that call for multidisciplinary research. For example, specialists in early childhood education could bring to such an effort the knowledge of how children acquire stigma information in controlled classroom settings. Psychologists could discuss the personality effects of the libidinal drive, parental control, and ego development, and how these affect the motivation of people to stigmatize others. Adult development specialists could add a rich perspective on the changing external and internal social learning needs of people over the life course. Sociologists, specializing in the study of stigma and deviance, could provide much needed information on how people become stigmatized and why others apparently feel a need to stigmatize. A research agenda for such a multidisciplinary team might encompass the investigation of many issues, such as the effects of stigma on the productivity of a work unit in a manufacturing plant, the effects of stigma on the national high school dropout rate, the effect of personal contacts with stigmatized persons, and attitudinal changes toward stigma over the life course.

CONCLUSION: THE PERPETUATION OF STIGMA IN SOCIETY

Stigmatized groups will probably continue their efforts to create a "stigma-free" social environment for themselves and their families. The factors that initiate and perpetuate stigma are many and complex, however. It is extremely difficult, if indeed not impossible, in a free society to control what people will learn, how they will learn, or what they will come to believe and value.

To halt the perpetuation of stigma in society, we might be tempted to call for drastic measures that would threaten the basic freedoms that comprise the centerpiece of American democracy. Suppose, for example, we wanted to effect a massive change in American values by controlling the stigma content of the print and broadcast media. If such control were imposed by legislation, it would amount to state censorship. This would not only violate the First Amendment but would set in place a mechanism that could easily be turned to destructive new purposes—such as the creation and perpetuation of new stigmas. Such a thought raises questions about what means we *can* use to move toward the goal of a stigma-free society. Is it possible to have both an open and a stigma-free society? Can educational institutions be used effectively as instruments of social change? Can we really expect teachers to play a more active role in providing values, particularly with respect to attitudes about stigma, to children in a society that stresses individualism and the primary importance of the family? These questions and others illustrate the difficulties encountered as new and old groups of stigmatized persons bring public attention to their condition. Although it appears that some forms of existing stigmas may be eliminated while others are being created, this examination of social learning and stigma suggests that the goal of full citizenship will likely always be a distant dream for many Americans.

CHAPTER 9

Family Experience of Stigma in Childhood Cancer

Oscar A. Barbarin

INTRODUCTION

Chronic childhood illnesses are often conceived as family crises because of their profound effect on various aspects of family life, such as role assignment, task allocation, marital quality, sibling relationships, and family cohesion (Barbarin, Hughes, & Chesler, 1985; Binger, 1973; Christ & Floumanhaft, 1984; Futterman & Hoffman, 1973). In contrast, stigma is ordinarily conceived as an individual experience. That is, the stigma is often related to some characteristic viewed as inherent in the individual.

The essence of stigma is a taint or a readily observable mark that signifies moral depravity, physical disfigurement, or membership in a denigrated group. A stigma assigns to an individual or group an unverifiable set of personal characteristics such as weakness, passivity, incompetence, and vileness. These characterizations result in feelings of self-deprecation, shame, or guilt, and they become the basis for denying full social acceptance to the stigmatized person (Goffman, 1963).

Stereotypes or typifications of the stigmatized group are asserted to be a feature of each individual. These stereotypes or typifications have often been described as overinclusive schemas that inaccurately reduce complex realities to simple formulas. This process ignores the wide variation existing among individuals who share similar stigmas. Although stigma is a significant problem in chronic childhood illness, with few exceptions (Travis, 1976; Waddell, 1983), the literature either ignores stigma completely or fails to describe it in adequate detail. In particular, the literature fails to address the ways in which social relations are marked and personal identity is compromised as a consequence of the illness diagnosis.

CHILDHOOD CANCER AS A FORM OF STIGMA

The widely accepted view of childhood cancer as a family experience leads naturally to questions about ways in which the stigma associated with the illness might also be construed from a family perspective. Just as family members vicariously share the pain and uncertainty of the medical threat to the child's life, they also vicariously experience the psychosocial threats associated with the illness.

The concept of stigma as a family phenomenon is both appealing and challenging. Although no two families are identical, most people have direct meaningful experience of some form of family life. The challenge in understanding family dynamics in relation to stigma arises from the need to account for the numerous individual, group, and system factors that make for diversity in family functioning. Families are embedded within a particular social and historical context, are shaped in response to a particular set of cultural norms and demands, and are heavily influenced by the unique personalities of their members. Moreover, racial, ethnic, religious, and economic differences contribute further to observed variation among families with respect to family values, functioning, structure, and life-style.

Variations also occur across time with respect to the principal functions of families and the roles of children. Dramatic increases in divorce rates and in life expectancy have significantly altered patterns of family relations and structure. For example, relationships with extended families have become complex as adults with children divorce, remarry someone with children, and have children in the second marriage. Members of reconstituted nuclear families like these are likely to have a somewhat different extended family with which to establish relationships.

To understand the dynamics of a family's experience of stigma in childhood cancer requires a multidisciplinary approach. The complexities engendered by changes in family structure and other historical changes are not easily understood and explained within the paradigm of a single discipline. Insights developed in several health and family-related disciplines suggest a multidimensional basis for thinking about stigma as a family experience. These include (a) the link between medical and psychosocial stress, provided by psychosocial oncology (Christ & Floumanhaft, 1984); (b) the processes and structures families use for their emotional and functional tasks, developed in family therapy and family psychiatry (Bowen, 1978; Minuchin, 1978); (c) the influence of the social and community environment on the family's response to stress, provided by community psychology (Barbarin, 1983); (d) approaches to understanding death and bereavement, provided by medical social work (McCollum & Schwartz, 1972); and (e) ways families reorganize to deal with chronic stress such as separation and loss, provided by family social science (Hill, 1949).

Perspectives such as these are useful because they illuminate the ways in which stigma occurs in childhood cancer and how stigma is a family experience. One such example is provided in the case of Myra.

Myra has many friends who consider her fun to be with because of her bubbly enthusiasm and her infectious sense of humor. Though not brilliant, she does very well academically through persistence and hard work. Soon she will graduate from junior high school and become part of a select honors program for students showing promise in the performing arts.

By all accounts her prospects of becoming an accomplished pianist are good. She was selected to be part of a young people's musical group which would soon give a major recital in New York. This was to be the crowning moment of her young musical career.

For now, her dreams must be postponed. It began a few weeks before the recital, with a recurring pain and swelling in her arm. Her parents thought that it was the result of a bruise received in a soccer game at school. But the soreness did not go away.

When doctors first told me it was osteogenic sarcoma [i.e., bone cancer], it scared me as it does most people. Now, the word doesn't scare me anymore. In some ways, knowing is a relief. I had always imagined the worst, and even though this is one of the worst things that it could be, it is better knowing. My future is a bit uncertain; I have totally stopped planning. I had planned out my whole life, but then I got the rug pulled out from under me. I'm not planning on anything because I don't want anyone bursting my balloon.

I hear my group talking excitedly about the recital, and it hurts a little bit. I ask myself why me, why at this time just before this important performance, just before entering this new program at a new school. I could have handled it afterwards, but why now? The doctors think they can treat me without removing my arm, but it will be a while before they know for sure. Losing an arm bothers me a lot, but I can't think about it much.

To make things worse, my friends don't come around as much as they used to. I don't feel any different now that I have cancer, but they treat me differently. When they come around, they act strange and don't seem to know what to say. My best friends are quiet and sad around me, and it makes me feel like I have to cheer them up. They try to ask about the cancer, but they don't know what to say. Other kids seem to pity me. After a few awkward moments, they make a quick exit.

It hurts not being a part of the gang anymore. It's like the cancer is a wall between us that is hard to tear down with most of the kids. It's strange, but the little kids in my neighborhood are the most honest and direct. They come right up and ask if the cancer hurts and if I'm scared to die. One little girl even admitted that her mother did not want me to baby-sit her anymore because I might give her cancer. That hurts!

Myra's mother gets worried because Myra is not very open with her feelings. Her mother comments that there are times when Myra does not show any emotions that one might expect her to show. Myra masks her sadness, despair, and fear so that her parents and friends will not know how much she is hurt by the disappointments, the loss of control, the withdrawal of friends, and the uncertainty about life. The family recognizes that to some extent they all try to protect each other by disguising their feelings.

My parents and I have decided that we can't hide all the pain and despair. So we made an agreement that when we have to cry, or to show our real feelings, we do. We sometimes get angry, and don't know who to blame.

Myra and her family have become much closer as they have tried to deal not only with the predictable problems associated with the illness and its treatment but also with the surprising uneasiness in contacts with friends and acquaintances. As a consequence of the illness, her status in the family and in the community is changed. Moreover, the effects of stigmatizing processes may not be limited to Myra. Persons who are closely associated with stigmatized individuals are often subjected to the same reactions as the stigmatized person (Goffman, 1963). The family keenly senses the pain of Myra's struggle to resist being treated as different. They have come to feel vulnerable for her and experience a degree of ambivalence in relations with their friends, whom they are reluctant to burden with their concerns about Myra.

Childhood cancer is seen as an outrage of nature that is especially disturbing because it juxtaposes the boundless energy of childhood with death's stillness, its undiminished optimism with death's despair, and its refreshing naivete with death's corruption (Schowalter, 1970). Children with cancer are stigmatized and isolated because they compel us to think about the unthinkable death of the innocent and our own deaths. An additional factor underlying stigma is boundary maintenance. The experience of stigma sets a boundary around those with life-threatening illness through social exclusion, and, thus, we are able to maintain the illusion that death is improbable.

Cancer's strong association with pain, disfigurement, and certain death makes it a dreaded disease. Learning that a relative or close friend has been diagnosed with cancer often leads to feelings of dread and terror that may, in turn, affect feelings about the newly diagnosed individual. Even though improved treatment methods have increased survival rates dramatically within the past 10 years (American Cancer Society, 1981), the word "cancer" conjures up in the minds of many people a sense of futility, despair, and death.

The thought of dying can be so disturbing that we actively suppress all reminders of death. In *The Denial of Death*, Becker argues that in order to reduce anxiety about death, society has formed a compact to disguise or remove from view any reminders of our mortality. This self-deceptive avoidance of death functions for individuals by making it possible to proceed with life with a semblance of purpose and meaning. The diagnosis of cancer violates our social compact, confronts us with the specter of presumably certain death and thereby infuses us with a sadness and terror we had hoped to avoid. Moreover, our sense of order in relation to the continuity of life dictates that children should grow to be adults, have their own children, and live a full and rewarding life. Consequently, the thought of a dying child constitutes a significant breach of the natural order, raises anxiety about personal mortality, and seriously threatens our ability to construe life as predictable and meaningful.

Until recently (i.e., until the enactment of federal legislation requiring access of disabled children to the normal classroom environment [Public Law 94-142]), children with cancer were rarely accorded the opportunity for complete participation in normal classroom activities. They were either limited to homebound instruction even when physically able to attend class, or they were dropped from the school's roster because administrators considered it a waste of resources to educate a child they assumed would die. Exclusion from school was often accompanied by unnecessary restrictions on participation in community-based recreational activities. The children were thus systematically excluded from contact with other children and adults. Often, administrators and other adults justified these exclusions on the basis of concern for the child and fear that he or she might be too fragile or vulnerable to participate in school or recreational activities.

Although a majority of children with cancer now reenter school soon after treatment induction, the problems of school reentry have not all been solved. Families of children with cancer and school personnel continue to report difficulties with peer acceptance of the ill child in the school and in the neighborhood (Barbarin & Chesler, 1983). Parents noted that most neighbors were gracious and accepting but that some avoided contact with the child and the family. We can speculate that social encounters with the ill child and family were avoided because such encounters confronted neighbors with disturbing thoughts of the mortality of their own children, and perhaps of themselves. For example, some parents of the ill child's classmates wanted children with cancer excluded so that their own children would not be exposed to morbid thoughts connected with serious illness and death. Parents thus hoped to protect their children and themselves from the discomfort associated with the thought of dying. One teacher quoted other parents as saying, "I don't like to talk about Billy [ill child]. It makes me think that my own child might get cancer and die!" Much of this analysis of the motivations for stigma is still in the preliminary stages, yet it establishes a foundation for arguing the categorization of childhood cancer as a stigmatized condition.

STIGMA AND FAMILY FUNCTIONING

Conceptions of family functioning developed by structural family theorists can be used to depict stigma as a family experience (Minuchin, 1978). Within these frameworks, families are viewed as organizations made up of functionally distinct subunits with overlapping rule-determined membership. Examples of subunits include the executive or parental subsystem, the martial subsystem, and the sibling subsystem.

The executive subsystem is the leadership unit that is often composed of two adults and is responsible for making decisions, acquiring and allocating resources, maintaining order, creating a stable and healthy climate, providing for the protection, nurturance, and development of individual family members, caring for family members in time of physical or emotional trauma, and preparing offspring for adult life. In families of children with cancer, the parental and executive functions may be more difficult to carry out because of the extensive demands of caring for the ill child. Normal family rituals, communal meals, holidays, leisure time, and vacations are frequently disrupted. Parents may decide to change homes in order to be closer to extended family or to permit easier access to medical care. Parents may work longer hours in order to meet medical expenses, or conversely, one partner may quit work entirely. Less time is available for both parents to care for their other children. Instead, the children may be cared for by neighbors, friends, extended family, or by one parent only. This role often falls to the father, who must reorganize his life in order to work and care for the healthy siblings while the mother is caring for the ill child in the hospital.

Under the weight of such stress and uncertainty, parents may come to feel that they have lost control over their own family's situation. These feelings often arise from the painful realization that the family's concern and arduous efforts will make little difference in the child's chances of long-term survival. In time, parents' inability to assure the well-being of their child may lead them to question their competence as parents and to poorly evaluate their own functioning in the executive subsystem (Cook, 1984).

The marital subsystem, usually composed of the husband and wife, is responsible for providing for the intimacy needs of parents. It provides both physical and emotional intimacy in a way that cannot be satisfied through friendships or relationships with the children. This subsystem also experiences tremendous disruption when a child is ill. There is little time for privacy and being together, with one spouse often viewing the other as emotionally withdrawn at a difficult time. Sexual intimacy deteriorates, and the frequency of sexual interaction falls precipitously (Cook, 1984; Kalnins, 1983).

The sibling subsystem usually consists of the offspring in a family. Members of this subsystem occupy roughly similar formal status within the family but have unequal informal status and power because older children usually carry more responsibilities and exercise a degree of informal control and influence over younger children. The sibling subsystem is the arena in which individuals learn to be intimate, to share, to cooperate, to experience and resolve conflict, and acquire social skills related to assertiveness, negotiation, and problem solving.

Siblings of children with cancer often feel ambivalent, worrying about the threat to the ill child's life while resenting the loss of attention from their parents. Children experience anger at their parents for abandoning them and spending so much time with the sick child. Moreover, siblings sometimes feel envy and anger when they observe the ill child receiving extra gifts and attention and getting away with behavior for which they themselves would be reprimanded. At times, they feel guilty and believe that they should have been the sick one. Occasionally, they feel closer to their sibling, and, like the parents, center their emotional energies around caring for the ill child.

In a crisis such as childhood cancer, the rules governing the boundaries—that is, who participates within these subsystems and the functions to be carried out by participants—may become vague and irrelevant. For example, the membership of the parental subsystem may shift, or the executive subsystem may alter, as one parent moves out to be more closely linked to the child in the hospital setting. The family life situation may alter so drastically that the rules governing how these subsystems function may require considerable change. The existence of these subsystems and the rules governing the participation in them largely dictates the nature of the relationship among family members. The alteration of these rules during a child's illness provides the terms to understanding how relationships among family members may be changed as a consequence of this stigmatizing condition.

STIGMA AS A FAMILY EXPERIENCE

Learning of the diagnosis of childhood cancer is so distressing that it leads to reactions such as fear, uncertainty, anger, horror, pity, and concern for the child's life. Parents describe the devastating effect of the diagnosis in terms of a sense of unreality, disbelief, shock, numbness, inability to eat or sleep, and "being in a deep black hole". Manifestations of stigma in families often arise because of the uncertainty of the child's survival, the painful, invasive nature of treatment, and the intensive protective care provided to the child by the family. Stigma as a family experience surfaces in the form of distorted perceptions of and ambivalence toward the ill child in the family members and in strained relations between the family and its social network.

ALTERED STATUS OF THE CHILD IN THE FAMILY

The uncertainty and fragility of life associated with cancer quite understandably alter parents' beliefs about their child's future and create ambivalence about how to view and treat their child. In spite of assurance from medical staff, some parents do not allow themselves to be optimistic but limit their focus to one day at a time.

> I hope he makes it to his 21st birthday. I don't think the odds are all that great. I never told my wife that, but from what I understand about cancer I don't think that he will make it much past his 21st birthday—no matter what the doctors say.

Family members themselves are not always immune to stigmatizing the child. Family members may view the child as fragile and focus on the physical aberrations resulting from the cancer or its treatment. In some cases, they internalize the values associated with the stigma and exemplify the same stigmatizing behavior exhibited by individuals outside of the family. The physical integrity of the child and how he or she might look to others seriously concern some families. For example, some parents worry that the child might be scarred or otherwise disfigured; others believe that their child will be sterile.

> His left shoulder may grow less than his right. He looks as though he could grow uneven. It would be nice when he is 16 that he looks fairly functional. There is a possibility that he won't.

> It would be nice if the dead skin on his neck would fall off. People always ask why he doesn't wash. I would rather see him grow normally for 15 years than grow abnormally and live for 30 or 40 years.

> One thing that I was impressed with were the nice operations that they sew. The scars are very thin. They did work like artists—no stitch marks.

Care of the sick child takes up a lion's share of the family's physical and emotional resources. Much of the family's energy and time is devoted to such tasks as carefully adhering to the medication schedule, taking care not to expose the child to bacterial or viral infections, transporting the child to clinic visits, and reassuring the child that painful procedures are necessary and helpful. The intensity of this activity elevates the child from a peripheral to a central role in the family and determines the frequency and nature of family interactions.

The child's presence can no longer be taken for granted, and thus he or she becomes a cause of major adjustments in family life. For example, family celebrations, outings, and vacations may be arranged to avoid conflict with the child's treatment. Even the form of these events may be modified to coordinate with or conform to the ill child's needs, abilities, and interests.

Although the channeling of so many resources into the ill child has benefits in terms of family solidarity and the adequacy of care, it also exacts a high price from the marital dyad and siblings. The needs of other family members may be put aside as the family establishes the health of the sick child as its major concern. The family's adaptation to cancer may thus affect the status of a child within the family and community. Family processes and functioning may alter, thereby influencing social relationships among family members. Ultimately, the status of the family in the community may be altered.

The fragile nature of the child's life at the time of diagnosis is a source of both concern and confusion. Parents are no longer clear about how much to expect and require of the ill child and the extent to which they should strictly enforce rules. They are especially perplexed with respect to standards of conduct, maturity demands, and expectations of achievement (Barbarin & Chesler, 1983). For example, they are uncertain about how to respond to the child's moodiness, listlessness, temper tantrums, and other undesirable behaviors. They are in conflict about insisting that their ill child complete school assignments, comply with family rules, perform household chores, and exhibit self-control. This uncertainty about expectations, performance standards, and strictness becomes pronounced when parents are convinced that the child will die.

Although most parents are certain that previous expectations and standards lack applicability to the child's current situation, they are not sure what ground rules to apply. Parents often resolve this dilemma by relaxing expectations, maturity demands, and performance standards. They often indulge the child's whims and accede to pleas for such things as candy and junk foods when they would ordinarily say "no." Not all parents are comfortable with this solution, however. Some parents worry that they might be creating a spoiled, self-indulgent child who will possess too little self-control if he or she survives to adulthood. Moreover, they feel caught in inconsistency if they permit behavior in the ill child that they do not tolerate in their other children.

An additional response to the perceived fragility of the child is incessant worry about potential physical or psychological harm. Parents report in retrospect that they initially viewed their child as more fragile and dependent and behaved more protectively than the situation may have required. Overprotection may also be expressed in reluctance to be totally honest with the child about the seriousness of the illness. Parents may avoid telling the child that he or she will die, and as a result, family members carry this around as a secret that stands between themselves and the child. The child is perceived as vulnerable, weak, and in need of protection from the excessive demands of the external world.

In time, many parents learn to moderate their inclination toward overprotection, develop new behavioral standards that challenge the child's competence rather than presume incompetence, and help the child lead as normal a life as possible. In aiming for a normal life for the ill child, however, parents must constantly resist their own and others' tendency to view and treat the child as "special" and to ignore the child's fundamental similarity to peers. In summary, the altered status of the child in the family is expressed in changed perceptions of the child, in the child's increased influence over family functioning, and in the family's overprotection, lowered performance expectations, and relaxed behavioral standards for the ill child.

ALTERED STATUS OF THE CHILD IN THE COMMUNITY

Early in the course of the illness, parents must decide whom to tell about the diagnosis and how much information to give about the child's progress. Although parents recognize the need of close friends and school personnel to know, there is a reluctance to say too much for fear that the child will be subjected to overprotection, social exclusion, and decreased performance expectations. Occasionally, children themselves will have concerns about being stigmatized and with parental cooperation may conceal the illness from teachers and peers.

Concealment is often possible because many common forms of pediatric cancer (e.g., leukemia, brain cancer, and lymphomas) are not externally visible. However, the side effects of treatment— alopecia, nausea, vomiting, mood fluctuations, diarrhea, constipation, loss of appetite, weight loss, halitosis, stomatitis, skin problems, fatigue, or loss of a limb—may disclose the child's condition and reinforce in the child a sense of being different. When the child's status as a cancer patient becomes evident, a progression of negative social events may occur that make his or her life even less tolerable.

STEREOTYPES OF CHILDREN WITH CANCER

The likelihood of stereotyping is increased when there is visible evidence of a child's cancer, such as limb amputation in cases of osteogenic sarcoma, or the side effects of chemotherapy of radiation. Stereotyping refers to the attribution of negative traits, behavior, or dispositions to an individual based solely on that person's membership in a disparaged category. Stereotypes can also be described as overinclusive schema or unsubstantiated generalizations by which an individual and group are characterized as morally inferior, even in the fact of disconfirming evidence. There is remarkable similarity in the content of the stereotypes about such divergent groups as those who are physically disabled, members of racial minorities, elderly, chronically ill, and developmentally disabled. Descriptors for such stereotypes include passive, childlike, helpless, dependent, happy-go-lucky, and weak (Jones, 1972).

In one study, teachers of 42 children with cancer rated an ill child and a typical classmate of the same sex and age on classroom behavior and the open expression of positive and negative emotions (Deasy-Spinetta & Spinetta, 1981). Generally, teachers made less favorable ratings of children with cancer than of their classroom peers. Teachers tended to view the child with cancer as self-conscious, easily embarrassed, less active, less able to concentrate, less willing to try new things, and less expressive of positive and negative emotions than the typical child who did not have cancer. These stereotypes are not uncommon. They result in at least two negative outcomes for long-term survivors: difficulty in obtaining affordable life and health insurance and refusal of the armed forces to accept survivors for military service.

Many people believe that children with cancer differ significantly from their counterparts. For example, there is a widespread belief that children with cancer perform more poorly in school, are more frequently absent, and exhibit a more depressed mood (Barbarin & Chesler, 1983). However, the evidence regarding these differences is inconclusive (Barbarin & Chesler, 1983; Koocher & O'Malley, 1984). Some parents of sick children's classmates who held such beliefs complained that seriously ill children should not be allowed into classrooms with their own children. They feared that their children might contract the illness after close contact with the ill child.

CHILDHOOD CANCER AS A MASTER STATUS

Stereotyping in children with cancer results not only in attributing negative qualities but also neutralizes the child's positive qualities. Many of the positive attributes of the child identified prior to the diagnosis are later qualified by the child's status as being chronically and seriously ill. In this way, the childhood cancer becomes a master status that becomes the most salient aspect of the child's identity. For example, although children may variously demonstrate themselves to be accomplished gymnasts, bright and high-achieving students, mischievous children, active, independent children, or passive students, they are viewed first and foremost as children with cancer. All other aspects of a child's behavior and character are ignored. In effect, the bright student is no longer a bright student but a student with cancer. The pranks and jokes of a mischievous child are to be overlooked or excused because of illness. When people respond not on the basis of the child's own actions but on the basis of characteristics of the illness, the child's uniqueness and personal identity are undermined. This reinforces the feeling in such children that they are different than they were before the diagnosis.

The effect of childhood cancer as a master status is illustrated in the case of an adolescent boy who had been a rather active but average student in a junior high school. Prior to the diagnosis, he was often sent to the principal's office for throwing airplanes around the room, getting out of his seat, or not paying attention in class. After the amputation of his leg, however, he was no longer punished for such offenses. The teacher responded to his behavior differently than in the past, which had the effect of isolating him from his peers. He behaved even more disruptively than he had before as a way of resisting the special treatment, by walking out of the classroom and refusing to do homework, until the teacher could no longer ignore him. Finally, in frustration, she sent him down to the principal's office. He savored his victory as he hobbled down the hall, reassuming his role as the active, mischievous child in the classroom.

The effect of the stigma as a master status was to force this child to be even more outrageous than he might ordinarily be, so that he could be accepted again as a member of his peer group. For him, peer acceptance and being perceived as normal were well worth the price of punishment.

SELF-PERCEPTIONS OF STIGMATIZED PERSONS

Over time, stigmatized individuals may internalize characteristics attributed to them in their social environment, a devastating aspect of stigma. The extent to which this phenomenon occurs among children with cancer is still unclear. Much of the evidence suggests, however, that these children, like other stigmatized populations, find subtle but effective ways to resist the stereotypes (Barbarin & Chesler, 1983). They often do so by resuming most of their preillness activities and thereby making their lives as autonomous and normal as possible.

Nevertheless, several aspects of the lives of these children make the maintenance of normalcy extremely difficult. Frequent, disruptive hospitalizations, the uncertain course of the illness, and the intrusiveness of the medical regime all interfere with normal activities and social contacts. Even those children who survive 5 or 10 years past the diagnosis have lingering doubts about the long-term effects of chemotherapy and radiation with respect to their fertility and cognitive functioning. Despite the uncertainly about their survival and the long-term effects of treatment, many children optimistically anticipate an active and long adult life.

Children with cancer avoid internalizations and negative attributes of the stigma, not only by acting in ways that contradict the stigma but by concealing their condition. For example, when adolescents go on to college or move on to a different school, they are often reluctant to tell others, even teachers, that they have been diagnosed as having cancer. This strategy has been used effectively by other stigmatized persons, who are accepted by the community as long as their stigmatized status is unknown (Travis, 1976).

REACTIONS TO SOCIAL ENCOUNTERS
WITH STIGMATIZED PERSONS

Observations of face-to-face interactions between stigmatized and nonstigmatized persons reveal an attraction toward and anxiety about social contact. This ambivalence is often reflected in uneasiness in the voice, tentativeness in statements, and a patronizing approach to dealing with stigmatized individuals. The uncertainty often centers around a lack of clarity about how to behave. The nonstigmatized person often is preoccupied with the visible manifestation of the stigma, as indicated in the verbal or visual attention given to it. The person may not be able to decide whether to confront the stigma directly or to pretend it does not exist. The ambivalent reaction, however, unambiguously conveys to stigmatized persons that they are "untouchable," "tainted," or "abnormal."

Adolescents with cancer are very sensitive to the awkwardness their peers exhibit in dealing with them immediately after the diagnosis. They report the difficulty in these ways: "My friends don't know what to say to me"; "They seem strained and unable to talk as easily"; "They are insensitive; they avoid asking how I feel or how I'm doing"; "They don't touch me as freely, and they avoid eye contact." One adolescent with osteogenic sarcoma described the awkwardness when friends came to visit her after surgical removal of her leg. They stared at her amputated leg but did not say anything. Finally, one person broke the ice and asked her what it felt like not having a leg. She replied candidly that it did not feel like anything and that as soon as she could she would learn to dance and tumble with one leg. Reconnecting with friends may occur more quickly when friends directly approach the child with cancer and inquire openly about the experience.

Stigmatization of children with visible forms of cancer is frequently regarded by the children themselves as a significant stressor. For example, Sourkes (1980) asked children to list the things that most upset them about having cancer. The most frequently mentioned items were associated with negative social reactions such as "not being permitted to play with the other children," "everyone calling me baldy," and "being called dummy because I can't read as well as the other second-graders."

Although most children with cancer experienced some form of social exclusion and avoidance, reactions to them were not uniformly negative. Many individuals—friends, neighbors, teachers, classmates—responded in a helpful and caring way. The social exclusion depicted here is often subtle and inadvertent. More often than not, it is perpetrated by individuals who care about the ill child but who are ambivalent in their feeling. Teachers' closeness to the ill child and family make them highly susceptible to these concerns. In fact, many describe their reactions to the diagnosis in the very same terms that the child's parents use: disbelief, anger, and depression. They account for this strong reaction by their close identification with the ill child's parents. Often, they report the unshakable fear that the same fate might befall their own children.

ALTERED FAMILY RELATIONS AND FUNCTIONING

Although having cancer may result in rejection and with-drawal by friends, the effect on interactions in the family is often quite different. The experience of childhood cancer may pro-foundly reshape family relationships by strengthening family co-hesion, identity, and emotional fusion. Parents often report that the family becomes much closer after the child is diagnosed with cancer (Barbàrin, Hughes, & Chesler, 1985). Thus, cultivation of family life may become ascendant over other life pursuits such as education, careers, and friendships. In some cases, mothers give up their jobs to care for the child. Older siblings may withdraw from college to be at home, and fathers may moderate their career aspirations. Although the adaptive function of family identity and cohesion is apparent, the distortion of family relations sometimes produced by this strong pull toward family unity may be over-looked.

In fact, family members may become so close that they vicari-ously experience the pain and distress, the successes and failures of other family members as their own. Accordingly, the social exclusion and vulnerability of the ill child are experienced in their fullness by the entire family. Parents and siblings strongly identi-fy with and agonize over the troubled relationships that the ill child has in school, the neighborhood, and the larger community; they feel a need to protect the ill child from teasing and rejection. Bowen (1978) uses the term *undifferentiated family ego mass* to describe this situation of emotional fusion in which family mem-bers are so connected and empathic that they are unable to sepa-rate their own feelings, thoughts, wishes, and fantasies from those of other family members.

The heightened sensitivity of family members to the sick child may paradoxically erect a barrier between family members, who feel compelled to disguise their sadness and pain in order to shield the others. Although well-intended, the secrecy and con-cealment of feelings strain and distort genuine intimacy in the family. A dying child may be denied the comfort and support of close family because parents do not want to increase the child's anxiety about death by talking about it. The child, in turn, may wish to protect the family from his or her own terror of dying. The unintended consequence of the lack of disclosure is experienced as withdrawal and estrangement at a time when family members most need support from one another.

ALTERED STATUS OF THE FAMILY IN THE COMMUNITY

The reluctance to tell others about the illness suggests a conviction on the part of the ill child and family that undesirable consequences are likely to occur when the child is identified as a cancer patient. An effort to conceal the illness can be interpreted as a tactic for avoiding stigma. This raises many interesting questions about the motivations for and the consequences of stigma in childhood cancer.

Families report that stigma associated with childhood cancer touches the child's parents and the siblings not only because they vicariously share the child's pain and rejection, but because they, too, are treated differently by others. For this reason, sharing the diagnosis with others is experienced as a dilemma for many families. Families worry that dissemination of this information will alter relations with extended family, friends, and others in the social network. Parents especially want to avoid being treated as special and exposing themselves to questions that might reveal their distress, make them appear weak, or result in their becoming a burden to friends (Barbarin & Chesler, 1983).

Relationships with friends become characterized by tentativeness and strain. Parents experience ambivalence because they desire emotional comfort but do not want to appear too needy or to burden or depress their friends. Friends also experience awkwardness because they do not know how much they can ask about the child's or the parents' condition without being judged intrusive, demanding, or voyeuristic. For this reason, friends hesitate to reach out to help too quickly and in too intimate a way. This ambivalence is stronger in individuals within the social network who were not very close to the family prior to the illness, such as neighbors, acquaintances, co-workers, the child's and siblings' schoolteachers, principals, and other school personnel.

The way a family is perceived and relates to the community may also be affected by the experience of childhood cancer. Parents and siblings may be treated as though they are tainted. Some people, believing that cancer is contagious, think that family members carry a communicable disease or virus. Other individuals may impute blame on the family for the illness by viewing it as a consequence of the family's neglect, defective genes, or moral transgressions. For example, some parents of children with cancer report criticism from their own parents for not taking proper precautions to avoid carcinogens in the child's diet. Others report criticism from religious leaders and church members who view the cancer as God's punishment for the sins of the parents.

The illness may alter the family's relationship with the community by increasing its visibility and involvement in a variety of social service agencies. In the child's school, they become a "special family," to be supported, pitied, or avoided. Moreover, a combination of decreased income and increased financial obligations may alter the economic status of the family and restrict the range of activities in which family members are able to participate. For example, some families accumulate debts of $80,000 to $100,000 and are forced to declare bankruptcy and accept welfare or seek assistance from charitable organizations. This change of status may damage the self-esteem of families who had taken pride in their ability to take care of themselves.

The work life and career development of family members may also be affected. Care of a seriously ill child often disrupts the continuity and quality of work performance. A family member may no longer be perceived as an efficient, productive, and reliable employee. Supervisors and fellow workers often convey sympathy and acceptance initially, then gradually give way to resentment at having to make adjustments to compensate for the family member's absence. Although the specific ways in which families of children with cancer are viewed may vary from situation to situation, that they are viewed and treated differently as a result of the diagnosis is indisputable.

CONCLUSION

Previous analyses of stigma directed our attention to the effects of stigmatizing processes on social relationships of individuals who possess the stigmatizing condition. These analyses have tended to focus on stigma as an individual process, and consequently they have overlooked the dynamic aspects of stigma as a shared experience. The family's identification with the child who has cancer, the intrusiveness of treatment, and attempts to deal with the emotional and instrumental demands of the illness substantially affect many aspects of family life such as social status, economic status, place of residence, work life, and task allocation. No one in the family is untouched by these demands that bind the family together in a common struggle and a common pattern of adaptation. The experience of stigma in childhood cancer is expressed in terms of the changes in the way the family relates to the child and to each other. In this regard, the family itself stigmatizes the child and shares in the effect of stigmatization by persons outside of the family. Unlike stigmatization by outsiders, the family's stigmatization of the child may be an outcome of their attempt to cope with the fragility of the ill child's life and the uncertainty of the outcome of treatment.

This aspect of stigma in childhood cancer leads to several interesting questions about the importance of the motivation and source of stigma to its stability and outcome over time. Family members, who share the stigma through their emotional attachment to the child, may stigmatize in different ways and for different reasons than persons who have no such attachment. Stigma within the family may result from a lack of information and a desire to protect the child, whereas for persons outside of the family the motive may be to protect oneself from contagion and death anxiety. Family and nonfamily members may differ considerably in the extent to which the child's incapacity is attributed to global, stable, and internal characteristics or to transient situational factors associated with the disease.

When stigmatization of the child by the family occurs, it is often more benign, pliable, and attributed to the illness. Low performance expectations of the child often are changed in response to new, contradictory information. Stigmatizing attitudes and behavior of persons outside of the family, however, often endure in spite of contradictory evidence. For example, the attitude of insurance companies and the U.S. military toward the disease-free adult who has a history of childhood cancer is intractable. Even when individuals have been in remission for 10 or 20 years, they are treated as though they are still diseased. Thus, differences in the motivation and genesis of stereotyped attitudes associated with stigma may influence the rigidity of attitudes and subsequent responses to stigma.

Although it is highly probably that family members' experience of stigma changes over time, the factors associated with that change are not obvious. Does the family stigma disappear if the child dies or survives into adulthood? Does the role-dependent nature of the family experience mean that each family member is affected differently by the stigma? Do some ordinarily healthy characteristics of family systems such as coordination of effort, mutuality, and cohesion make it more difficult for family members to forge a separate identity and reject the stigma? Do siblings give up the stigma when they move away from their family of origin and go on to form their own families of procreation?

Still another set of questions emerges regarding the potentially positive effects of stigma. Some of the immediate effects have already been discussed. For example, in many cases the quality of family life, especially in relation to cohesion and mutual support, seems to be strengthened by the experience. It is possible that other long-term effects of the stigma may occur. Does the early experience of stigma and the confrontation with death inoculate family members against harmful effects of different stigmatizing conditions in later life? Much more will be understood about stigma in general by exploring the answers to these questions about family experiences.

CHAPTER 10

Stigmatization in Childhood
A SURVEY OF DEVELOPMENTAL TRENDS AND ISSUES

Carol K. Sigelman and Louise C. Singleton

"Hey, ape man, what you got tied to your feet, boxing gloves?" So went the first day of school for Henry Viscardi (1952, p. 14), born with severely deformed legs. Experiences like Viscardi's stun those of us who imagine young children free of the hatred and prejudice that plague adulthood, and who, like Rodgers and Hammerstein, assume that "you've got to be carefully taught," presumably by prejudiced adults, in order to hate. When do children first show tendencies to stigmatize those who are different in some way? How do such tendencies evolve over the childhood years? Why do some children come to tolerate differences, whereas others hate with passion? What does the study of human development contribute to a multidisciplinary view of stigma? It is questions such as these that the present chapter addresses.

DEVELOPMENTAL ISSUES

Psychologists, sociologists, educators, and others within the multidisciplinary field of child development have long been concerned with children's reactions to various human differences. We believe that a developmental perspective offers something unique to the understanding of stigma. Developmental research cannot tell us about the historical and social forces that give root to stigmatization, but it can help tell us how we as individuals come to stigmatize others as a function of both our maturation as humans and our specific learning experiences.

Students of child development continually grapple with the classic nature–nurture, or maturation versus experience, issue. It would be one thing to view stigmatization primarily as the natural outgrowth of normal, genetically guided maturational processes, for then we would be implying that the fundamental processes involved in stigmatization are universal, even if the targets of stigma vary from society to society. It would be quite another thing to view stigmatization primarily as the product of specific learning experiences that only some children have, for then we would view stigma as an environment-specific phenomenon and see more possibilities for preventing and eliminating it. Researchers of child development have arrived at a consensus that both nature and nurture are important and interact to make us what we are. There is still room for debate, however, about the relative influences of maturation and learning on specific aspects of development. Although environmental influences should not be neglected, biology is a force to consider as well.

Developmental studies also attempt to understand the shape or form of development, some demonstrating distinct stages emerging in orderly sequence over childhood, others demonstrating gradual and continuous accumulations of capacities that might differ markedly from one child to the next. Could there be predictable stages in the development of stigmatization that make it quite a different phenomenon in early childhood from what it is in later childhood or adulthood? If such stages exist, a multidisciplinary understanding of stigma would have to include the recognition that the very meaning of stigma changes over the life span. Developmental research can help us understand how and when the components of stigma—thought (e.g., negative stereotypes), emotion (e.g., dislike), and behavior (e.g., discrimination against an out-group)—first take form and when they become intertwined to form a coherent response tendency.

In this chapter, we begin by looking at three major theories of development—psychoanalytic theory, social learning theory, and cognitive-developmental theory—that offer broad frameworks for examining the origins and development of stigmatization. To our knowledge, there is no developmental theory of stigma, but broad developmental theories can be, and have been, applied to the study of stigmatization. Then we search for the earliest roots of stigmatization in the infant years. Centering our attention on the two topics of racial prejudice and negative reactions to physical and mental disabilities, we then selectively review developmental trends and issues in stigmatization over childhood. Finally, we attempt to integrate the material in light of developmental theory and to identify issues for future theory building, research, and intervention.

DEVELOPMENTAL THEORY AND STIGMA

PSYCHOANALYTIC THEORY

Psychoanalytic theory, originated by Freud and shaped by many others, has had its impact on conceptualizations of stereotyping and prejudice (see Ashmore & Del Boca, 1976). Rather than tracing developmental trends, psychoanalytically oriented researchers have attempted to account for individual differences in the tendency to stigmatize by examining differences in personality. Stigmatization is thought to reflect internal personality conflicts rooted in early childhood experiences, possibly in parental punitiveness. Underlying conflict can be expressed through defense mechanisms such as displacement (expressing frustrations against an out-group when one cannot express them against the actual sources of the frustration) and projection (attributing to an out-group urges that one cannot admit in oneself). Personality conflict can also give rise to an "authoritarian personality," a hostile, rigid, and conforming world view rooted in early childhood and resulting in prejudice toward a range of groups. In short, prejudice reflects personality development gone astray.

Imagine children whose parents restrict their natural biological urges through stingy feeding practices in infancy, harsh toilet training, or punishment for sexual curiosity. Such children, according to the psychoanalytic view, would harbor unconscious anxiety and would need to develop ways to cope with it. If they could not admit to and express hostilities toward their parents for thwarting their urges, they might lash out instead at an accessible out-group. If they could not accept their own sexual urges, they might attribute those very urges to an out-group. The nature of the conflict between biological urges and rational and social controls would change with age, and the subtlety of defenses against anxiety would increase with age, but the basic idea of stigmatizing others in order to cope with internal personality conflicts would remain constant.

Actual evidence regarding relationships between child-rearing practices and prejudice has been inconsistent (Ashmore & Del Boca, 1976), and the psychoanalytic approach is not as widely embraced as it once was. However, it is currently regaining the attention of developmental researchers because it so nicely highlights the role of emotion in development—and in stigma as well.

SOCIAL LEARNING THEORY

The social learning approach associated with Albert Bandura, Walter Mischel, and others (e.g., Bandura, 1977) uses the same principles to explain sex-role attitudes or racial prejudice as it does to explain other complex behaviors. One essential way children learn is through observing behaviors modeled by others (e.g., prejudiced remarks made by their parents). Social learning theorists stress a distinction between acquisition (or learning) and performance because children do not imitate every behavior they see and may acquire information even if they do not imitate what they see. The likelihood that children will directly or indirectly imitate what they observe is influenced by the consequences of behavior, which create expectancies of future consequences that then guide future behavior. It should be emphasized that social learning theory, although it pays attention to cognition, puts primary emphasis on behavior. Moreover, it is not a stage theory, though it does indicate that children's facility in observational learning gradually increases over childhood.

Thus, social learning theorists would view stigmatizing reactions as sets of learned behaviors that develop through the interaction among the modeled behaviors to which the child is exposed, the expectancy of reinforcement for those behaviors, and the current physical/cognitive skill level of the child. For example, a sexist little boy might be shaped if the boy's father and male peers consistently model "male" behaviors and sexist attitudes, reinforce "male" behaviors and sexist attitudes, and punish the slightest signs of "female" behavior. Development would be expected to vary from child to child depending on each child's experiences, and changes in behavior could readily occur if different behaviors were modeled and reinforced (Huston, 1983). Thus, social learning theorists would be the first to emphasize that our social environment is critical in determining whether or not we stigmatize, whom we stigmatize, and how we stigmatize. Social learning theorists also remind us that when we detect systematic stages in development it could be because the social environments of children change as they move from infancy to adulthood.

COGNITIVE-DEVELOPMENTAL THEORY

The cognitive-developmental perspective associated with Jean Piaget and extended by others has dominated developmental psychology in recent years (see Kohlberg, 1969, for an overview). Among its themes are the following:

- Children actively develop themselves, arriving at their own understandings of the world rather than merely absorbing adult understandings.
- Maturation and experience interact during development, with current understandings influencing what children seek and take from their environments, and new experiences pushing them toward more advanced levels of understanding.
- Development proceeds through qualitatively different stages, each reflecting a coherent, but distinctive, way of viewing and dealing with the world.
- Differences in experiences among children lead primarily to differences in rates of development through stages that are basically universal.

Stigmatization of certain groups of people might be related to the development of social cognition, or thinking about people (e.g., Serafica, 1982). It might be linked, for example, to growing capacities to discriminate among people, categorize them into groups, form one's identity in relation to others, and interpret the behavior of others. If this is correct, stigmatizing reactions might evolve through predictable stages. One might then see evidence of stigmatization in most children, not just those who have had their personalities twisted in ways that Freud might have described or those who have undergone distinctive learning experiences. At the very least, the cognitive-developmental perspective would expect stigmatization as expressed by a 5-year-old to be different in kind from stigmatization expressed by a 20-year-old, a lesson of some importance to adults who insist on judging children in adult terms.

Consider sex roles from the cognitive-developmental approach. Lawrence Kohlberg (1966) proposed that the child's own efforts to construct an identity as male or female, as opposed to socialization efforts by parents and others, are critical. Once children are able to categorize themselves as male or female at the age of 2 or 3, they actively seek out knowledge of how to be a boy or a girl. As understanding increases, children become even more attentive to same-sex models and committed to all that is sex-appropriate. Children are hypothesized to pass through stages in sex-role development at roughly the same ages. Parents and others need not indoctrinate children; they will do the hard work themselves (e.g., Huston, 1983).

Clearly the psychoanalytic, social learning, and cognitive-developmental perspectives all contribute something to our understanding of the development of stigmatization. Just as clearly, they differ in emphasis. Psychoanalytic theory places stigmatization in the context of emotions, especially emotional conflicts growing out of the child's biological urges and early experiences with parents. Social learning theory stresses behavior and puts more weight on the power of different social environments to push children in one developmental direction or another. Finally, cognitive-developmental theorists emphasize predictable stages in understanding such concepts as gender and racial identity and building knowledge of stereotypes, stages that are actively "constructed" by all normal children. Emotion, behavior, and thought, as they are shaped by maturation and learning, must all be understood if we are to grasp the nature and origins of stigma.

THE EARLY ORIGINS OF STIGMATIZATION IN INFANCY

How early in life can we detect the origins of stigmatization? Newborns do not stigmatize people. Before stigmatization is even conceivable, infants have a number of important discriminations to make: self versus nonself, people versus nonpeople, one person versus another, and so on. Then they must learn to respond differentially based on such discriminations or social categorizations. Research on the development of close attachments and wariness of strangers in infancy tells us much about this maturational process and its implications.

The development of an attachment to a parent or other significant person unfolds in an orderly way during infancy (e.g., Schaffer & Emerson, 1964). In the first 2 months of life, social stimulation is not much more interesting than nonsocial stimulation, but newborns do appear to have an interest in faces and an ability to distinguish normal from abnormal faces (e.g., see Sherrod, 1981). By 3 to 5 months of age, a clear preference for social stimulation emerges, but infants are as unprejudiced as they could be, promiscuously enjoying the company of both familiar and strange humans. It is with the formation of the first genuine attachment at roughly 7 months that signs of wariness of strangers begin to appear. Such signs continue to heighten over the first year, waning in the second and third years.

Stranger anxiety is of obvious relevance to the search for early roots of stigmatization. The literature (e.g., Sroufe, 1977) suggests that not all strangers are equally threatening. Infants are more wary of adults than of children (Brooks & Lewis, 1976), and of men than of women (Greenberg, Hillman & Grice, 1973). Moreover, white infants are more wary of blacks than of whites (Feinman, 1980). Stranger anxiety is by no means stigmatization, for it is quickly overcome after a period of familiarization. Nonetheless, it appears to be a universal phenomenon in the first year of life, and one wonders what underlies it.

Unfamiliarity, dissimilarity to self, and uncertainty have been suggested as bases for stranger wariness. Infants might be especially wary of people who are different from most people they have encountered. They might form what cognitive-developmentalists call schemas, or cognitive models, for the self; categorize themselves as children rather than adults, female rather than male, and so on; and attach positive meaning to "like me" and negative meaning to "not like me" (Lewis & Brooks, 1974). Finally, they might be wary when they are unsure what to expect in an encounter with an unfamiliar person and cannot answer the questions they raise to reduce their uncertainty (Kagan, Kearsley, & Zelazo, 1975). It is likely that unfamiliarity, dissimilarity to self, and unresolved uncertainty all play some role in stranger anxiety—and may be important considerations in stigmatization across the life span as well.

Research on attachment also tells us that infants are already capable of assessing situational cues in deciding whether to react positively or negatively toward others. For example, Sroufe, Waters, and Matas (1974) found that infants smiled and laughed when their mothers put on a strange mask but frowned, turned away, and sometimes cried when a stranger did the same thing. An infant's reactions to unfamiliar people may be especially influenced by cues provided by significant others such as parents (e.g., Feinman, 1982). Even very young infants will look to others for such cues. Thus, a parent's discomfort in the presence of a disabled person could easily influence an infant's reactions.

In summary, we have suggested that, as part of their social-cognitive maturation, infants enter a period of heightened stranger wariness; that some strangers are more threatening than others; and that situational cues, as interpreted by infants, help shape responses in predominantly positive or negative directions. But if stranger anxiety fades with age, how can it help account for stigmatization later in life? Perhaps it cannot. However, it may serve as a prototype of stigmatization, illustrating the roles of both cognitive capacity and environment in stigmatization.

As children develop, their schemas and expectations regarding people become increasingly complex and information-rich, but children continue to encounter individuals who are unfamiliar, are dissimilar to themselves, or are sources of uncertainty, and their responses differ. Individual differences in the tendency to stigmatize could, of course, be rooted in genetically influenced differences in temperament. Moreover, as Freud long maintained, the roots of a child's style of relating to people may lie in infancy and the security of the parent–child relationship (see Waters, Wippman, & Sroufe, 1979). Finally, one can easily imagine some infants learning a predominantly negative response to new or different people through social learning processes— for example, experiences in which parents signal their own aversions. The widespread, perhaps universal, tendency of infants to be wary of people who are different implies that the potential for stigmatization lies in everyone. Whether or not that potential is realized later in life, however, may come to depend less on cognitive universals and more on social experience as the child moves out of infancy and into childhood.

DEVELOPMENTAL TRENDS IN STIGMATIZATION OVER CHILDHOOD

When during childhood do negative responses first emerge toward peers who are different? How do they evolve over childhood? Logically, it would seem that the child's first task in developing stigmatizing responses is to cognitively differentiate classes of people. The cognitive component of attitudes also involves forming stereotypes or beliefs about characteristics associated with social categories (e.g., mentally retarded people are dangerous). The affective component of attitudes consists of emotional responses, preferences, and evaluative judgments. Finally, the behavioral component involves learning to act differentially toward members of different social categories. The literature on the development of stigmatization includes some attention to all three components, enough for us to conclude that the roots of stigmatization are evident in the preschool years. We will illustrate some of the messages of developmental research by examining children's reactions to peers of a different race and to peers with physical and mental disabilities.

RACIAL PREJUDICE

Race is one visible characteristic that can set a child apart as different and result in stigmatization by peers. Goodman (1964) proposed three stages in the development of racial attitudes: (a) *ethnic awareness*, at ages 3 to 5, when the focus in on the cognitive processes of differentiating among groups and establishing one's own racial or ethnic identity; (b) *ethnic orientation*, ages 5 to 7, when the focus is on the affective component of attitudes as children begin to make positive and negative evaluations of racial groups: and (c) *ethnic attitudes*, ages 7 to 10, when the cognitive, affective, and behavioral aspects of attitudes become more congruent and prejudice generally increases.

More recently, Katz (1976) has set forth an expanded, eight-stage version of Goodman's model. Like Goodman, she emphasizes the early emergence of prejudice and the increasing consistency of the three components of attitudes with age. Katz takes into account data showing that awareness of racial differences emerges before the age of 3, however, and that negative evaluations of certain racial groups emerge simultaneously with the ability to classify racial groups. She concludes that the cognitive, affective, and behavioral aspects of prejudice do not follow one another in a clear developmental progression as Goodman suggested. Instead, the three components may be acquired relatively independently and may depend on different social learning experiences. Katz reminds us, then, to consider thought, feeling, and behavior both separately and jointly if we are to understand stigma.

THE PRESCHOOL YEARS

Before a child can stigmatize racial groups, he or she must be able to perceive racial differences. The ability to discriminate between racial groups has its roots in infancy and so may a preference for white over black, at least among white infants (Feinman, 1980; Hershenson, 1964). Williams and Morland (1976) have proposed that a preference for the color *white* over the color *black* in children as young as 2 and 3 years of age may be biologically based. They hypothesize that color and race bias may originate in a child's natural tendency to prefer light over darkness because disorientation occurs in the dark, whereas major need satisfactions occur during the day. This prolight bias, they say, is further reinforced by cultural norms that associate light with good and dark with bad, and it generalizes directly to a preference for light-skinned over dark-skinned people, even though it is not initially a racial bias.

Does research support this view? One measure of prejudice often used by researchers is the doll preference task (Clark & Clark, 1947) and its variants. It measures racial classification ability, racial stereotyping, and racial preferences. Two dolls, one black and one white, are presented to the child, who is asked such questions as, "Which is the white doll?" and "Which doll looks nice?" Clark and Clark (1947) found that most black and white children can correctly identify black and white dolls by age 3 and that this racial classification ability improves over the preschool years.

What does research tell us about affect and behavior? Although early research indicated that both black and white children preferred the white doll (Asher & Allen, 1969; Clark & Clark, 1947), more recent studies indicate that white children prefer white dolls, but black children show no preference or prefer black dolls (e.g., Hraba & Grant, 1970). These inconsistencies in black children's preferences may be linked to such factors as the black pride movement of the 1970s, geographic variations in attitudes, or methodological variations among studies (Katz, 1976). Few studies have examined the actual behavior of preschoolers. Stevenson and Stevenson (1960) found no race bias in play patterns observed in a nursery school, whereas Finkelstein and Haskins (1983), observing a slightly older sample of kindergarten children, found significant own-race preference by both black and white children.

Overall, then, racial preference appears to emerge early and simultaneously with racial classification ability, and both increase with age over the preschool years. However, we must be skeptical of this research and its implications. The fact that recent studies reveal less prolight bias among black children than earlier studies casts doubt on Williams and Morland's theory that prolight bias is biologically based. Perhaps social forces are at work, making today's black children less likely to internalize negative societal views of blacks. Any biological hypothesis of stigma is undermined to the extent that children in different subcultural settings or historical periods show different tendencies toward stigmatization. Williams and Morland may underestimate the human tendency, whether one is black or white, to be attracted toward those who are similar to oneself.

Moreover, serious questions can be raised about our ability to conceptualize and measure prejudice in young children (Katz, 1976). For example, Porter (1971) found that playmate preferences were largely unrelated to responses on doll preference tasks. Lerner and Schroeder (1975) compared different versions of the doll preference task in a sample of white kindergarten children. Forced to choose, children associated positive traits with the white doll and negative traits with the black doll, but when asked to describe what each doll was like, children never derogated the black doll. Thus, the commonly used forced-choice method may elicit more racial bias than children display when they are given more freedom of choice. Possibly different components of prejudice are simply independent in early childhood, in which case we would not expect consistency among different measures. Or possibly we have encountered a problem that is especially challenging when young children are involved but applies at any age: How does one develop measures that adequately tap the multifaceted nature of stigma? We can conclude that prejudice originates in and strengthens over the preschool years, but we cannot claim to have a good grasp on the nature of racial stigmatization in early childhood.

LATER DEVELOPMENT

Studies of older children have increasingly focused on the cognitive aspects of attitudes. Tajfel and his colleagues (e.g., Tajfel, 1969) have proposed that we naturally categorize people into groups. Once people are grouped, there is a fundamental cognitive tendency to exaggerate between-group differences and to minimize within-group ones. For example, Billig and Tajfel (1973) found that when older elementary-school children are arbitrarily divided into groups to which labels are applied, children will value their own group and discriminate against the out-group. Most of Tajfel's research has been done with older children and adults. The effects of categorization might be even stronger among younger children, whose cognitive abilities are just developing. Moreover, Billig and Tajfel used arbitrary criteria to form groups, and even stronger in-group/out-group feelings might be generated if race were the criterion.

Does racial categorization bias perception? Katz (1973) examined the ability of black and white children to discriminate among faces of their own or another race. Because children hear racial labels applied more frequently to people of other races than to people of their own race, Katz expected that it would be more difficult for them to learn to discriminate among other-race faces than among own-race faces. This was the case for both black and white children. More learning trials were not needed when faces were green, suggesting that it was racial labeling itself, not unfamiliarity with other-race members, that was interfering with discrimination between other-race faces. Black children learned more quickly than white children did, suggesting that black children have been more strongly socialized to attend to skin color differences.

Collectively, the studies of Tajfel and Katz and their colleagues suggest that prejudice may be partly rooted in a natural tendency to divide people into groups and label them. Once this happens, perceptions of group members are shaped by the group label, and individual differences among group members are ignored, even though it is the very process of attending to individual differences that could best help to break down cultural stereotypes. Stigmatization, then, is partly based in the information-processing capacities of all humans. However, societal influences can make a specific attribute like skin color more salient to some children than to others (Katz, 1973).

Another line of research on the cognitive aspects of older children's racial attitudes has focused on stereotypes. Studying black and white children in grades 4 through 12, Brigham (1974) found that by fourth grade most children were aware of what traits are stereotyped as black or white traits. However, children's stereotypes did not follow the simple "white is good, black is bad" rule evident among preschoolers. Rather, both black and white children attributed favorable traits to their own race. In addition, agreement within each racial group on the content of stereotypes increased with age, suggesting that race-specific social learning experiences were influential.

Interestingly, Brigham's study also revealed a tendency for older white children to attribute more positive traits to blacks than younger children did. Although this may indicate that stereotypes become more complex with age, it may also reflect greater awareness of socially desirable responses with age—greater awareness that it is unacceptable to express prejudice. A study by Katz, Johnson, and Parker (1970) supports this view. They found a decrease in prejudice from second to sixth grade on a questionnaire measure, but no such decrease on a projective measure for which socially desirable responses were less obvious (see also Silverman & Shaw, 1973).

We should also be suspicious of developmental declines in prejudice revealed in measures of cognition because they are not mirrored in affective and behavioral measures. The affective component of racial attitudes has been studied extensively, using sociometric measures that ask children to nominate preferred friends or playmates or rate how much they like to play or work with each of their classmates (e.g., Singleton & Asher, 1977, 1979). In general, sociometric studies find that children prefer peers of their own race to peers of the other race (e.g., Singleton & Asher, 1977, 1979). However, these studies—in direct contradiction to the research on cognitive stereotypes—also show increased preference for own-race peers as children get older (e.g., Asher, Singleton, & Taylor, 1982). This developmental trend toward increased racial polarization may be due to such factors as the development of racial identity, the emergence of interest in dating in early adolescence, or the growing achievement gap between black and white children.

Just as expressions of positive racial attitudes in older children are accompanied by little cross-race friendship, they are accompanied by little cross-race behavioral interaction. As noted earlier, nursery-school children appear to show no own-race bias in their play, whereas kindergarten children show some. Third-graders engage in a considerable amount of cross-race interaction (Singleton & Asher, 1977), whereas older children and adolescents show increasingly strong own-race preferences (Schofield & Sagar, 1977; Silverman & Shaw, 1973).

Having traced the developmental course of children's racial attitudes, we are left with many unanswered questions. Perceptual awareness and evaluation of color differences begin at such an early age that we cannot entirely dismiss Williams and Morland's theory that color preference is partly biologically based. In addition, the work of Tajfel and Katz points to the power of racial labeling and universal cognitive processes in the development of prejudice. This does not imply that prejudice is inevitable. Indeed, we have uncovered much evidence that social learning experiences shape children's preferences, create differences between black and white children's attitudes, and become increasingly influential as children mature. Our problems lie in determining which of these influences on development are most critical and how they interact. Moreover, we must account for the fact that prejudice appears to decline with age when cognitions are assessed but appears to increase with age when affect and behavior are assessed. If pressures to give socially desirable answers were reduced, older children might stigmatize as much as or even more than younger children do. However, we will not be sure until we unravel the complex relationships among cognition, affect, and behavior as they evolve over childhood.

REACTIONS TO PHYSICAL AND MENTAL DISABILITIES

Does the development of negative reactions to children with physical and mental disabilities resemble the development of racial prejudice? Because many disabilities are rare, little is known about reactions to children who have them, though one suspects that the nature and symptoms of a specific impairment partially shape peer responses to it.

The Preschool Years

Exploring the cognitive component of attitudes toward several disabilities, Conant and Budoff (1983) reported that preschoolers first became at least somewhat aware of the meaning of both blindness and deafness and then developed awareness of orthopedic disability. Awareness of mental retardation emerged only in elementary-school years, and awareness of psychological disorder still later. Not surprisingly, then, children are aware of visible differences before they are aware of problems such as low intellectual ability that must be inferred from behavior.

Several researchers have shown preschoolers pictures or drawings of disabled children and questioned them about their preferences. Although their studies illustrate once more the challenges of assessing and interpreting young children's attitudes, they also indicate at least mild preference for the ablebodied over the nonablebodied. For example, Weinberg (1978) found no clear signs of rejection of a wheelchair-bound child among 3- to 5-year-olds until a forced-choice method was used—that is, until children were asked whether they would rather play with the disabled child or an ablebodied child.

Studies of the behavioral component of attitudes also suggest preference for those without disabilities. Most research has centered on mentally retarded children, who, in this age range, often also have visible disabilities or abnormalities (e.g., Down's syndrome appearance). Studies of peer interactions in preschool settings consistently show that nonretarded preschoolers prefer to interact with other nonretarded preschoolers, whereas retarded children may or may not prefer other retarded children (e.g., Porter, Ramsey, Tremblay, Iaccobo, & Crawley, 1978). Because the concept of mental retardation means nothing to preschoolers, they must be reacting to concrete signs of behavioral or physical similarity and difference. Nonretarded children might be expressing both a preference for those who are similar to themselves and a wariness of those who are dissimilar. Whatever the reasons, children who are disabled, although they do not face active hostility, are less than fully accepted quite early in life.

LATER DEVELOPMENT

Although preschoolers are not highly negative toward disabled peers, a number of studies suggest that consciously expressed attitudes become more positive with age. Spillers (1982), for example, asked preschoolers and third-graders to respond to photos of ablebodied and wheelchair-bound children. Both groups were highly accepting of disabled children when not forced to choose, but on a forced-choice task there was a developmental shift: Preschoolers preferred the ablebodied children, whereas third-graders preferred the wheelchair-bound ones. Spillers suspected that the older children were making socially desirable responses. Similarly, verbally expressed attitudes toward mentally retarded children appear to become more positive, starting in the later elementary-school years (e.g., Gottlieb & Switzky, 1982). If older children hold negative attitudes toward disabled peers, they apparently have learned to suppress them while responding to reactive attitudinal measures, just as we saw was the case in the development of racial attitudes.

Similar themes emerge from studies conducted by Stephen Richardson and his colleagues, in which children ranked drawings of ablebodied and disabled children (see Richardson, 1983, for a review). Richardson (1970) used this ranking methodology to examing age trends from kindergarten to 12th grade. Kindergarteners did not show a clear perference for the ablebodied target and may not have understood the task fully, whereas older children clearly preferred the ablebodied child to the others. Liking for a wheelchair-bound child increased with age, whereas liking for certain other children decreased. With age, children's preferences also became more like those of their parents. Thus, Richardson suggested that younger children most disliked the targets who most diverged from normal appearance, whereas older ones based their preferences on learned cultural values.

We must note that this kind of ranking methodology forces children to make choices that they might not otherwise make.

Indeed, Matthews and Westie (1966) commented that many of their high-school subjects objected strenuously to Richardson's ranking procedure, saying, for example, "I will not be prejudiced." This response is consistent with the well-documented tendency of adults to display, not stigmatization, but positive prejudice toward both successful and unsuccessful physically disabled persons under many circumstances (e.g., Carver, Glass, & Katz, 1978). Similarly, studies of college students suggest that when a person is labeled mentally retarded, he or she is not blamed as much as a nonretarded person for failure. Unlike a physically disabled person, however, he or she gets less rather than more credit for successes (e.g., Gibbons, 1981). In both cases, adults seem to be reflecting an understanding that disability makes certain achievements very difficult and explains failure.

When does this sympathy arise during childhood? Elementary-school children generally appear to like competent peers more than incompetent peers, but their reactions to the presence of a physical or mental disability range from the stigmatizing to the sympathetic and most often are not strong one way or the other (Gottlieb, 1974). Possibly sympathy for physically disabled children is in the making as early as the middle elementary school years (cf., Spillers, 1982). However, in a study patterned after those of Carver *et al.* (1978), Sigelman and McGrail (1985) detected stigmatization of both a wheelchair-bound child and a mentally retarded child who were incompetent among third- and fourth-graders. Like adults, both junior and senior high school students tended to evaluate the incompetent disabled children more positively than an incompetent ablebodied child. All age groups were unaffected by the presence of a disability when a person was successful (see also Elam and Sigelman, 1983). Thus, we see a developmental shift in reactions to hypothetical disabled peers who are poorly adjusted: Elementary-age children stigmatize, but adolescents grant what has been called "special dispensation," tolerating failure in a disabled person more than they tolerate failure in a person who is not disabled.

We must be cautious about these apparently heartening findings, however, for they may mislead us into thinking that from adolescence on, disabled persons can expect sympathy rather than stigmatization. Although Carver *et al.* (1978) demonstrated that socially desirable responding was not the source of sympathetic response to physically disabled persons, other studies do document aversive reactions to such people on the part of adults, especially when pressures toward socially desirable responding are reduced (e.g., Snyder, Kleck, Strenta, & Mentzer, 1979). Moreover, sociometric studies asking children to name liked and disliked peers tend to reveal that physically disabled children, although not strongly rejected, are less well-liked than their ablebodied peers (Kleck & DeJong, 1983). Similarly, mentally retarded children have low sociometric status from early childhood through adolescence (e.g., Semmel, Gottlieb, & Robinson, 1979). In completing sociometric surveys, children are not aware that their attitudes toward disabled peers are at issue, and that may be a critical factor in explaining the low social acceptance that such surveys reveal. Alternatively, children may respond to real individuals who are disabled differently than they respond to hypothetical ones.

In summary, the evidence presents a confusing, but possibly interpretable, picture. Certain reactions to physically and mentally disabled people do become more positive with age, just as certain aspects of racial attitudes do. What is unclear is how favorable such reactions really are. Both older children and adults will express sympathetic and positive attitudes when verbal measures are used. This evidence suggests that children acquire adult social norms demanding sympathy for those who are disabled through no fault of their own.

Yet one suspects that attitudinal studies paint too rosy a picture. Sociometric choices and behavioral interaction patterns from the preschool years on, along with the tendency of children to prefer ablebodied to disabled children when forced to choose, offer hints of a negative attitudinal undercurrent that warrants further plumbing. We can be cheered by the fact that children come to understand the limits that disabilities impose and to hold, at a conscious level at least, primarily sympathetic attitudes. We must also acknowledge, however, that even adolescents and adults continue to value competence and to experience aversion toward people with physical and mental disabilities.

Once again, then, we are struck by the complexity of the relationships among the cognitive, affective, and behavioral components of stigma.

SUMMARY AND IMPLICATIONS

What can we conclude about the development of stigmatization? What is the current state of knowledge, and what must be done to improve on it? What are the prospects for preventing or reducing stigmatization? What does a developmental perspective contribute to a multidisciplinary understanding of stigma?

The study of stigmatization in childhood has come a long way since early, and largely unsuccessful, attempts to test the psychoanalytic hypothesis that prejudice is rooted in personality conflict. Research in this area still has a long way to go, however. We wish that less research were descriptive and more tested hypotheses derived from major developmental theories. We wish that more research were genuinely developmental, charting transitions in stigmatization longitudinally from infancy to adolescence.

We call for more research comparing reactions to different stigmatizing attributes and comparing children in different subcultural and cultural settings to help sort out which developmental trends are generalized and perhaps even universal and which are peculiar to specific stigmas and social contexts. Having raised numerous questions about the methods used to study children's reactions, we challenge future researchers to assess more systematically the different components of stigma and devise ways to tap the same components in both younger and older children. We encourage more attention to individual differences in stigmatizing reactions, as they are shaped by both personal and social influences. Finally, we wish that more researchers would rise above a particular theoretical bias and integrate perspectives gained from multiple theories and disciplines.

We need to attend more to the possible biological as well as psychological and sociocultural influences on the development of stigmatization. The recent dominance of cognitive-developmental theory in the field of child development may have blinded us to the emotional aspects of stigma emphasized by Freud and the sociocultural influences on development emphasized by social learning theorists, as well as to the need to view stigma, not as cognition, but as a complex interaction of cognition, emotion, and behavior.

Limited as the existing research is, it gives us a foundation for thinking about the origins and development of stigmatizing tendencies in childhood. Starting in infancy, children notice at least visible physical and behavioral differences among peers and form social categories that guide their thought, feelings, and behavior. The social categorizations made by preschoolers reflect their level of cognitive development by being rigid, all-or-none distinctions. In their effort to "construct" a meaningful social world, preschoolers can ill afford to dwell on similarities between social categories. Instead, their first step appears to be to form gross distinctions between the normal and the abnormal, between the "like me" and the "not like me," and to prefer the former to the latter. Only after the preschool years do differential preferences for various "not like me" peers appear to emerge (Sigelman, Miller, & Whitworth, in press). The identification of differences between oneself and another person or group is a fundamental basis for any form of stigmatization, and perhaps this process is necessary if young children are to find their places in the social world.

We question whether preschoolers truly display the multifaceted response we recognize as stigmatization in older children and adults. Preschoolers notice differences and establish preferences, but they do not appear to strongly stigmatize anyone. After the preschool years, thought, affect, and behavior become more complex. Two trends are evident: marked changes in children's thought processes and increased awareness of culturally approved and disapproved responses. Advances in cognitive development are illustrated by the fact that, although preschoolers' stereotypes are one-sided, older children's stereotypes include both positive and negative traits. Children also accumulate social learning experiences as they develop. On the one hand, it is true that learning appears to make them more sensitive to what one should not say about children who are different, thus accounting for positive responses on attitude measures for which socially desirable responses are obvious. On the other hand, cumulative social learning experiences give children greater exposure to and reinforcement for stigmatizing responses that continue to be revealed in their peer preferences and behavior.

Our survey of the development of stigmatization thus leads us to examine broader issues in child development, issues addressed by the dominant theoretical perspectives in the field. In support of the cognitive-developmental position, we have seen that broad maturational changes may underlie stigmatization, especially early in life. Stigmatization may first evolve from the child's attempts to understand the social world. Limitations in the young child's cognitive capacities may render their stereotypes simple and one-sided, and stigma may be a qualitatively different phenomenon among preschoolers than it is among older children. Generally, the cognitive-developmental perspective reminds us that a complete account of stigma requires attention to biological and maturational forces as well as to environmental ones, and increases our awareness that stigma means different things at different ages.

The social learning perspective also has merit, however. Because this perspective emphasizes individual differences in learning experiences, it is well-equipped to account for individual and cross-cultural differences in stigmatization. Moreover, solid support for the notion of clear-cut, universal stages in the development of stigmatization has not yet emerged. As we have seen, the cognitive, affective, and behavioral components of attitudes appear to follow different developmental paths. In addition, although developmental increases in cognitive complexity might be expected to foster greater tolerance of differences—and do indeed increase understanding of the nature and effects of disabilities—prejudice, especially as revealed by actual behavior, appears to increase rather than decrease with age, possibly due to the cumulative effects of social learning. Generally, then, social learning theory reminds us that children always develop in a social context, and that social contexts vary from child to child, culture to culture, and historical period to historical period.

Overall, then, although the cognitive-developmental perspective seems especially useful in accounting for the early origins of stigmatization, observational learning and reinforcement become more important as children get older. We may also need to revive Freud to remind us that some children may stigmatize others as a means of coping with emotional conflicts that arise out of their early difficulties in expressing biological urges.

We cannot afford to ignore either nature or nurture, either biological maturation or cumulative social learning experiences. We must attempt to identify universal maturational stages underlying the development of stigmatization if they exist, but we cannot dismiss the fact that children gradually amass knowledge of what their own society values and disvalues. If society deems overt expressions of prejudice against particular groups unacceptable, children will learn to suppress them, and if society strongly stigmatizes particular groups, children will steadily master the social learning "curriculum" to which they are exposed, particularly as it is conveyed to them by parents and peers.

Even as a sounder understanding of the development of stigmatization is being built, children are continuing to stigmatize peers who are different. To the extent that stigmatization is rooted in universal maturational processes, it may be unrealistic to expect much improvement, though social changes undoubtedly alter the specific content of stereotypes and the relative stigmatization of different attributes. To the extent that social learning theory is correct, there are grounds for more optimism about the prospects for reducing stigmatization in childhood. Indeed, acceptance of stigmatized children can be increased through carefully planned interventions, especially those that encourage cooperation among children (e.g., see Rosenfield & Stephan, 1981). Tolerance for many stigmatized groups has been increasing in recent years, and black and white children as well as disabled and nondisabled children are increasingly interacting with each other as a result of legislated school desegregation and mainstreaming of special education students. Hopefully, these social changes will foster the development of positive attitudes in children.

To be sure, developmental theory and research tell us that all human beings, by virtue of being human, mature in predictable steps. But Rodgers and Hammerstein may have been right: "You've got to be carefully taught." The emergence and strengthening of stigmatizing reactions during childhood may not be inevitable. Yet the evolution of those reactions will continue to fascinate researchers who seek to understand and optimize child development. And those researchers will continue to enrich our broader understanding of the nature of stigma and its biological and social roots.

PART **III**

STIGMA, CONTINUITY, AND CHANGE

CHAPTER 11

Stigma

AN ENIGMA DEMYSTIFIED

Lerita M. Coleman

> Nature caused us all to be born equal; if fate is
> pleased to disturb this plan of the general law,
> it is our responsibility to correct its caprice, and
> to repair by our attention the usurpations of the
> stronger.
>
> —Maurice Blanchot

We began this volume with the two basic questions: What is stigma and why does stigma remain? Because stigmas mirror culture and society, they are in constant flux, and therefore the answers to these two questions continue to elude social scientists. Viewing stigma from multiple perspectives exposes its intricate nature and helps us to disentangle its web of complexities and paradoxes. Stigma represents a view of life; a set of personal and social constructs; a set of social relations and social relationships; a form of social reality. Stigma has been a difficult concept to conceptualize because it reflects a property, a process, a form of social categorization, and an affective state.

Two primary questions, then, that we as social scientists have addressed in these chapters are how and why during certain historical periods, in specific cultures or within particular social groups, some human differences are valued and desired, and other human differences are devalued, feared, or stigmatized. In attempting to answer these questions, I propose another view of stigma, one that takes into account its behavioral, cognitive, and affective components and reveals that stigma is a response to the dilemma of difference.

THE DILEMMA

No two human beings are exactly alike; there are countless ways to differ. Shape, size, skin color, gender, age, cultural background, personality, and years of formal education are just a few of the infinite number of ways in which people can vary. Perceptually, and in actuality, there is greater variation on some of these dimensions than on others. Age and gender, for example, are dimensions with limited and quantifiable ranges; yet they interact exponentially with other physical or social characteristics that have larger continua (e.g., body shape, income, cultural background) to create a vast number of human differences. Goffman states, though, that "stigma is equivalent to an undesired differentness" (see Stafford & Scott, Chapter 5). The infinite variety of human attributes suggests that what is undesired or stigmatized is heavily dependent on the social context and to some extent arbitrarily defined. The large number of stigmatizable attributes and several taxonomies of stigmas in the literature offer further evidence of how arbitrary the selection of undesired differences may be (see Ainlay & Crosby, Chapter 2; Becker & Arnold, Chapter 3; Solomon, Chapter 4; Stafford & Scott, Chapter 5).

What is most poignant about Goffman's description of stigma is that it suggests that all human differences are potentially stigmatizable. As we move out of one social context where a difference is desired into another context where the difference is undesired, we begin to feel the effects of stigma. This conceptualization of stigma also indicates that those possessing power, the dominant group, can determine which human differences are desired and undesired. In part, stigmas reflect the value judgments of a dominant group.

Many people, however, especially those who have some role in determining the desired and undesired differences of the zeitgeist, often think of stigma only as a property of individuals. They operate under the illusion that stigma exists only for certain segments of the population. But the truth is that any "nonstigmatized" person can easily become "stigmatized." "Nearly everyone at some point in life will experience stigma either temporarily or permanently. . . . Why do we persist in this denial?" (Zola, 1979, p. 454). Given that human differences serve as the basis for stigmas, being or feeling stigmatized is virtually an inescapable fate. Because stigmas differ depending upon the culture and the historical period, it becomes evident that it is mere chance whether a person is born into a nonstigmatized or severely stigmatized group.

Because stigmatization often occurs within the confines of a psychologically constructed or actual social relationship, the experience itself reflects relative comparisons, the contrasting of desired and undesired differences. Assuming that flawless people do not exist, relative comparisons give rise to a feeling of superiority in some contexts (where one possesses a desired trait that another person is lacking) but perhaps a feeling of inferiority in other contexts (where one lacks a desired trait that another person possesses). It is also important to note that it is only when we make comparisons that we can feel different. Stigmatization or feeling stigmatized is a consequence of social comparison. For this reason, stigma represents a continuum of undesired differences that depend upon many factors (e.g., geographical location, culture, life cycle stage) (see Becker & Arnold, Chapter 3).

Although some stigmatized conditions appear escapable or may be temporary, some undesired traits have graver social consequences than others. Being a medical resident, being a new professor, being 7 feet tall, having cancer, being black, or being physically disfigured or mentally retarded can all lead to feelings of stigmatization (feeling discredited or devalued in a particular role), but obviously these are not equally stigmatizing conditions. The degree of stigmatization might depend on how undesired the difference is in a particular social group.

Physical abnormalities, for example, may be the most severely stigmatized differences because they are physically salient, represent some deficiency or distortion in the bodily form, and in most cases are unalterable. Other physically salient differences, such as skin color or nationality, are considered very stigmatizing because they also are permanent conditions and cannot be changed. Yet the stigmatization that one feels as a result of being black or Jewish or Japanese depends on the social context, specifically social contexts in which one's skin color or nationality is not a desired one. A white American could feel temporarily stigmatized when visiting Japan due to a difference in height. A black student could feel stigmatized in a predominantly white university because the majority of the students are white and white skin is a desired trait. But a black student in a predominantly black university is not likely to feel the effects of stigma. Thus, the sense of being stigmatized or having a stigma is inextricably tied to social context. Of equal importance are the norms in that context that determine which are desirable and undesirable attributes. Moving from one social or cultural context to another can change both the definitions and the consequences of stigma.

Stigma often results in a special kind of downward mobility. Part of the power of stigmatization lies in the realization that people who are stigmatized or acquire a stigma lose their place in the social hierarchy. Consequently, most people want to ensure that they are counted in the nonstigmatized "majority." This, of course, leads to more stigmatization.

Stigma, then, is also a term that connotes a relationship. It seems that this relationship is vital to understanding the stigmatizing process. Stigma allows some individuals to feel superior to others. Superiority and inferiority, however, are two sides of the same coin. In order for one person to feel superior, there must be another person who is perceived to be or who actually feels inferior. Stigmatized people are needed in order for many nonstigmatized people to feel good about themselves.

On the other hand, there are many stigmatized people who feel inferior and concede that other persons are superior because they possess certain attributes. In order for the process to occur (for one person to stigmatize another and have the stigmatized person feel the effects of stigma), there must be some agreement that the differentness is inherently undesirable. Moreover, even among stigmatized people, relative comparisons are made, and people are reassured by the fact that there is someone else who is worse off. The dilemma of difference, therefore, affects both stigmatized and nonstigmatized people.

Some might contend that this is the very old scapegoat argument, and there is some truth to that contention. But the issues here are more finely intertwined. If stigma is a social construct, constructed by cultures, by social groups, and by individuals to designate some human differences as discrediting, then the stigmatization process is indeed a powerful and pernicious social tool. The inferiority/superiority issue is a most interesting way of understanding how and why people continue to stigmatize.

Some stigmas are more physically salient than others, and some people are more capable of concealing their stigmas or escaping from the negative social consequences of being stigmatized. The ideal prototype (e.g., young, white, tall, married, male, with a recent record in sports) that Stafford cites in his chapter may actually possess traits that would be the source of much scorn and derision in another social context. Yet, by insulating himself in his own community, a man like the one described in the example can ensure that his "differentness" will receive approbation rather than rejection, and he will not be subject to constant and severe stigmatization. This is a common response to stigma among people with some social influence (e.g., artists, academics, millionaires). Often, attributes or behaviors that might otherwise be considered "abnormal" or stigmatized are labeled as "eccentric" among persons of power or influence. The fact that what is perceived as the "ideal" person varies from one social context to another, however, is tied to Martin's notion that people learn ways to stigmatize in each new situation.

In contrast, some categories of stigmatized people (e.g., the physically disabled, members of ethnic groups, poor people) cannot alter their stigmas nor easily disguise them. People, then, feel permanently stigmatized in contexts where their differentness is undesired and in social environments that they cannot easily escape. Hence, power, social influence, and social control play a major role in the stigmatization process.

In summary, stigma stems from differences. By focusing on

differences we actively create stigmas because any attribute or difference is potentially stigmatizable. Often we attend to a single different attribute rather than to the large number of similar attributes that any two individuals share. Why people focus on differences and denigrate people on the basis of them is important to understanding how some stigmas originate and persist. By reexamining the historical origins of stigma and the way children develop the propensity to stigmatize, we can see how some differences evolve into stigmas and how the process is linked to the behavioral (social control), affective (fear, dislike), and cognitive (perception of differences, social categorization) components of stigma.

THE ORIGINS OF STIGMA

The phrase *to stigmatize* originally referred to the branding or marking of certain people (e.g., criminals, prostitutes) in order to make them appear different and separate from others (Goffman, 1963). The act of marking people in this way resulted in exile or avoidance. In most cultures, physical marking or branding has declined, but a more cognitive manifestation of stigmatization—social marking—has increased and has become the basis for most stigmas (Jones *et al.*, 1984). Goffman points out, though, that stigma has retained much of its original connotation. People use differences to exile or avoid others. In addition, what is most intriguing about the ontogenesis of the stigma concept is the broadening of its predominant affective responses such as dislike and disgust to include the emotional reaction of fear. Presently, *fear* may be instrumental in the perpetuation of stigma and in maintaining its original social functions. Yet as the developmental literature reveals, fear is not a natural but an acquired response to differences of stigmas.

Sigelman and Singleton offer a number of insightful observations about how children learn to stigmatize. Children develop a natural wariness of strangers as their ability to differentiate familiar from novel objects increases (Sroufe, 1977). Developmental psychologists note that stranger anxiety is a universal phenomenon in infants and appears around the age of seven months. This reaction to differences (e.g., women versus men, children versus adults, blacks versus whites) is an interesting one and, as Sigelman and Singleton point out, may serve as a prototype for stigmatizing. Many children respond in a positive (friendly) or negative (fearful, apprehensive) manner to strangers. Strangers often arouse the interest (Brooks & Lewis, 1976) of children but elicit negative reactions if they intrude on their personal space (Sroufe, 1977). Stranger anxiety tends to fade with age, but when coupled with self-referencing it may create the conditions for a child to learn how to respond to human differences or how to stigmatize.

Self-referencing, or the use of another's interpretation of a situation to form one's own understanding of it, commonly occurs in young children. Infants often look toward caregivers when encountering something different, such as a novel object, person, or event (Feinman, 1982). The response to novel stimuli in an ambiguous situation may depend on the emotional displays of the caregiver; young children have been known to respond positively to situations if their mothers respond reassuringly (Feinman, 1982). Self-referencing is instrumental to understanding the development of stigmatization because it may be through this process that caregivers shape young children's responses to people, especially those who possess physically salient differences (Klinnert, Campos, Sorce, Emde, & Svejda, 1983). We may continue to learn about how to stigmatize from other important figures (e.g., mentors, role models) as we progress through the life cycle. Powerful authority figures may serve as the source of self-referencing behavior in new social contexts (Martin, Chapter 8).

Sigelman and Singleton also point out that preschoolers notice differences and tend to establish preferences but do not necessarily stigmatize. Even on meeting other children with physical disabilities, children do not automatically eschew them but may respond to actual physical and behavioral similiarities and differences. There is evidence, moreover, indicating that young children are curious about human differences and often stare at novel stimuli (Brooks & Lewis, 1976). Children frequently inquire of their parents or of stigmatized persons about their distinctive physical attributes. In many cases, the affective response of young children is interest rather than fear.

Barbarin offers a poignant example of the difference between interest and fear in his vignette about Myra, a child with cancer. She talks about young children who are honest and direct about her illness, an attitude that does not cause her consternation. What does disturb her, though, are parents who will not permit her to baby-sit with their children for *fear* that she might give them cancer. Thus, interest and curiosity about stigma or human differences may be natural for children, but they must *learn* fear and avoidance as well as which categories or attributes to dislike, *fear,* or stigmatize. Children may learn to stigmatize without ever grasping "why" they do so (Martin, Chapter 8), just as adults have beliefs about members of stigmatized groups without ever having met any individuals from the group (Crocker & Lutsky, Chapter 6). The predisposition to stigmatize is passed from one generation to the next through social learning (Martin, Chapter 8) or socialization (Crocker & Lutsky, Chapter 6; Stafford & Scott, Chapter 5).

Sigelman and Singleton agree with Martin that social norms subtly impinge upon the information-processing capacities of young children so that negative responses to stigma later become automatic. At some point, the development of social cognition must intersect with the affective responses that parents or adults display toward stigmatized people. Certain negative emotions become attached to social categories (e.g., *all* ex-mental patients are dangerous, *all* blacks are angry or harmful). Although the attitudes (cognitions) about stigma assessed in paper-and-pencil tasks may change in the direction of what is socially acceptable, the affect and behavior of elementary- and secondary-school children as well as adults reflect the early negative affective associations with stigma. The norms about stigma, though, are ambiguous and confusing. They teach young children to avoid or dislike stigmatized people, even though similar behavior in adults is considered socially unacceptable.

STIGMA AS A FORM OF COGNITIVE PROCESSING

The perceptual processing of human differences appears to be universal. Ainlay and Crosby suggest that differences arouse us; they can please or distress us. From a phenomenological perspective, we carry around "recipes" and "typifications" as structures for categorizing and ordering stimuli. Similarly, social psychologists speak of our need to categorize social stimuli in such terms as *schemas* and *stereotypes* (Crocker & Lutsky, Chapter 6). These approaches to the perception of human differences indirectly posit that stigmatizing is a natural response, a way to maintain order in a potentially chaotic world of social stimuli. People want to believe that the world is ordered.

Although various approaches to social categorization may explain how people stereotype on the basis of a specific attribute (e.g., skin color, religious beliefs, deafness), they do not explain the next step—the negative imputations. Traditional approaches to sociocognitive processing also do not offer ideas about how people can perceptually move beyond the stereotype, the typification, or stigma to perceive an individual. Studies of stereotyping and stigma regularly reveal that beliefs about the inferiority of a person predominate in the thoughts of the perceiver (Crocker & Lutsky, Chapter 6).

Stigma appears to be a special and insidious kind of social categorization or, as Martin explains, a process of generalizing from a single experience. People are treated categorically rather than individually, and in the process are devalued (Ainlay & Crosby, Chapter 2; Barbarin, Chapter 9; Crocker & Lutsky, Chapter 6; Stafford & Scott, Chapter 5). In addition, as Crocker and Lutsky point out, coding people in terms of categories (e.g., "X is a redhead") instead of specific attributes ("X has red hair") allows people to feel that stigmatized persons are fundamentally different and establishes greater psychological and social distance.

A discussion of the perceptual basis of stigma inevitably leads back to the notion of master status (Goffman, 1963). Perceptually, stigma becomes the master status, the attribute that colors the perception of the entire person. All other aspects of the person are ignored except those that fit the stereotype associated with the stigma (Kanter, 1979). Stigma as a form of negative stereotyping has a way of neutralizing positive qualities and undermining the identity of stigmatized individuals (Barbarin, Chapter 4). This kind of social categorization has also been described by one sociologist as a "discordance with personal attributes" (Davis, 1964). Thus, many stigmatized people are not expected to be intelligent, attractive, or upper class.

Another important issue in the perception of human differences or social cognition is the relative comparisons that are made between and within stigmatized and nonstigmatized groups. Several authors discuss the need for people to accentuate between-group differences and minimize within-group differences as a requisite for group identity (Ainlay & Crosby, Chapter 2; Crocker & Lutsky, Chapter 6; Sigelman & Singleton, Chapter 10). Yet these authors do not explore in depth the reasons for denigrating the attributes of the out-group members and elevating the attributes of one's own group, unless there is some feeling that the out-group could threaten the balance of power. Crocker and Lutsky note, however, that stereotyping is frequently tied to the need for self-enhancement. People with low self-esteem are more likely to identify and maintain negative stereotypes about members of stigmatized groups; such people are more negative in general. This line of reasoning takes us back to viewing stigma as a means of maintaining the status quo through social control. Could it be that stigma as a perceptual tool helps to reinforce the differentiation of the population that in earlier times was deliberately designated by marking? One explanation offered by many theorists is that stereotypes about stigmatized groups help to maintain the exploitation of such groups and preserve the existing societal structure.

Are there special arrangements or special circumstances, Ainlay and Crosby ask, that allow people to notice differences but not denigrate those who have them? On occasion, nonstigmatized people are able to "break through" and to see a stigmatized person as a real, whole person with a variety of attributes, some similar traits and some different from their own (Davis, 1964). Just how frequently and in what ways does this happen?

Ainlay and Crosby suggest that we begin to note differences within a type when we *need* to do so. The example they give about telephones is a good one. We learn differences among types of telephones, or appliances or schools or even groups of people when we need to. Hence stereotyping or stigmatizing is not necessarily automatic; when we want to perceive differences we perceive them, just as we perceive similarities when we *want* to. In some historical instances, society appears to have recognized full human potential when it was required, while ignoring certain devalued traits. When women were needed to occupy traditionally male occupations in the United States during World War II, gender differences were ignored as they have been ignored in other societies when women were needed for combat. Similarly, the U.S. armed forces became racially integrated when there was a need for more soldiers to fight in World War II (Terry, 1984).

Thus, schemas or stereotypes about stigmatized individuals can be modified but only under specific conditions. When stigmatized people have essential information or possess needed expertise, we discover that some of their attributes are not so different, or that they are more similar to us than different. "Cooperative interdependence" stemming from shared goals may change the nature of perceptions and the nature of relationships (Crocker & Lutsky, Chapter 6). Future research on stigma and on social perception might continue to investigate the conditions under which people are less likely to stereotype and more likely to respond to individuals rather than categories (cf., Locksley, Borgida, Brekke, & Hepburn, 1980; Locksley, Hepburn & Ortiz, 1982).

THE MEANING OF STIGMA FOR SOCIAL RELATIONS

I have intimated that "stigmatized" and "nonstigmatized" people are tied together in a perpetual inferior/superior relationship. This relationship is key to understanding the meaning of stigma. To conceptualize stigma as a social relationship raises some vital questions about stigma. These questions include (a) when and under what conditions does an attribute become a stigmatized one? (b) can a person experience stigmatization without knowing that a trait is devalued in a specific social context? (c) does a person feel stigmatized even though in a particular social context the attribute is not stigmatized or the stigma is not physically or behaviorally apparent? (d) can a person refuse to be stigmatized or destigmatize an attribute by ignoring the prevailing norms that define it as a stigma?

These questions lead to another one: Would stigma persist if stigmatized people did not feel stigmatized or inferior? Certainly, a national pride did not lessen the persecution of the Jews, nor does it provide freedom for blacks in South Africa. These two examples illustrate how pervasive and powerful the social control aspects of stigma are, empowering the stigmatizer and stripping the stigmatized of power. Yet a personal awakening, a discovery that the responsibility for being stigmatized does not lie with oneself, is important. Understanding that the rationale for discrimination and segregation based on stigma lies in the mind of the stigmatizer has led people like Mahatma Gandhi and civil rights activist Rosa Parks to rise above the feeling of stigmatization, to ignore the norms, and to disobey the existing laws based on stigma. There have been women, elderly adults, gays, disabled people, and many others who at some point realized that their fundamental similarities outweighed and outnumbered their differences. It becomes clear that, in most oppressive situations the primary problem lies with the stigmatizer and not with the stigmatized (Sartre, 1948; Schur, 1980, 1983). Many stigmatized people also begin to understand that the stigmatizer, having established a position of false superiority and consequently the need to maintain it, is enslaved to the concept that stigmatized people are fundamentally inferior. In fact, some stigmatized individuals question the norms about stigma and attempt to change the social environments for their peers.

In contrast, there are some stigmatized persons who accept their devalued status as legitimate. Attempting to "pass" and derogating others like themselves are two ways in which stigmatized people effectively accept the society's negative perceptions of their stigma (Goffman, cited in Gibbons, Chapter 7). It is clear, especially from accounts of those who move from a nonstigmatized to a stigmatized role, that stigmatization is difficult to resist if everyone begins to reinforce the inferior status with their behavior. Two of the most common ways in which nonstigmatized people convey a sense of fundamental inferiority to stigmatized people are social rejection or social isolation and lowered expectations.

There are many ways in which people communicate social rejection such as speech, eye contact, and interpersonal distance. The stigmatized role, as conceptualized by the symbolic interactionism approach, is similar to any other role (e.g., professor, doctor) in which we behave according to the role expectations of others and change our identity to be congruent with them. Thus, in the case of stigma, role expectations are often the same as the stereotypes. Some stigmatized people become dependent, passive, helpless, and childlike because that is what is expected of them.

Social rejection or avoidance affects not only the stigmatized individual but everyone who is socially involved, such as family, friends, and relatives (Barbarin, Chapter 9). This permanent form of social quarantine forces people to limit their relationships to other stigmatized people and to those for whom the social bond outweighs the stigma, such as family members. In this way, avoidance or social rejection also acts as a form of social control or containment (Edgerton, 1967; Goffman, 1963; Schur, 1983; Scott, 1969). Social rejection is perhaps most difficult for younger children who are banned from most social activities of their peers.

Social exile conveys another message about expectations. Many stigmatized people are not encouraged to develop or grow, to have aspirations or to be successful. Barbarin reports that children with cancer lose friendships and receive special, lenient treatment from teachers. They are not expected to achieve in the same manner as other children. Parents, too, sometimes allow stigmatized children to behave in ways that "normal" children in the same family are not permitted to do. Social exclusion as well as overprotection can lead to decreased performance. Lowered expectations also lead to decreased self-esteem.

The negative identity that ensues becomes a pervasive personality trait and inhibits the stigmatized person from developing other parts of the self. Another detrimental aspect of stigmatization is the practice of treating people, such as the ex-con and ex-mental patient who are attempting to reintegrate themselves into society, as if they still had the stigma. Even the terms we use to describe such persons suggest that role expectations remain the same despite the stigmatized person's efforts to relinquish them. It seems that the paradoxical societal norms that establish a subordinate and dependent position for stigmatized people while ostracizing them for it may stem from the need of nonstigmatized people to maintain a sense of superiority. Their position is supported and reinforced by their perceptions that stigmatized people are fundamentally inferior, passive, helpless, and childlike.

The most pernicious consequence of bearing a stigma is that stigmatized people may develop the same perceptual problems that nonstigmatized people have. They begin to see themselves and their lives through the stigma, or as Sartre (1948) writes about the Jews, they "allow themselves to be poisoned by the stereotype and live in fear that they will correspond to it" (p. 95). As Gibbons observes, stigmatized individuals sometimes blame their difficulties on the stigmatized trait, rather than confronting the root of their personal difficulties. Thus, normal issues that one encounters in life often act as a barrier to growth for stigmatized people because of the attributional process involved.

The need to maintain one's identity manifests itself in a number of ways, such as the mischievous behavior of the adolescent boy with cancer cited in Barbarin's chapter. "Attaining normalcy within the limits of stigma" (Tracy & Gussow, 1978) seems to be another way of describing the need to establish or recapture one's identity (Weiner, 1975).

Stigma uniquely alters perceptions in other ways, especially with respect to the notion of "normality", and raises other questions about the dilemma of difference. Most people do not want to be perceived as different or "abnormal." Becker and Arnold and Gibbons discuss normalization as attempts to be "not different" and to appear "normal." Such strategies include "passing" or disguising the stigma and acting "normal" by "covering up"—keeping up with the pace of nonstigmatized individuals (Davis, 1964; Gibbons, Chapter 7; Goffman, 1963; Weiner, 1975). For stigmatized people, the idea of normality takes on an exaggerated importance. Normality becomes the supreme goal for many stigmatized individuals until they realize that there is no precise definition of normality except what they would be without their stigma. Given the dilemma of difference that stigma reflects, it is not clear whether anyone can ever feel "normal."

Out of this state of social isolation and lowered expectations, though, can arise some positive consequences. Although the process can be fraught with pain and difficulty, stigmatized people who manage to reject the perceptions of themselves as inferior often come away with greater inner strength (Jones et al., 1984). They learn to depend on their own resources and, like the earlier examples of Mahatma Gandhi and Rosa Parks, they begin to question the bases for defining normality. Many stigmatized people regain their identity through redefining normality and realizing that it is acceptable to be who they are (Ablon, 1981b; Barbarin, Chapter 9; Becker, 1980; Becker & Arnold, Chapter 3).

FEAR AND STIGMA

Fear is important to a discussion of how and why stigma persists. In many cultures that do not use the term *stigma*, there is some emotional reaction beyond interest or curiosity to differences such as children who are born with birthmarks, epilepsy, or a caul. Certain physical characteristics or illnesses elicit fear because the etiology of the attribute or disease is unknown, unpredictable, and unexpected (Sontag, 1979). People even have fears about the sexuality of certain stigmatized groups such as persons who are mentally retarded, feeling that if they are allowed to reproduce they will have retarded offspring (Gibbons, Chapter 7). It seems that what gives stigma its intensity and reality is fear.

The nature of the fear appears to vary with the type of stigma. For most stigmas stemming from physical or mental problems, including cancer, people experience fear of contagion even though they know that the stigma cannot be developed through contact (see Barbarin, Chapter 9). This fear usually stems from not knowing about the etiology of a condition, its predictability, and its course.

The stigmatization of certain racial, ethnic, and gender categories may also be based on fear. This fear, though, cannot stem from contagion because attributes (of skin color, ethnic background, and gender) cannot possibly be transmitted to nonstigmatized people. One explanation for the fear is that people want to avoid "courtesy stigmas" or stigmatization by association

(Goffman, 1963). Another explanation underlying this type of fear may be the notion of scarce resources. This is the perception that if certain groups of people are allowed to have a share in all resources, there will not be enough: not enough jobs, not enough land, not enough water, or not enough food. Similar explanations from the deviance literature suggest that people who stigmatize feel threatened and collectively feel that their position of social, economic, and political dominance will be dismantled by members of stigmatized groups (Schur, 1980, 1983). A related explanation is provided by Hughes, who states, "that it may be that those whose positions are insecure and whose hopes for the higher goals are already fading express more violent hostility to new people" (1945, p. 356). This attitude may account for the increased aggression toward members of stigmatized groups during dire economic periods.

Fear affects not only nonstigmatized but stigmatized individuals as well. Many stigmatized people (e.g., ex-cons, mentally retarded adults) who are attempting to "pass" live in fear that their stigmatized attribute will be discovered (Gibbons, Chapter 7). These fears are grounded in a realistic assessment of the negative social consequences of stigmatization and reflect the long-term social and psychological damage to individuals resulting from stigma.

At some level, therefore, most people are concerned with stigma because they are fearful of its unpredictable and uncontrollable nature. Stigmatization appears uncontrollable because human differences serve as the basis for stigmas. Therefore, *any* attribute can become a stigma. No one really ever knows when or if he or she will acquire a stigma or when societal norms might change to stigmatize a trait he or she already possesses. To deny this truth by attempting to isolate stigmatized people or escape from stigma is a manifestation of the underlying fear.

The unpredictability of stigma is similar to the unpredictability of death. Both Gibbons and Barbarin note that the development of a stigmatized condition in a loved one or in oneself represents a major breach of trust—a destruction of the belief that life is predictable. In a sense, stigma represents a kind of death—a social death. Nonstigmatized people, through avoidance and social rejection, often treat stigmatized people as if they were invisible, nonexistent, or dead. Many stigmas, in particular childhood cancer, remove the usual disguises of mortality. Such stigmas can act as a symbolic reminder of everyone's inevitable death (see Barbarin's discussion of Ernest Becker's [1973] *The Denial of Death*). These same fears can be applied to the acquisition of other stigmas (e.g., mental illness, physical disabilities) and help to intensify and perpetuate the negative responses to most stigmatized categories. Thus, irrational fears may help stigmatization to be self-perpetuating with little encouragement needed in the form of forced segregation from the political and social structure.

The ultimate answers about why stigma persists may lie in an examination of why people fear differences, fear the future, fear the unknown, and therefore stigmatize that which is different and unknown. An equally important issue to investigate is how stigmatization may be linked to the fear of being different.

CONCLUSION

Stigma is clearly a very complex multidisciplinary issue, with each additional perspective containing another piece of this enigma. A multidisciplinary approach allowed us as social scientists to perceive stigma as a whole; to see from within it rather than to look down upon it. Our joint perspectives have also demonstrated that there are many shared ideas across disciplines, and in many cases only the terminology is different.

Three important aspects of stigma emerge from this multidisciplinary examination and may forecast its future. They are fear, stigma's primary affective component; stereotyping, its primary cognitive component; and social control, its primary behavioral component. The study of the relationship of stigma to fear, stereotyping, and social control may elucidate our understanding of the paradoxes that a multidisciplinary perspective reveals. It may also bring us closer to understanding what stigma really is—not primarily a property of individuals as many have conceptualized it to be but a humanly constructed perception, constantly in flux and legitimizing our negative responses to human differences (Ainlay & Crosby, Chapter 2). To further clarify the definition of stigma, one must differentiate between an "undesired differentness" that is likely to lead to feelings of stigmatization and actual forms of stigmatization. *It appears that stigmatization occurs only when the social control component is imposed, or when the undesired differentness leads to some restriction in physical and social mobility and access to opportunities that allow an individual to develop his or her potential. This definition combines the original meaning of stigma with more contemporary connotations and uses.*

In another vein, stigma is a statement about personal and social responsibility. People irrationally feel that, by separating themselves from stigmatized individuals, they may reduce their own risk of acquiring the stigma (Barbarin, Chapter 9). By isolating individuals, people feel they can also isolate the problem. If stigma is ignored, the responsibility for its existence and perpetuation can be shifted elsewhere. Making stigmatized people feel responsible for their own stigma allows nonstigmatized people to relinquish the onus for creating or perpetuating the conditions that surround it.

Changing political and economic climates are also important to the stigmatization and destigmatization process. What is economically feasible or politically enhancing for a group in power will partially determine what attributes are stigmatized, or at least how they are stigmatized. As many sociologists have suggested, some people are stigmatized for violating norms, whereas others are stigmatized for being of little economic or political value (Birenbaum & Sagarin, 1976, cited in Stafford & Scott, Chapter 5). We should admit that stigma persists as a social problem because it continues to have some of its original social utility as a means of controlling certain segments of the population and ensuring that power is not easily exchanged. Stigma helps to maintain the existing social hierarchy.

One might then ask if there will ever be societies or historical periods without stigma. Some authors hold a positive vision of the future. Gibbons, for example, suggests that as traditionally stigmatized groups become more integrated into the general population, stigmatizing attributes will lose some of their onus. But historical analysis would suggest that new stigmas will replace old ones. Educational programs are probably of only limited help, as learning to stigmatize is a part of early social learning experiences (Martin, Chapter 8; Sigelman & Singleton, Chapter 10). The social learning of stigma is indeed very different from learning about the concept abstractly in a classroom. School experiences sometimes merely reinforce what children learn about stigmatization from parents and significant others.

From a sociological perspective, the economic, psychological and social benefits of stigma sustain it. Stigmas will disappear when we no longer need to legitimize social exclusion and segregation (Zola, 1979). From the perspective of cognitive psychology, when people find it necessary or beneficial to perceive the fundamental similarities they share with stigmatized people rather than the differences, we will see the beginnings of a real elimination of stigma. This process may have already occurred during some particular historical period or within particular societies. It is certainly an important area for historians, anthropologists, and psychologists to explore.

Although it would seem that the core of the problem lies with the nonstigmatized individuals, stigmatized people also play an important role in the destigmatization process. Stigma contests, or the struggles to determine which attributes are devalued and to what extent they are devalued, involve stigmatized and nonstigmatized individuals alike (Schur, 1980). Stigmatized people, too, have choices as to whether to accept their stigmatized condition and the negative social consequences or continue to fight for more integration into nonstigmatized communities. Their cognitive and affective attitudes toward themselves as individuals and as a group are no small element in shaping societal responses to them. As long as they continue to focus on the negative, affective components of stigma, such as low self-esteem, it is not likely that their devalued status will change. Self-help groups may play an important role in countering this tendency.

There is volition or personal choice. Each stigmatized or nonstigmatized individual can choose to feel superior or inferior, and each individual can make choices about social control and about fear. Sartre (1948) views this as the choice between authenticity or authentic freedom, and inauthenticity or fear of being oneself. Each individual can choose to ignore social norms regarding stigma. Personal beliefs about a situation or circumstance often differ from norms, but people usually follow the social norms anyway, fearing to step beyond conformity to exercise their own personal beliefs about stigma (see Ainlay & Crosby, Chapter 2, and Stafford & Scott, Chapter 5, discussions of personal versus socially shared forms of stigma). Changing human behavior is not as simple as encouraging people to exercise their personal beliefs. As social scientists, we know a number of issues may be involved in the way personal volition interacts with social norms and personal values.

The multidisciplinary approach could be used in a variety of creative ways to study stigma and other social problems. Different models of how stigma has evolved and is perpetuated could be subject to test by a number of social scientists. They could combine their efforts to examine whether stigma evolves in a similar manner in different cultures, or among children of differing cultural and social backgrounds, or during different historical periods. The study of stigma encompasses as many factors and dimensions as are represented in a multidisciplinary approach. Some of these factors, dimensions, and the responses they produce are presented in Figure 2. All of the elements are interactive and in constant flux. The affective, cognitive, and behavioral dimensions are subject to the current cultural, historical, political, and economic climates, which are in turn linked to the norms and laws. Although, in Figure 2, the responses of stigmatized and nonstigmatized individuals appear to be separate, we know that they are also interconnected and may produce other responses when considered together. This graphic portrayal of the issues vital to the study of stigma is neither exhaustive nor definitive. It does suggest, however, that a multidimensional model of stigma is needed to understand how these factors, dimensions, and responses co-vary.

We need more cross-disciplinary research from researchers who do not commonly study stigma. For example, a joint project among historians, psychologists, economists, and political scien-

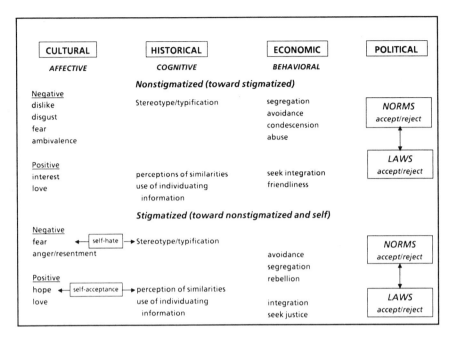

FIGURE 2. Stigmatization—factors, dimensions, and responses.

tists might examine the relationship between economic climate, perceptions of scarcity, and stigmatization. Other joint ventures by anthropologists and economists could design research on how much income is lost over a lifetime by members of a stigmatized category (e.g., blind, deaf, overweight), and how this loss adversely affects the GNP and the overall economy. Another example would be work by political scientists and historians or anthropologists to understand the links between the stigmatization of specific attributes and the maintenance of social control and power by certain political groups. Psychologists might team up with novelists or anthropologists to use case studies to understand individual differences or to examine how some stigmatized persons overcome their discredited status. Other studies of the positive consequences of stigma might include a joint investigation by anthropologists and psychologists of cultures that successfully integrate stigmatized individuals into nonstigmatized communities and utilize whatever resources or talents a stig-

matized person has to offer (as the shaman is used in many societies) (Halifax, 1979, 1982).

The study of stigma by developmental and social psychologists, sociologists, anthropologists, economists, and historians
may also offer new insights into the evolution of sex roles and sex
role identity across the life cycle and during changing economic
climates. Indeed, linguists, psychologists, and sociologists may
be able to chronicle the changes in identity and self-concept of
stigmatized and nonstigmatized alike, by studying the way people
describe themselves and the language they use in their interactions with stigmatized and nonstigmatized others (Coleman,
1985; Edelsky & Rosegrant, 1981).

The real challenge for social scientists will be to better understand the need to stigmatize; the need for people to reject rather
than accept others; the need for people to denigrate rather than
uplift others. We need to know more about the relationship between stigma and perceived threat, and how stigma may represent "the kinds of deviance that [a society] fears and perhaps even
the amount of deviance that it seeks out" (Schur, 1980, p. 22).
Finally, social scientists need to concentrate on designing an op-
timal system in which every member of society is permitted to
develop one's talents and experience one's full potential regardless
of any particular attribute. If such a society were to come about,
then perhaps some positive consequences would arise from the
dilemma of difference.

References

Ablon, J. (1981). Dwarfism and social identity: Self-help group participation. *Social Science and Medicine, 15,* 25–30. (a)

Ablon, J. (1981). Stigmatized health conditions. *Social Science and Medicine, 15,* 5–9. (b)

Ablon, J. (1981). Implications of cultural patterning for the delivery of alcohol services. *Journal of Studies on Alcohol, 9,* 185–206. (c)

Ablon, J. (1984). *Little people in America.* New York: Praeger.

Adorno, T. W., Frenkel-Brunswik, E., Levinson, D. J., & Sanford, R. N. (1950). *The authoritarian personality.* New York: Harper & Row.

Agnew, J. C. (1979). The threshold of exchange: Speculations on the market. *Radical History Review, 21,* 99–118.

Allport, G. W. (1954). *The nature of prejudice.* Reading, MA: Addison-Wesley.

American Cancer Society. (1981). *Cancer facts.* New York: ACS, Inc.

Archombault, R. D. (1969). Learning as understanding. In D. Vandenberg (Ed.), *Teaching and learning: Readings in the philosophy of education* (pp. 260–263). Chicago: University of Illinois Press.

Arluck, E. W. (1941). A study of some personality characteristics of epileptics. *Archives of Psychology, 37,* 263.

Arnold, R. (1979). *Socio-structural determinants of self-esteem and the relationship between self-esteem and criminal behavioral patterns of imprisoned minority women.* Unpublished doctoral dissertation, Bryn Mawr College.

Aronson, E., & Bridgeman, D. (1979). Jigsaw groups and the desegregated classroom: In pursuit of common goals. *Personality and Social Psychology Bulletin, 5,* 438–446.

Asher, S. R., & Allen, V. L. (1969). Racial preference and social comparison processes. *Journal of Social Issues, 25,* 157–166.

Asher, S. R., Singleton, L. C., & Taylor, A. R. (1982). Acceptance versus friendship: A longitudinal study of racial integration. In C. Chan (Chair), *Racial integration and mainstreaming: Methodological and substantive issues.* Symposium conducted at the meeting of the American Educational Research Association, New York.

Ashmore, R. D. (1981). Sex stereotypes and implicit personality theory. In D. L. Hamilton (Ed.), *Cognitive processes in stereotyping and intergroup behavior* (pp. 37–81). Hillsdale, NJ: Erlbaum.

Ashmore, R. D., & Del Boca, F. K. (1976). Psychological approaches to understanding intergroup conflicts. In P. A. Katz (Ed.), *Towards the elimination of racism* (pp. 73–123). New York: Pergamon.

Ashmore, R. D., & Del Boca, F. K. (1981). Conceptual approaches to stereotypes and stereotyping. In D. L. Hamilton (Ed.), *Cognitive processes in stereotyping and intergroup behavior* (pp. 1–35). Hillsdale, NJ: Erlbaum.

Bandura, A. (1977). *Social learning theory.* Englewood Cliffs, NJ: Prentice-Hall.

Bandura, A., & Walters, R. H. (1963). *Social learning and personality development.* Chicago, IL: Holt, Rinehart & Winston.

Barbarin, O. (1983). Coping with ecological transitions by black families: A psychosocial model. *Journal of Community Psychology, 11,* 308–322.

Barbarin, O., & Chesler, M. (1984). *Children with cancer.* Oak Park, IL: Eterna Press.

Barbarin, O., Hughes, D., & Chesler, M. (1985). Stress, coping and marital functioning among parents of children with cancer. *Journal of Marriage and the Family, 47,* 473–480.

Becker, E. (1973). *The denial of death.* New York: Free Press.

Becker, G. (1980). *Growing old in silence.* Berkeley: University of California Press.

Becker, G. (1981). Coping with stigma: Lifelong adaptation of deaf people. *Social Science and Medicine, 15,* 21–24.

Becker, H. S. (1963). *Outsiders: Studies in the sociology of deviance.* New York: Free Press.

Becker, H. S. (1964). Introduction. In H. Becker (Ed.), *The other side* (pp. 1–6). New York: Free Press.

Beisser, A. (1979). Denial and affirmation in health and illness. *American Journal of Psychiatry, 136,* 1026–1030.

Bem, D. J. (1970). *Beliefs, attitudes and human affairs.* Belmont, CA: Brooks/Cole Publishing Company.

Bem, D. J. (1972). Self-perception theory. In L. Berkowitz (Ed.), *Advances in experimental social psychology* (Vol. 6, pp. 2–62). New York: Academic Press.

Bender, R. E. (1960). *The conquest of deafness.* Cleveland: Case Western Reserve University Press.

Berger, P. (1967). *The sacred canopy.* New York: Doubleday.

Berger, P., & Luckmann, T. (1966). *The social construction of reality.* New York: Doubleday.

Berger, P., Berger, B., & Kellner, H. (1973). *The homeless mind.* New York: Vintage.

Bernard, J. (1957). The sociocultural study of conflict. In J. Bernard, T. H. Pear, R. Aron, & R. C. Angell (Eds.), *The nature of conflict* (pp. 33–117). Paris: UNESCO.

Berndt, R. M. (1962). *Excess and restraint.* Chicago: University of Chicago Press.

Bever, E. (1982). Old age and witchcraft in early modern Europe. In P. N. Stearns (Ed.), *Old age in pre-industrial society* (pp. 150–190). New York: Holmes & Meier.

Billig, M., & Tajfel, H. (1973). Social categorization and similarity in intergroup behaviour. *European Journal of Social Psychology, 3,* 27–51.

Binger, C. (1973). Childhood leukemia: Emotional impact on the siblings. In E. J. Anthony & E. Koupernick (Eds.), *The child and his family:Impact of disease and death.*(pp.195–210). New York: Wiley.

Birenbaum, A. (1970). On managing a courtesy stigma. *Journal of Health and Social Behavior, 11,* 196–206.

Birenbaum, A., & Sagarin, E. (1976). *Norms and human behavior.* New York: Praeger.

Bizière, J. M. (1984). Psychohistory and histoire des mentalités. *The Journal of Psychohistory, 11,* 89–109.

Blake, J., & Davis, K. (1964). Norms, values, and sanctions. In R. E. L. Faris (Ed.), *Handbook of modern sociology* (pp. 456–484). Chicago: Rand McNally.

Boswell, J. (1977). *The royal treasure: Muslim communities under the crown of Aragon in the fourteenth century.* New Haven: Yale University Press.

Boswell, J. (1980). *Christianity, social tolerance, and homosexuality.* Chicago: University of Chicago Press.

Bourdieu, P. (1977). *Outline of a theory of practice* (R. Nice, trans.). Cambridge, England: Cambridge University Press.

Bowen, M. (1978). *Family therapy in clinical practice.* New York: Jason Aronson.

Bowsma, W. J. (1973). Lawyers and early modern culture. *American Historical Review, 78,* 303–327.

Boyd, R. D. (1966, November). A psychological definition of adult education. *Adult Leadership,* 160–162, 180–181.

Braudel, P. (1980). History and the social sciences: The "Longue Durée." In S. Mathews (Trans.) *On history* (pp. 25–54). Chicago: University of Chicago Press.

Bray, A. (1982). *Homosexuality in Renaissance England.* London: Gay Men's Press.

Bree, G. (1966). *The world of Marcel Proust.* Boston: Houghton-Mifflin.

Brewer, M. B., Dull, V., & Lui, L. (1981). Perceptions of the elderly: Stereotypes as prototypes. *Journal of Personality and Social Psychology, 41,* 656–670.

Brewer, M. B., & Miller, N. (1984). *Beyond the contact hypothesis: Theoretical perspectives on desegregation.* New York: Academic Press.

Brickman, P., & Bulman, R. J. (1977). Pleasure and pain in social comparison. In J. M. Suls & R. L. Miller (Eds.), *Social comparison processes: Theoretical and empirical perspectives* (pp. 171–198). Washington, DC: Hemisphere.

Brigham, J. C. (1971). Ethnic stereotypes. *Psychological Bulletin, 76,* 15–38.

Brigham, J. C. (1974). Views of black and white children concerning the distribution of personality characteristics. *Journal of Personality, 42,* 144–158.

Brighouse, G. (1946). *The physically handicapped worker in industry.* Pasadena: California Institute of Technology.

Brody, S. N. (1974). *The disease of the soul: Leprosy in medieval literature.* Ithaca: Cornell University Press.

Brooks, J., & Lewis, M. (1976). Infants' responses to strangers: Midget, adult, and child. *Child Development, 47,* 323–332.

Brown, P. (1971). The rise and function of the holy man in late antiquity. *Journal of Roman Studies, 61,* 80–101.

Brown, R. (1965). *Social psychology.* New York: Free Press.

Brownmiller, S. (1975). *Against our will: Men, women and rape.* New York: Simon & Schuster.

Broyard, A. (1950). Portrait of the Negro. *Commentary, 10,* 59–60.

Budoff, M., & Siperstein, G. N. (1980). *Attitudes of EMRs toward mentally retarded peers: The effects of clinical label and academic competence.* Unpublished manuscript, University of Massachusetts, Boston.

Bullough, V. L., & Brundage, J. (1982). *Sexual practices and the medieval church.* Buffalo, NY: Prometheus Books.

Burg, B. R. (1980). Ho hum, another work of the Devil: Buggery and sodomy in early Stuart England. *Journal of Homosexuality, 6,* 69–78.

Burguière, A. (1980). The Charivari and religious repression in France during the ancient regime. In R. Wheaton & T. Hareven (Eds.), *Family and sexuality in French history* (pp. 84–110). Philadelphia: University of Pennsylvania Press.

Burke, P. (1978). *Popular culture in early modern Europe.* New York: Harper & Row.

Bynum, C. W. (1982). *Jesus as mother: Studies in the spirituality of the High Middle Ages.* Berkeley: University of California Press.

Byrne, D. (1971). *The attraction paradigm.* New York: Academic Press.

Cahnman, W. J. (1968). The stigma of obesity. *The Sociological Quarterly, 9*, 283–299.

Carson, R. (1962). *Silent spring*. Boston: Houghton-Mifflin.

Carver, C. S., Glass, D. C., & Katz, I. (1978). Favorable evaluations of blacks and the handicapped: Positive prejudice, unconscious denial, or social desirability? *Journal of Applied Social Psychology, 8*, 97–106.

Chambliss, W. (1964). A sociological analysis of the law of vagrancy. *Social Problems, 12*, 67–77.

Chesler, M., & Barbarin, O. (1984). Difficulties of providing help in a crisis: Friends' roles with parents of children with cancer. *Journal of Social Issues, 40*, 113–135.

Chinn, L. (1982). *One of the lucky ones*. New York: Doubleday.

Chodorow, N. (1978). *The reproduction of mothering*. Berkeley: University of California Press.

Christ, A., & Floumanhaft, K. (1984). *Childhood cancer: Impact on the family*. New York: Plenum.

Christie, R., & Jahoda, M. (1954). *Studies in the scope and methodology of the authoritarian personality*. New York: Free Press.

Clark, A., & Gibbs, J. P. (1965). Social control: A reformulation. *Social Problems, 12*, 398–415.

Clark, K. B., & Clark, M. P. (1947). Racial identification and racial preference in Negro children. In T. M. Newcomb & E. L. Hartley (Eds.), *Readings in social psychology* (pp. 239–252). New York: Holt, Rinehart & Winston.

Clark, S. (1980). Inversion, misrule and the meaning of witchcraft. *Past and Present, 87*, 98–127.

Clinard, M. B., & Meier, R. F. (1979). *Sociology of deviant behavior*. New York: Holt, Rinehart & Winston.

Coates, D., & Winston, T. (1983). Counteracting the deviance of depression: Peer support groups for victims. *Journal of Social Issues, 39*, 169–194.

Cohen, A. K. (1966). *Deviance and control*. Englewood Cliffs, NJ: Prentice-Hall.

Cohen, J. (1982). *The friars and the Jews: The evolution of medieval anti-Judaism*. Ithaca: Cornell University Press.

Cohn, N. (1975). *Europe's inner demons: An enquiry inspired by the great witch-hunt*. New York: Basic Books.

Coleman, L. (1983, July). *Social cognitions about group membership: Marking social distance in speech*. Paper presented at the 2nd International Conference on Language and Social Psychology, Bristol, England.

Coleman, L. (in press). Language and the evolution of identity and self-concept. In F. Kessel (Ed.), *The development of language and language researchers: Essays in honor of Roger Brown*. Hillsdale, NJ.: Erlbaum.

Coleman, R. L. (1973). Organ inferiority and personality. *Dissertation Abstracts international, 22,* 5373B.

Comer, R. J., & Piliavin, J. A. (1972). The effects of physical deviance upon face-to-face interaction: The other side. *Journal of Personality and Social Psychology, 23,* 33–39.

Conant, S., & Budoff, M. (1983). Patterns of awareness in children's understanding of disabilities. *Mental Retardation, 21,* 119–125.

Cook, J. (1984). Influence of gender on the problems of parents of fatally ill children. *Journal of Psychosocial Oncology, 2,* 71–91.

Cook, S. (1984). *Experimenting on social issues: The case of school desegregation.* Paper presented at the annual meeting of the American Psychological Association, Toronto, Canada.

Cox, O. C. (1984). *Caste, class and race.* Garden City, NY: Doubleday.

Criddle, R. (1953). *Love is not blind.* New York: W. W. Norton & Co.

Crocker, J. (1983). *Changing stereotypes about stigmatized groups.* Paper presented at the annual meeting of the American Psychological Association, Anaheim, CA.

Crocker, J., & Schwartz, I. (1985). Prejudice and ingroup favoritism in a minimal intergroup situation: Effects of self-esteem. *Personality and Social Psychology Bulletin, 11,* 379–386.

Crocker, J., Fiske, S. T., & Taylor, S. E. (1984). Schematic bases of belief change. In J. R. Eiser (Ed.), *Attitudinal judgment* (pp. 197–226). New York: Springer.

Culler, J. (1982). *On deconstruction: Theory and criticism after structuralism.* Ithaca: Cornell University Press.

Darley, J. M., & Fazio, R. H. (1980). Expectancy confirmation processes arising in the social interaction sequence. *American Psychologist, 35,* 867–881.

Darnton, R. (1984). Peasants tell tales: The meaning of Mother Goose. In R. Darton (Ed.), *The great cat massacre and other episodes in French cultural history* (pp. 9–74). New York: Basic Books.

Davies, C. (1982). Sexual taboos and social boundaries. *American Journal of Sociology, 87,* 1032–1063.

Davis, F. (1961). Deviance disavowal: The management of strained interaction by the visibly handicapped. *Social Problems, 9,* 120–132.

Davis, F. (1964). Deviance disavowal: The management of strained interaction by the visibly handicapped. In H. Becker (Ed.), *The other side* (pp. 119–138). New York: Free Press.

Davis, N. J. (1980). *Sociological constructions of deviance: Perspectives and issues in the field.* Dubuque, IA: William C. Brown.

Davis, N. Z. (1971). The reasons of misrule: Youth groups and charivaris in sixteenth-century France. *Past and Present, 50,* 41–75.

Davis, N. Z. (1973). *Living with multiple sclerosis: A social psychological analysis.* Springfield, IL: Charles C Thomas.

Davis, N. Z. (1983). *The return of Martin Guerre.* Cambridge, MA: Harvard University Press.

Davis, N. Z. (1984). Charivari, honor and community in seventeenth-century Lyon and Geneva. In J. J. MacAloon (Ed.), *Rite, drama, festival, spectacle: Rehearsals toward a theory of cultural performance* (pp. 42–57). Philadelphia: ISHI.

Deasy-Spinetta, P., & Spinetta, J. (1981). The child with cancer in school: Teachers' appraisals. In J. Spinetta & P. Deasy-Spinetta (Eds.), *Living with childhood cancer* (pp. 153–168). St. Louis: Mosby.

Deaux, K., & Emswiller, T. (1974). Explanation of successful performance on sex-linked tasks: What is skill for the male is luck for the female. *Journal of Personality and Social Psychology, 29,* 80–85.

Deaux, K., Winton, W., Crowley, M., & Lewis, L. (1985). Level of categorization and the content of gender stereotypes. *Social Cognition, 8,* 13–18.

Demos, J. P. (1982). *Entertaining Satan: Witchcraft and the culture of early New England.* New York: Oxford University Press.

Derrida, J. (1981). Plato's pharmacy. In B. Johnson (Trans.), *Dissemination.* Chicago: University of Chicago Press.

Deutsch, M. (1975). Equality, equity and need: What determines which value will be used as the basis of distributive justice? *Journal of Social Issues, 31,* 137–149.

Deutsch, M. (1985). *Distributive justice.* New Haven, CT: Yale University Press.

Doob, A. N., & Ecker, B. P. (1970). Stigma and compliance. *Journal of Personality and Social Psychology, 14,* 302–304.

Douglas, J. (1970). Understanding everyday life. In J. Douglas (Ed.), *Understanding everyday life* (pp. 3–44). Chicago: Aldine.

Douglas, M. (1966). *Purity and danger: An analysis of concepts of pollution and taboo.* London: Routledge & Kegan Paul.

Douglas, M. (1970). *Natural symbols: Explorations in cosmology.* New York: Pantheon.

Dumont, L. (1970). *Homo hierarchicus: An essay on the caste system.* Chicago: University of Chicago Press.

Dunkel-Schetter, C., & Wortman, C. (1982). The interpersonal dynamics of cancer: Problems in social relationships and their impact on the patient. In H. S. Friedman & M. R. DiMatteo (Eds.), *Interpersonal issues in health care* (pp. 69–100). New York: Academic Press.

Edelsky, C., & Rosegrant, T. (1981). Interactions with handicapped children: Who's handicapped? *Sociolinguistic Working Paper 92.* Austin, TX: Southwest Educational Development Laboratory.

Edgerton, R. (1976). *Deviance: A cross-cultural perspective.* Menlo Park, CA: Cummings.

Edgerton, R. G. (1967). *The cloak of competence: Stigma in the lives of the mentally retarded.* Berkeley: University of California Press.

Ehrlich, H. J. (1974). *The social psychology of prejudice.* New York: Wiley.

Elam, J. J., & Sigelman, C. K. (1983). Developmental differences in reactions to children labeled mentally retarded. *Journal of Applied Developmental Psychology, 4,* 303–315.

El Ghatit, A., & Hanson, R. (1976). Marriage and divorce after spinal cord injury. *Archives of Physical and Medical Rehabilitation, 57,* 470–472.

Eliade, M. (1959). *The sacred and the profane: The nature of religion.* New York: Harcourt, Brace & World.

Elliott, G. C., Ziegler, H. L., Altman, B. M., & Scott, D. R. (1982). Understanding stigma: Dimensions of deviance and coping. *Deviant Behavior, 3,* 275–300.

Erber, R., & Fiske, S. T. (1984). Outcome dependency and attention to inconsistent information. *Journal of Personality and Social Psychology, 47,* 709–726.

Erikson, K. (1966). *Wayward Puritans.* New York: Wiley.

Estroff, S. (1983). *Making it crazy.* Berkeley: University of California Press.

Fazio, R. H., Powell, M. C., & Herr, P. M. (1983). Toward a process model of the attitude/behavior relation: Accessing one's attitude upon mere observation of the attitude object. *Journal of Personality and Social Psychology, 44,* 723–735.

Febvre, L. (1982). *The problem of unbelief in the sixteenth century, the religion of Rabelais.* Cambridge, MA: Harvard University Press.

Feild, H. S. (1978). Attitudes toward rape: A comparative analysis of police, rapists, crisis counselors, and citizens. *Journal of Personality and Social Psychology, 36,* 156–179.

Feinman, S. (1980). Infant response to race, size, proximity and movement of strangers. *Infant Behavior and Development, 3,* 187–204.

Feinman, S. (1982). Social referencing in infancy. *Merrill-Palmer Quarterly, 28,* 445–470.

Festinger, L. (1954). A theory of social comparison processes. *Human Relations, 7,* 117–140.

Fine, M. J., & Caldwell, T. E. (1967). Self-evaluation of school-related behavior of educable mentally retarded children: A preliminary report. *Exceptional Children, 33,* 324.

Finkelstein, N. W., & Haskins, R. (1983). Kindergarten children prefer same-color peers. *Child Development, 54,* 502–508.

Finucane, R. C. (1977). *Miracles and pilgrims: Popular beliefs in medieval England.* Totowa, NJ: Rowman and Littlefield.

Fishbein, M., & Ajzen, I. (1975). *Belief, attitude, intention and behavior: An introduction to theory and research.* Reading, MA: Addison-Wesley.

Fiske, S. T. (1981). Social cognition and affect. In J. Harvey (Ed.), *Cogni-*

tion, *social behavior, and the environment* (pp. 227–264). Hillsdale, NJ: Erlbaum.

Fiske, S. T., & Taylor, S. E. (1984). *Social cognition.* Reading, MA: Addison-Wesley.

Foucault, M. (1965). *Madness and civilization: A history of insanity in the age of reason.* New York: Pantheon.

Foucault, M. (1975). *The birth of the clinic: An archaeology of medical perception.* New York: Vintage.

Foucault, M. (1978). *The history of sexuality. Volume I: An introduction.* New York: Vintage.

Foucault, M. (1979). *Discipline and punish: The birth of the prison.* New York: Vintage.

Fox, R. (1980). *The red lamp of incest.* New York: E. P. Dutton.

Freidson, E. (1965). Disability as social deviance. In M. B. Sussman (Ed.), *Sociology and rehabilitation* (pp. 71–99). Washington, DC: American Sociological Association.

French, R. D. (1984). The long term relationships of marked people. In E. E. Jones, A. Farina, A. H. Hastorf, H. Markus, D. T. Miller, & R. A. Scott (Eds.), *Social stigma: The psychology of marked relationships* (pp. 254–294). New York: W. H. Freeman.

Futterman, E., & Hoffman, I. (1973). Crisis and adaptation in families of fatally ill children. In. E. J. Anthony & J. Koupernik (Eds.), *The child in his family: The impact of disease and death* (pp. 127–144). New York: Wiley.

Gabbay, J. (1982). Asthma attacked: Tactics for the reconstruction of a disease concept. In P. Wright & A. Treacher (Eds.), *The problem of medical knowledge: Examining the social construction of medicine* (pp. 23–47). Edinburgh: Edinburgh University Press.

Garfinkel, H. (1956). Conditions of successful degradation ceremonies. *American Journal of Sociology, 65,* 420–424.

Gartner, A., & Riessman, F. (1977). *Self-help in the human services.* San Francisco: Jossey-Bass.

Geremek, B. (1976). *Les marginaux parisiens aux XIVe et XVe siècles [Marginal Parisians in the fourteenth and fifteenth centuries].* Paris: Flammarion.

Gergen, K. J., & Jones, E. E. (1963). Mental illness, predictability, and affective consequences as stimulus factors in person perception. *Journal of Abnormal and Social Psychology, 67,* 95–104.

Gibbons, F. X. (1981). The social psychology of mental retardation: What's in a label? In S. S. Brehm, S. M. Kassin, & F. X. Gibbons (Eds.), *Developmental social psychology: Theory and research* (pp. 249–270). New York: Oxford University Press.

Gibbons, F. X. (1985). Stigma perception: Social comparison among mentally retarded persons. *American Journal of Mental Deficiency, 90,* 98–106.

Gibbons, F. X., & Kassin, S. M. (1982). Behavioral expectations of retarded and nonretarded children. *Journal of Applied Developmental Psychology, 3*, 85–104.

Gibbons, F. X., Stephen, W. G., Stephenson, B. O., & Petty, C. R. (1980). Reactions to stigmatized others: Response amplification vs. sympathy. *Journal of Experimental Social Psychology, 16*, 591–605.

Gibbs, J. P. (1965). Norms: The problem of definition and classification. *American Journal of Sociology, 70*, 586–594.

Gibbs, J. P. (1972). Issues in defining deviant behavior. In R. A. Scott & J. D. Douglas (Eds.), *Theoretical perspectives on deviance* (pp. 39–68). New York: Basic Books.

Gibbs, J. P. (1981). *Norms, deviance, and social control: Conceptual matters.* New York: Elsevier.

Gilligan, C. (1982). *In a different voice: Psychological theory and women's development.* Cambridge, MA: Harvard University Press.

Ginzburg, C. (1980). *The cheese and the worms: The cosmos of a sixteenth-century miller.* Baltimore: Johns Hopkins University Press.

Girard, R. (1977). *Violence and the sacred.* Baltimore: Johns Hopkins University Press.

Goffman, E. (1961). *Asylums: Essays on the social situation of mental patients and other inmates.* Garden City, NY: Anchor.

Goffman, E. (1963). *Stigma: Notes on the management of spoiled identity.* Englewood Cliffs, NJ: Prentice-Hall.

Goffman, E. (1967). *Interaction ritual.* Garden City, NY: Pantheon.

Goldstein, H. (1981). *Social learning and change: A cognitive approach to human services.* Columbia: University of South Carolina Press.

Goodman, M. E. (1964). *Race awareness in young children* (rev. ed.). New York: Collier Books.

Goodnow, J. (1984). On being judged "intelligent." *International Journal of Psychology, 19*, 391–406.

Goody, J. (1983). *The development of the family and marriage in Europe.* Cambridge, UK: Cambridge University Press.

Gottlieb, J. (1974). Attitudes toward retarded children: Effects of labeling and academic performance. *American Journal of Mental Deficiency, 79*, 168–273.

Gottlieb, J., & Switzky, H. N. (1983). Development of school-age children's stereotypic attitudes toward mentally retarded children. *American Journal of Mental Deficiency, 86*, 596–600.

Gould, S. J. (1981). *The mismeasure of man.* New York: W. W. Norton.

Green, T. F. (1969). The concept of teaching. In D. Vandenberg (Ed.), *Teaching and learning: Readings in the philosophy of education* (pp. 5–14). Chicago: University of Illinois Press.

Greenberg, D. J., Hillman, D., & Grice, D. (1973). Infant and stranger variables related to stranger anxiety in the first year of life. *Developmental Psychology, 9,* 207–212.

Gruder, C. L. (1977). Choice of comparison persons in evaluating oneself. In J. M. Suls & R. L. Miller (Eds.), *Social comparison processes: Theoretical and empirical perspectives* (pp. 21–42). Washington, DC: Hemisphere.

Gusfield, J. (1975). Moral passage: The symbolic process in public designations of deviance. In J. Davis & R. Stivers (Eds.), *The collective definition of deviance* (pp. 85–113). New York: Free Press.

Gussow, Z., & Tracy, G. S. (1968). Status ideology and adaptation to stigmatized illness: A study of leprosy. *Human Organization, 27,* 316–325.

Halifax, J. (1979). *Shamanic voices: A survey of visionary narratives.* New York: Dutton.

Halifax, J. (1982a). *The healing journey.* New York: Crossroads New York.

Halifax, J. (1982b). *Shaman: The wounded healer.* London: Thames & Hudson.

Hamilton, D. L. (1976). Cognitive biases in the perception of social groups. In J. S. Carroll & J. W. Payne (Eds.), *Cognition and social behavior* (pp. 81–94). Hillsdale, NJ: Erlbaum.

Hamilton, D. L. (1979). A cognitive-attributional analysis of stereotyping. In L. Berkowitz (Ed.), *Advances in Experimental Social Psychology* (Vol. 12, pp. 53–84) New York: Academic Press.

Hamilton, D. L. (1981). *Cognitive processes in stereotyping and intergroup behavior.* Hillsdale, NJ: Erlbaum.

Hastorf, A. H., & Isen, A. M. (1982). *Cognitive social psychology.* New York: Elsevier North Holland.

Herman, J. (1981). *Father–daughter incest.* Cambridge, MA: Harvard University Press.

Hershenson, M. (1964). Visual discrimination in the human newborn. *Journal of Comparative and Physiological Psychology, 58,* 270–276.

Hexter, J. H. (1972). Fernand Braudel and the "Monde Braudellien." *Journal of Modern History, 44,* 480–539.

Higgins, P. C. (1980). *Outsiders in a hearing world: A sociology of deafness.* Beverly Hills, CA: Sage.

Hill, R. (1949). *Families under stress.* New York: Harper & Row.

Hilton, J. L., & Darley, J. M. (1984). Constructing other persons: Some limits on the effect. *Journal of Experimental Social Psychology, 21,* 1–18.

Hoebel, E. A. (1954). *The law of primitive man.* Cambridge, MA: Harvard University Press.

Hofstadter, R. (1955). *Social Darwinism in American thought.* Boston: Beacon Press.

Homans, G. C. (1961). *Social behavior: Its elementary forms.* New York: Harcourt, Brace, & World.

Hraba, J., & Grant, J. (1970). Black is beautiful: A re-examination of racial preference and identification. *Journal of Personality and Social Psychology, 16,* 398–402.

Hughes, D. O. (1978). From brideprice to dowry in Mediterranean Europe. *Journal of Family History, 3,* 262–296.

Hughes, E. C. (1945). Dilemmas and contradictions of status. *American Journal of Sociology, 50,* 353–359.

Husserl, E. (1970). *Cartesian meditations.* The Hague, Netherlands: Martinus Nijhoff.

Huston, A. C. (1983). Sex typing. In E. M. Hetherington (Ed.), *Handbook of child psychology (4th ed), Vol. 4: Socialization, personality, and social development* (pp. 387–467). New York: Wiley.

Ingham, R. J., & Nelson, R. M. (1984). *How does a person learn? Using life history analysis to answer the question.* Paper presented at the National Adult Education Conference, Louisville, KY.

Ingleby, D. (1982). The social construction of mental illness. In P. Wright & A. Treacher (Eds.), *The problem of medical knowledge: Examining the social construction of medicine* (pp. 123–143). Edinburgh: Edinburgh University Press.

Isen, A. M., & Hastorf, A. H. (1982). Some perspectives on cognitive social psychology. In A. H. Hastorf & A. M. Isen (Eds.), *Cognitive social psychology* (pp. 1–31). New York: Elsevier North Holland.

Jackson, D. (1966). Family rules: Marital quid pro quo. *Archives of General Psychiatry, 12,* 589–594.

Jones, E. E., Farina, A., Hastorf, A. H., Markus, H., Miller, D. T., & Scott, R. A. (1984). *Social stigma: The psychology of marked relationships.* New York: Freeman.

Jones, J. (1972). *Prejudice and racism.* Reading, MA: Addison-Wesley.

Jones, R. A. (1982). Perceiving other people: Stereotyping as a process of social cognition. In A. G. Miller (Ed.), *In the eye of the beholder: Contemporary issues in stereotyping* (pp. 41–91). New York: Praeger.

Kagan, J. (1970). The determinants of attention in the infant. *American Scientist, 58,* 298–306.

Kagan, J. (1972). Do infants think? *Scientific American, 226,* 74–82.

Kagan, J., Kearsley, R. B., & Zelazo, P. R. (1975). The emergence of initial apprehension to unfamiliar peers. In M. Lewis & L. Rosenblum (Eds.), *Friendship and peer relations* (pp. 187–206). New York: Wiley.

Kalnins, I. V. (1983). Cross-illness comparisons of separation and divorce among parents having a child with a life-threatening illness. *Children's Health Care, 12,* 72–77.

Kanter, R. M. (1977). Some effects of proportions on group life: Skewed sex ratios and responses to token women. *American Journal of Sociology, 82,* 965–990.

Kanter, R. M. (1979). *Men and women of the corporation.* New York: Basic Books.

Katz, I. (1981). *Stigma: A social psychological analysis.* Hillsdale, NJ: Erlbaum.

Katz, P. A. (1973). Perception of racial cues in preschool children: A new look. *Developmental Psychology, 8,* 295–299.

Katz, P. A. (1976). The acquisition of racial attitudes in children. In P. A. Katz (Ed.), *Towards the elimination of racism* (pp. 125–154). New York: Pergamon.

Katz, P. A., Johnson, J., & Parker, D. (1970). Racial attitudes and perception in black and white urban school children. In *Proceedings of the 78th Annual Convention of the American Psychological Association, 5,* 311–312.

Kazantzakis, N. (1952). *Zorba the Greek.* New York: Touchstone Press.

Kelly, G. (1955). *The psychology of personal constructs* (Vols. 1–2). New York: Norton.

Kelly-Gadol, J. (1976). The social relations of the sexes: Methodological implications of women's history. In E. Abel & E. K. Abel (Eds.), *The signs reader: Women, gender, and scholarship* (pp. 11–26). Chicago: University of Chicago Press.

Keohane, N. O., Rosaldo, M. Z., & Gelpi, B. C. (1982). *Feminist theory: A critique of ideology.* Chicago: University of Chicago Press.

Kieckhefer, R. (1976). *European witch trials: Their foundations in popular and learned culture, 1300–1500.* Berkeley: University of California Press.

Kieckhefer, R. (1979). *Repression of heresy in medieval Germany.* Philadelphia: University of Pennsylvania Press.

Kinder, D. R., & Sears, D. O. (1981). Prejudice and politics: Symbolic racism vs. racial threats to the good life. *Journal of Personality and Social Psychology, 40,* 414–431.

Kinder, D. R., & Sears, D. O. (1985). Public opinion and political action. In G. Lindzey & E. Aronson (Eds.), *The Handbook of Social Psychology* (pp. 659–742). Hillsdale, NJ: Erlbaum.

Kleck, R. E. (1969). Physical stigma and task oriented interaction. *Human Relations, 22,* 53–60.

Kleck, R. E., & DeJong, W. (1983). Physical disability, physical attractiveness, and social outcomes in children's small groups. *Rehabilitation Psychology, 28,* 79–91.

Kleck, R. E., Ono, H., & Hastorf, A. H. (1966). The effects of physical deviance upon face-to-face interaction. *Human Relations, 19,* 425–436.

Klein, D., & Kress, J. (1976). Any woman's blues: A critical overview of women, crime and the criminal justice system. *Crime and Social Justice, 5,* 34–49.

Kleinberg, J., & Galligan, B. (1983). Effects of deinstitutionalization on adaptive behavior of mentally retarded adults. *American Journal of Mental Deficiency, 88,* 21–27.

Klinnert, M. D., Campos, J. J., Sorce, J. F., Emde, R., & Svejda, M. (1983). Emotions as behavior regulators: Social referencing in infancy. In R. Plutchik & H. Kellerman (Eds.), *Emotions theory, research, and experience, Vol. II, Emotions in early development* (pp. 57–86). New York: Academic Press.

Kohlberg, L. (1966). A cognitive-developmental analysis of children's sex-role concepts and attitudes. In E. E. Maccoby (Ed.), *The development of sex differences* (pp. 82–172). Stanford, CA: Stanford University Press.

Kohlberg, L. (1969). Stages and sequence: The cognitive-developmental approach to socialization. In D. Goslin (Ed.), *Handbook of socialization theory and research* (pp. 347–480). Chicago: Rand McNally.

Koocher, G. P., & O'Malley, J. (1983). *The Damocles syndrome: Psychosocial consequences of surviving childhood cancer.* New York: McGraw-Hill.

Kristeva, J. (1982). *Powers of horror: An essay on abjection.* New York: Columbia University Press.

Ladner, J. (1973). *The death of white sociology.* New York: Random House.

Langbein, J. H. (1974). *Prosecuting crime in the Renaissance: England, Germany, France.* Chicago: University of Chicago Press.

Langbein, J. H. (1976). *Torture and the law of proof: Europe and England in the ancien regime.* Chicago: University of Chicago Press.

Langer, E. J., & Abelson, R. P. (1974). A patient by any other name . . . : Clinician group difference in labeling bias. *Journal of Consulting and Clinical Psychology, 42,* 4–9.

Langer, E. J., Taylor, S. E., Fiske, S. T., & Chanowitz, B. (1976). Stigma, staring, and discomfort: A novel stimulus hypothesis. *Journal of Experimental Social Psychology, 12,* 451–463.

Larner, C. (1981). *Enemies of God: The witch-hunt in Scotland.* Baltimore: Johns Hopkins University Press.

Lauderdale, P. (1976). Deviance and moral boundaries. *American Sociological Review, 41,* 660–675.

Legoff, J. (1980). Licit and illicit trades in the medieval West. In *Time, work, and culture in the Middle Ages* (pp. 58–70). Chicago: University of Chicago Press.

Lerner, M. (1980). *The belief in a just world.* New York: Plenum Press.

Lerner, M., & Miller, D. (1978). Just world research and the attribution process: Looking back and ahead. *Psychological Bulletin, 85,* 1030–1051.

Lerner, M. J. (1970). The desire for justice and reactions to victims. In J. Macaulay and L. Berkowitz (Eds.), *Altruism and helping behavior.* (pp. 205–229). New York: Academic Press.

Lerner, R. E. (1972). *The heresy of the Free Spirit in the later Middle Ages.* Berkeley: University of California Press.

Lerner, R. M., & Schroeder, C. (1975). Racial attitudes in young white children: A methodological analysis. *Journal of Genetic Psychology, 127,* 3–12.

LeRoy Ladurie, E. (1978). *Montaillou: The promised land of error.* New York: Braziller.

Levine, R. A., & Campbell, D. T. (1972). *Ethnocentrism: Theories of conflict, ethnic attitudes and group behavior.* New York: Wiley.

Levinson, D. J., Darrow, C. N., Klein, E. B., Levinson, M. H., & Braxton, M. (1978). *The seasons of a man's life.* New York: Ballantine Books.

Levinson, R. M., & Starling, D. M. (1981). Retardation and the burden of stigma. *Deviant Behavior, 2,* 371–390.

Lewin, K. (1948). *Resolving social conflicts, Part III.* New York: Harper & Row.

Lewis, M., & Brooks, J. (1974). Self, other and fear: Infants' reactions to people. In M. Lewis & L. Rosenblum (Eds.), *The origins of fear: The origins of behavior* (Vol. 2, pp. 195–227). New York: Wiley.

Lis, C., & Soly, H. (1979). *Poverty and capitalism in pre-industrial Europe.* Atlantic Highlands, NJ: Humanities Press.

Little, L. K. (1971). Pride goes before Avarice: Social change and the vices in Latin Christendom. *American Historical Review, 76,* 16–49.

Little, L. K. (1978). *Religious poverty and the profit economy in medieval Europe.* Ithaca: Cornell University Press.

Locksley, A., Borgida, E., Brekke, N., & Hepburn, C. (1980). Sex stereotypes and social judgment. *Journal of Personality and Social Psychology, 39,* 821–831.

Locksley, A., Hepburn, C., & Ortiz, V. (1982). Social stereotypes and judgments of individuals: An instance of the base-rate fallacy. *Journal of Experimental Social Psychology, 18,* 23–42.

Lofland, J. (1969). *Deviance and identity.* Englewood Cliffs, NJ: Prentice-Hall.

Lomax, L. (1962). *The Negro revolt.* New York: Harper & Row.

Lutsky, N. S. (1980). Attitudes toward old age and elderly persons. *Annual Review of Gerontology and Geriatrics, 1,* 287–336.

Lutsky, N. S. (1983). *Attributes and categories with special references to age constructs.* Paper presented at the annual meeting of the American Psychological Association, Anaheim, CA.

MacAloon, J. J. (1984). *Rite, drama, festival, spectacle: Rehearsals toward a theory of cultural performance.* Philadelphia: ISHI.

MacFarlane, A. (1970). *Witchcraft in Tudor and Stuart England.* New York: Harper & Row.

MacGregor, F. (1979). *After plastic surgery*. South Hadley, MA: Bergin.

MacLeod, R. (1958). The phenomenological approach to social psychology. In R. Tagiuri & L. Petrullo (Eds.), *Person perception and interpersonal behavior* (pp. 33–53). Stanford, CA: Stanford University Press.

McArthur, L. Z. (1981). What grabs you? The role of attention in impression formation and causal attribution. In E. T. Higgins, C. P. Herman, & M. P. Zanna (Eds.), *Social cognition: The Ontario Symposium* (Vol. 1, pp. 201–246). Hillsdale, NJ: Erlbaum.

McArthur, L. Z. (1982). Judging a book by its cover: A cognitive analysis of the relationship between physical appearance and stereotyping. In A. Hastorf & A. Isen (Eds.), *Cognitive social psychology*. (pp. 149–211). New York: Elsevier North-Holland.

McCauley, C., Stitt, C. L., & Sega, M. (1980). Stereotyping: From prejudice to prediction. *Psychological Bulletin, 87,* 195–208.

McCollum, A., & Schwartz, A. H. (1972, January). Social work and the mourning patient. *Social Work,* 25–37.

McHugh, P. (1970). A common-sense conception of deviance. In J. D. Douglas (Ed.), *Deviance and respectability* (pp. 61–88). New York: Basic Books.

McMurray, F. (1969). Learning as appropriating. In D. Vandenberg (Ed.), *Teaching and learning: Readings in the philosophy of education* (pp. 39–44). Chicago: University of Chicago Press.

Mankoff, M. (1971). Societal reaction and career deviance: A critical analysis and introduction to the political economy of law enforcement. *Sociological Quarterly, 12,* 204–218.

Marshall, M. (1979). *Weekend warriors: Alcohol in a Melanesian culture*. Palo Alto, CA: Mayfield.

Martin, L. G. (1984). Adult high school noncompleters: Toward a typology of psychosocial development. *Adult Literacy and Basic Education, 8,* 1–20.

Matthews, V., & Westie, C. (1966). A preferred method for obtaining rankings: Reactions to physical handicaps. *American Sociological Review, 31,* 851–854.

Maurer, D. & Barrera, M. (1981). Infants' perception of natural and distorted arrangements of a schematic face. *Child Development, 52,* 196–202.

Mazur, A., Mazur, J., & Keating, C. (1984). Military rank attainment of a West Point class: Effects of cadets' physical features. *American Journal of Sociology, 90,* 125–150.

Mehta, V. (1982). *Vedi*. New York: Oxford University Press.

Mehta, V. (1985, February 18). Personal history: Sound shadows of the New World-II. *The New Yorker,* 46–85.

Meier, R. F. (1981). Norms and the study of deviance: A proposed research strategy. *Deviant Behavior, 3,* 1–25.

Meier, R. F. (1982). Prospects for control theories and research. In J. P.

Gibbs (Ed.), *Social control: Views from the social sciences* (pp. 265–276). Beverly Hills: Sage.

Merleau-Ponty, M. (1963). *Phenomenology of perception.* London: Routledge & Kegan Paul. (a)

Merleau-Ponty, M. (1963). *The structure of behavior.* Boston: Beacon Press. (b)

Merton, R. (1972). Insiders and outsiders: A chapter in the sociology of knowledge. *American Journal of Sociology, 78,* 9–47.

Midelfort, H. C. E. (1972). *Witchhunting in southwestern Germany, 1562–1684.* Stanford, CA: Stanford University Press.

Miller, J. (1976). *Toward a new psychology of women.* Boston: Beacon Press.

Millman, M. (1980). *Such a pretty face: Being fat in America.* New York: Berkeley Press.

Minuchin, S. (1978). *Families and family therapy.* Cambridge, MA: Harvard University Press.

Mithun, J. S. (1973). Cooperation and solidarity as survival necessities in a black urban community. *Urban Anthropology, 2,* 25–34.

Monbeck, M. (1973). *The meaning of blindness.* Bloomington: Indiana University Press.

Monter, E. W. (1976). *Witchcraft in France and Switzerland: The borderlands during the Reformation.* Ithaca: Cornell University Press.

Monter, E. W. (1983). *Ritual, myth and magic in early modern Europe.* Brighton, UK: Harvester Press.

Morris, R. T. (1956). A typology of norms. *American Sociological Review, 21,* 610–613.

Mundy, J. H. (1955). Hospitals and leprosaries in twelfth and early thirteenth century Toulouse. In J. H. Mundy, R. W. Emery, & B. N. Nelson (Eds.), *Essays in medieval life and thought presented in honor of A. P. Evans* (pp. 181–205). New York: Columbia University Press.

Newman, G. (1978). *The punishment response.* Philadelphia: Lippincott.

Norris, C. (1972). *Deconstruction: Theory and practice.* New York: Methuen.

Oberman, H. A. (1984). *The roots of anti-Semitism in the age of Renaissance and Reformation.* Philadelphia: Fortress Press.

Ong, W. J. (1981). *Fighting for life: Context, sexuality, and consciousness.* Ithaca: Cornell University Press.

Ong, W. J. (1982). *Orality and literacy: The technologizing of the Word.* New York: Methuen.

Otto, R. (1957). *The idea of the holy.* Oxford, UK: Oxford University Press.

Park, K., & Daston, L. J. (1981). Unnatural conceptions: The study of monsters in sixteenth and seventeenth century France and England. *Past and Present, 92,* 20–54.

Pasternak, J. L. (1981). An analysis of social perceptions of epilepsy: Increasing rationalization as seen through the theories of Comte and Weber. *Social Science and Medicine, 15,* 223–229.

Perelman, C. (1977). *The idea of justice and the problem of argument.* Atlantic Highlands, NJ: Academic Press.

Pfuhl, E. H., Jr. (1980). *The deviance process.* New York: D. Van Nostrand.

Poliakov, L. (1965). *The history of anti-Semitism.* New York: Vanguard.

Porter, J. (1971). *Black child, white child: The development of racial attitudes.* Cambridge, MA: Harvard University Press.

Porter, R. H., Ramsey, B., Tremblay, A., Iaccobo, M., & Crawley, S. (1978). Social interactions in heterogeneous groups of retarded and normally developing children: An observational study. In G. P. Sackett (Ed.), *Observing behavior, Vol. 1: Theory and applications in mental retardation* (pp. 311–328). Baltimore, MD: University Park Press.

Prager, D. & Telushkin, J. (1983). *Why the Jews?: The reason for anti-Semitism.* New York: Simon & Schuster.

Pullan, B. (1983). *The Jews of Europe and the Inquisition of Venice, 1555–1670.* Totowa, NJ: Barnes & Noble.

Rabin, D. L., Barnett, C. R., Arnold, W. D., Freiberger, R. H., & Brooks, G. (1965). Untreated congenital hip disease: A study of the epidemiology, natural history, and social aspects of the disease in a Navajo population. *American Journal of Public Health, 55,* 1–44.

Rasinski, K., Crocker, J., & Hastie, R. H. (1985). Another look at sex stereotypes and social judgment. *Journal of Personality and Social Psychology, 49,* 317–326.

Rawls, J. (1971). *A theory of justice.* Cambridge, MA: Harvard University Press.

Reeder, G., & Brewer, M. B. (1979). A schematic model of dispositional attribution in interpersonal perception. *Psychological Review, 86,* 61–79.

Reiss, D. (1981). *The family's construction of reality.* Cambridge, MA: Harvard University Press.

Richardson, S. A. (1970). Age and sex differences in values toward physical handicaps. *Journal of Health and Social Behavior, 11,* 207–214.

Richardson, S. A. (1983). Children's values in regard to disabilities: A reply to Yuker. *Rehabilitation Psychology, 28,* 131–140.

Rosch, E. (1981). Principles of categorization. In E. Rosch & B. B. Lloyd (Eds.), *Cognition and categorization* (pp. 27–48). Hillsdale, NJ: Erlbaum.

Rosenfield, D., & Stephan, W. G. (1981). Intergroup relations among children. In S. S. Brehm, S. M. Kassin, & F. X. Gibbons (Eds.), *Developmental social psychology: Theory and research* (pp. 271–297). New York: Oxford University Press.

Rothbart, M. (1981). Memory processes and social beliefs. In D. L. Hamilton (Ed.), *Cognitive processes in stereotyping and intergroup behavior* (pp. 145–182). Hillsdale, NJ: Erlbaum.

Rothbart, M., & John, O. (1985). Social categorization and behavioral episodes: A cognitive analysis of the effects of intergroup contact. *Journal of Social Issues, 41*, 81–104.

Rothbart, M. & Park, B. (1986). On the confirmability and disconfirmability of trait concepts. *Journal of Personality and Social Psychology, 50*, 131–142.

Rothkrug, L. (1980). Religious practices and collective perceptions: Hidden homologies in the Renaissance and Reformation. *Historical Reflections, 7*, 1–264.

Rubin, S. (1974). *Medieval English medicine.* New York: Barnes & Noble.

Russell, J. B. (1965). *Dissent and reform in the early Middle Ages.* Berkeley: University of California Press.

Russell, J. B. (1977). *The devil: Perceptions of evil from antiquity to primitive Christianity.* Ithaca: Cornell University Press.

Russell, J. B. (1981). *Satan: The early Christian tradition.* Ithaca: Cornell University Press.

Ryan, M. (1982). *Marxism and deconstruction.* Baltimore: Johns Hopkins University Press.

Ryan, W. (1971). *Blaming the victim.* New York: Vintage Books.

Rysman, A. (1977). How the "gossip" became a woman. *Journal of Communication, 27*, 176–180.

Sabini, J., & Silver, M. (1982). *Moralities of everyday life.* Oxford: Oxford University Press.

Sagar, H. A., & Schoenfeld, J. W. (1980). Racial and behavioral cues in black and white children's perceptions of ambiguously aggressive acts. *Journal of Personality and Social Psychology, 39*, 590–598.

Sagarin, E. (1975). *Deviants and deviance: An introduction to the study of disvalued people and behavior.* New York: Praeger.

Sagarin, E. (1979). Deviance without deviants: The temporal quality of patterned behavior. *Deviant Behavior, 1*, 1–13.

Sanday, P. R. (1981). *Female power and male dominance: On the origins of sexual inequality.* New York: Cambridge University Press.

Sartre, J. (1948). *Anti-Semite and Jew.* New York: Schocken Books.

Schachter, J. (1959). *The psychology of affiliation.* Stanford, CA: Stanford University Press.

Schaffer, H. R., & Emerson, P. E. (1964). The development of social attachments in infancy. *Monographs of the Society for Research in Child Development, 29.*

Scheerenberger, R. C. (1983). *A history of mental retardation.* Baltimore: Brooks Publishing.

Schoenberg, B., Carr, A. C., Peretz, D. C., Kutscher, A. (1970). *Loss and grief: Psychological management*. New York: Columbia University Press.

Schofield, J. W., & Sagar, H. A. (1977). Peer interaction patterns in an integrated middle school. *Sociometry, 40,* 130–138.

Schowalter, J. E. (1970). The child's reaction to his own terminal illness. In J. W. Schoenberg, A. C. Carr, D. Peretz, & A. T. Kutscher (Eds.), *Loss and grief: Psychological management* (pp. 53–59). New York: Columbia University Press.

Schur, E. (1971). *Labeling deviant behavior: Its sociological implications*. New York: Harper & Row.

Schur, E. (1979). *Interpreting deviance: A sociological introduction*. New York: Harper & Row.

Schur, E. (1980). *The politics of deviance: Stigma contests and the uses of power*. Englewood Cliffs, NJ: Prentice-Hall.

Schur, E. (1983). *Labeling women deviant: Gender, stigma, and social control*. Philadelphia: Temple University Press.

Schutz, A. (1964). *Collected papers, Volume 2: Studies in social theory*. The Hague, Netherlands: Martinus Nijhoff.

Schutz, A. (1971). *Collected papers, Volume 1: The problem of social reality*. The Hague, Netherlands: Martinus Nijhoff.

Schwartz, C. G. (1956). The stigma of mental illness. *Journal of Rehabilitation, 22,* 7–29.

Schwartz, R. D., & Skolnick, J. H. (1962). Two studies of legal stigma. *Social Problems, 10,* 133–142.

Scott, R. (1969). *The making of blind men*. New York: Russell Sage Foundation.

Semmel, M. I., Gottlieb, J., & Robinson, N. M. (1979). Mainstreaming: Perspectives on educating handicapped children in the public schools. In D. C. Berliner (Ed.), *Review of research in education* (pp. 241–279). Washington, DC: American Educational Research Association.

Senac, P. (1983). *L'image de l'autre: Histoire de l'Occident medieval face à l'Islam* [The image of the other: History of the medieval West in the face of Islam]. Paris: Flammarion.

Seneca (1963). *Moral essays*. Cambridge, MA: Harvard University Press.

Serafica, F. C. (Ed.). (1982). *Social-cognitive development in context*. New York: Guilford.

Shears, L. M., & Jensema, C. J. (1969). Social acceptability of anomalous persons. *Exceptional Children, 36,* 91–96.

Sherif, M., Harvey, O. J., White, B. J., Hood, W. R., & Sherif, C. W. (1961). *Intergroup conflict and cooperation: The Robber's Cave experiment*. Norman: University of Oklahoma Press.

Sherrod, L. R. (1981). Issues in cognitive-perceptual development: The special case of social stimuli. In M. E. Lamb & L. R. Sherrod (Eds.), *Infant social cognition: Empirical and theoretical considerations* (pp. 11–36). Hillsdale, NJ: Erlbaum.

Sigelman, C. K., & McGrail, L. E. (1985). Developmental differences in evaluative reactions to physically and mentally handicapped children. *Journal of Social and Clinical Psychology, 3,* 352–366.

Sigelman, C. K., Miller, T. E., & Whitworth, L. A. (in press). The early development of stigmatizing reactions to physical differences. *Journal of Applied Developmental Psychology.*

Silverman, I., & Shaw, M. E. (1973). Effects of sudden mass school desegregation on interracial interaction and attitudes in one southern city. *Journal of Social Issues, 29,* 133–142.

Singleton, L. C., & Asher, S. R. (1977). Peer preferences and social interaction among third-grade children in an integrated school district. *Journal of Educational Psychology, 69,* 330–336.

Singleton, L. C., & Asher, S. R. (1979). Racial integration and children's peer preferences: An investigation of developmental and cohort differences. *Child Development, 50,* 936–941.

Skipper, J. K., Fink, S. L., & Hallenbeck, P. N. (1968). Physical disability among married women. *Journal of Rehabilitation, 34,* 16–19.

Snyder, M., & Swann, W. B., Jr. (1976). When actions reflect attitudes: The politics of impression management. *Journal of Personality and Social Psychology, 34,* 1034–1042.

Snyder, M. L., Kleck, R. E., Strenta, A., & Mentzer, S. J. (1979). Avoidance of the handicapped: An attributional ambiguity analysis. *Journal of Personality and Social Psychology, 37,* 2297–2306.

Solomon, H. M. (1982). *Shame and chemise: Ceremonies of dressing and undressing in early modern culture.* Unpublished manuscript.

Sontag, S. (1979). *Illness as metaphor.* New York: Random House.

Sourkes, B. M. (1980). All the things that I don't like about having leukemia: Children's lists. In J. Kellerman (Ed.), *Psychological aspects of childhood cancer* (pp. 289–291). Springfield, IL: Charles C Thomas.

Spillers, C. (1982). An investigation of children's attitudes towards physically disabled peers. *Mid-American Review of Sociology, 7,* 55–69.

Spradley, J. (1970). *You owe yourself a drunk.* Boston: Little, Brown.

Sroufe, L. A. (1977). Wariness of strangers and the study of infant development. *Child Development, 48,* 731–746.

Sroufe, L. A., Waters, E., & Matas, L. (1974). Contextual determinants of infant affective response. In M. Lewis & L. Rosenblum (Eds.), *The origins of fear* (pp. 49–72). New York: Wiley.

Stack, C. (1974). *All our kin.* New York: Harper & Row.

Steinberg, L. (1984). *The sexuality of Christ in Renaissance art and modern oblivion.* New York: Pantheon.

Stern, L. D., Marrs, S., Millar, M. G., & Cole, E. (1984). Processing time and the recall of inconsistent and consistent behaviors of individuals and groups. *Journal of Personality and Social Psychology, 47,* 253–262.

Stevenson, H. W., & Stevenson, N. G. (1960). Social interaction in an interracial nursery school. *Genetic Psychology Monographs, 61,* 37–75.

Stoianovitch, T. (1976). *French historical method: The "Annales" paradigm.* Ithaca: Cornell University Press.

Stone, L. (1979). The revival of narrative: Reflections on a new old history. *Past and present, 85,* 3–25.

Stone, L. (1981). Family history in the 1980s. *Journal of Interdisciplinary History, 12,* 51–87.

Strang, L., Smith, M. D., & Rogers, C. M. (1978). Social comparison, multiple reference groups, and the self-concepts of academically handicapped children before and after mainstreaming. *Journal of Educational Psychology, 20,* 487–497.

Sumption, J. (1975). *Pilgrimage: An image of medieval religion.* London: Faber & Faber.

Sussman, M. B. (1977). The family life of old people. In R. H. Binstock & E. Shanas (Eds.), *Handbook of Aging and the Social Sciences* (pp. 218–243. New York: Van Nostrand Reinhold.

Swann, W. B., Jr., & Ely, R. J. (1984). A battle of wills: Self-verification versus behavioral confirmation. *Journal of Personality and Social Psychology, 46,* 1287–1302.

Szasz, T. (1970). *The manufacture of madness: A comparative study of the Inquisition and the modern mental health movement.* New York: Harper & Row.

Tajfel, H. (1969). Cognitive aspects of prejudice. *Journal of Social Issues, 25,* 79–97.

Taylor, S. E. (1981). A categorization approach to stereotyping. In D. L. Hamilton (Ed.), *Cognitive processes in stereotyping and intergroup behavior* (pp. 83–114). Hillsdale, NJ: Erlbaum.

Taylor, S. E. (1983). Adjustment to threatening events: A theory of cognitive adaptation. *American Psychologist, 38,* 1161–1173.

Taylor, S. E., & Fiske, S. T. (1978). Salience, attention and attribution: Top-of-the-head phenomena. In L. Berkowitz (Ed.), *Advances in Experimental Social Psychology,* (Vol. 11, pp. 250–288). New York: Academic Press.

Taylor, S. E., Wood, J. V., & Lichtman, R. R. (1983). It could be worse: Selective evaluation as a response to victimization. *Journal of Social Issues, 39,* 19–40.

Terry, W. (1984). *Bloods: An oral history of the Vietnam War by black veterans.* New York: Random House.

Thomas, K. (1971). *Religion and the decline of magic.* New York: Charles Scribner's Sons.

Thompson, E. P. (1972). "Rough Music": Le charivari anglais ["Rough Music": The English charivari]. *Annales: Economies, Sociétés, Civilisations, 27,* 285–312.

Toby, J. (1981). Deterrence without punishment. *Criminology, 19,* 195–209.

Toch, H. (1965). *The social psychology of social movements*. Indianapolis: Bobbs-Merrill.

Tracy, G. S., & Gussow, Z. (1978). Self-help health groups: A grass-roots response to a need for services. *Journal of Applied Behavioral Science, 381–396.*

Travis, G. (1976). *Chronic illness in children: Its impact on child and family*. Stanford, CA: Stanford University Press.

Trumbach, R. (1977). London's sodomites: Homosexual behavior and Western culture in the eighteenth century. *Journal of Social History, 10*, 1–33.

Truzzi, M. (1968). Lilliputians in Gulliver's land: The social role of the dwarf. In M. Truzzi (Ed.), *Sociology of everyday life* (pp. 197–211). Englewood Cliffs, NJ: Prentice-Hall.

Turnbull, C. (1962). *The forest people*. New York: Simon & Schuster.

Turner, V. (1973). The center out there: The pilgrim's goal. *History of Religions, 12*, 191–230.

Turner, V. (1977). Variations on a theme of liminality. In S. F. Moore & B. G. Myerhoff (Eds.), *Secular ritual* (pp. 37–40). Assen: Van Gorcum.

Valentine, B. (1978). *Hustling and other hard work: Lifestyles in the ghetto*. New York: Free Press.

Vann, D. H. (1970). Components of attitudes toward the obese including presumed responsibility for the condition. *Proceedings of the 78th Annual Convention of the American Psychological Association, 5*, 695–696.

Vauchez, A. (1975). *La spiritualité du moyen age occidental (VIIIe -XIIe siècles)* [Spirituality in the western Middle Ages (eighth through the twelfth centuries)]. Paris: Presses universitaires de France.

Vickers, B. (1984). Analogy versus identity: The rejection of occult symbolism, 1580–1680. In B. Vickers (Ed.), *Occult and scientific mentalities in the Renaissance* (pp. 95–164). New York: Cambridge University Press.

Viscardi, H., Jr. (1952). *A man's stature*. New York: John Day.

Waddell, C. (1983). *Faith, hope and luck: A sociological study of children growing up with a life-threatening illness*. Washington, DC: University Press of America.

Waite, R. G. L. (1977). *The psychopathic god Adolf Hitler*. New York: Signet.

Warfield, F. (1948). *Cotton in my ears*. New York: Viking Press.

Warner, M. (1981). *Joan of Arc: The image of female heroism*. New York: Knopf.

Waters, E., Wippman, J., & Sroufe, L. A. (1979). Attachment, positive affect, and competence in the peer group: Two studies in construct validation. *Child Development, 50*, 821–829.

Weber, R., & Crocker, J. (1983). Cognitive processes in the revision of stereotypic beliefs. *Journal of Personality and Social Psychology, 45*, 961–977.

Wedemeyer, C. A. (1981). *Learning at the back door: Reflections on non-traditional learning in the lifespan.* Madison: The University of Wisconsin Press.

Weidner, G., & Griffitt, W. (1983). Rape: A sexual stigma? *Journal of Personality, 51,* 152–166.

Weigert, A. (1981). *The sociology of everyday life.* New York: Longmans.

Weinberg, N. (1978). Preschool children's perceptions of orothopedic disability. *Rehabilitation Counseling Bulletin, 21,* 183–189.

Weiner, C. L. (1975). The burden of rheumatoid arthritis: Tolerating the uncertainty. *Social Science and Medicine, 99,* 97–104.

Weinstein, D., & Bell, R. M. (1982). *Saints and society: The two worlds of western Christendom, 1000–1700.* Chicago: University of Chicago Press.

Wilden, A. (1972). *System and structure: Essays in communication and exchange.* London: Tavistock.

Williams, J. E., & Morland, J. K. (1976). *Race, color, and the young child.* Chapel Hill: University of North Carolina Press.

Williams, J. F. (1972). Manifest anxiety and self-concept: A comparison of blind and sighted adolescents. *Developmental Psychology, 6,* 349–352.

Wills, T. A. (1981). Downward comparison principles in social psychology. *Psychological Bulletin, 90,* 245–271.

Willy, N. R., & McCandless, B. R. (1973). Social stereotypes for educable mentally retarded and orthopedically handicapped children. *Journal of Special Education, 7,* 283–288.

Wilson, W. (1980). *The declining significance of race: Blacks and changing American institutions.* Chicago: University of Chicago Press.

Wolff, R. P. (1977). *Understanding Rawls.* Princeton: Princeton University Press.

Wright, B. (1960). *Physical disability: A psychological approach.* New York: Harper & Row.

Wright, B. A. (1983). *Physical disability—A psychosocial approach.* New York: Harper & Row.

Wylie, R. C. (1979). *The self-concept* (Vol. 2). Lincoln: University of Nebraska Press.

Zajonc, R. B. (1980). Feeling and thinking: Preferences need no inferences. *American Psychologist, 35,* 151–175.

Zola, I. Z. (1979). Helping one another: A speculative history of the self-help movement. *Archives of Physical Medicine and Rehabilitation, 60,* 452–456.

Index

Alcoholics Anonymous, 142
Ambivalence, 4, 127–128, 143
Anti-Defamation League, 91
"Appresentation," 24
Attitudes
  attitude defined, 158
  "cognitive component," 158–159
Attributes
  contingent, 83
  defined, 97
  nonrecognition of, 219
The Authoritarian Personality
  (Adorno), 103
Authoritarian personality theory,
  102–103, 115, 187

BaBira Society, 29, 30
Bandura, Albert, 188–189
Becker, Ernest
  The Denial of Death, 168, 227
Becker, H. S., 45, 47, 147
Beliefs
  constructivist perspective on, 99
  development of, 153–159
  generalizations and stereotypes,
    101, 155–156
  higher-order, 156–158
    centrality of, 157
    horizontal structures, 157
    vertical structures, 156

Beliefs (*cont.*)
  logic of, 157–158
  normative
    perceived, 85
    personal, 85
  primitive, 154–155
    first-order, 155, 159
    zero-order, 154–155, 159
Bentham, Jeremy, 36
Blanchot, Maurice, 111
Body image, 48, 61–64
Bourdieu, Pierre, 65
Braudel, Fernand, 59
Brown, Peter, 62

Cancer, Stigmatizing effects
  See Cancer, childhood
Cancer, childhood
  case study, 165–167, 218
  child's altered status
    in community, 168–169, 174–175
    in family, 172–174
  family functioning, 169–171,
    180–182
  as master status, 164–169, 176–177
  relationships, 178–179
  self-perceptions 177–178
  stereotypes, 175–176
  See also Family experience

Carson, Rachel, 1
Categorization, 79, 104, 108–110,
   219
   See also Typification
Center for Advanced Study in the
   Behavioral Sciences, x, xvi
Childhood, stigmatization in/and,
   126, 155, 185–208
   disabilities, reactions to, 199–204
   infants, 26, 191–293
   differentiation and, 26
   later development, 196–199, 201–
   204
   preschool years, 194–196, 200–
   201, 217
   racial prejudice, 194, 195–196,
   197–199
   self-referencing, 217
   summary and implications, 204–
   208
China, 44, 48
Christianity and stigmatization, 61–
   75
Coding
   See categorization
Cognition, social, 106–114, 114–
   120
   cognitive analyses, 116–120
   cognitive recognition, 107–111
   consequences, 111–114
   defined, 107–111
   motivational analyses, 115–116,
   118–119
   sociocultural analyses, 114
Cognitive processing, 218–221
Cooperative interdependence, 119–
   120, 221
Courtesy stigma, 7, 87, 126, 225–
   226
   See also Family experience
Cultural universals, 29–30, 40–41
Culture
   basis of stigma, 41–42, 55, 146
   perceptions, 43–44, 106
   Western, 59–76

Davis, N. J., 35, 80
Death, 167–168, 226–227
Deconstructionism, 73

Default values/assumptions, 109,
   117
Deinstitutionalization, 125, 168
The Denial of Death (Becker), 168
Derrida, Jacques, 73
Destigmatization, 5, 53–55, 91,
   160–161
   changing cognition, 114–120
   current attitudes, 143–144
   deinstitutionalization, 125
   equal status contacts, 91
   future, 228–230
   individuality and, 229–230
   legal mandates, 125, 128, 168
   mainstreamlined classes, 115, 126
   See also Social change
Deutsch, Morton, 36
Developmental issues, 185–187
   theory, 187–191
   authoritarian personality, 102–
   103, 115, 187
   cognitive, 189–191
   psychoanalytic, 187–188
   psychosexual, 102
   social learning, 188–189, 216–
   218
   trends, 193–199
   See also Childhood, stigmatization in/and
Deviance, 8, 34, 77, 80–84
   defined, 81
   responsibility and, 83
   See also Stigma
Differences, 21–23
   background, 25
   class, 46, 47
   defined, 21
   foreground, 25–28, 34
   human, typology of, 23–31, 32
   See also Social learning
Disabilities, 49, 214
   children's reactions to, 199–204
Disconfirmability
   logical, 117, 118
   practical, 117, 118
Discrepancy hypothesis, 26
Disorientation, 27
Disvaluation
   See Stigma; Stigmatization

Expectancy confirmation processes, 113–114

Family experience of stigma, 164–165, 171–172, 223
altered status, 181–182
family functioning, 169–171, 180–181
executive subsystem, 169–170
general dynamics, 164–165
marital subsystem, 170
sibling subsystem, 170–171
interfamily stigmatization, 180–181, 183–184
See also Cancer, childhood
Febvre, Lucien, 72–73
Foucault, Michael, 66
Freud, Sigmund, 187, 190, 193
psychosexual development theories, 102
Friedson, E., 82, 83
on deviance, 34

Gay Activist Alliance, 91
Ghandi, Mahatma, 222
Girard, René, 73
Goffman, Erving, ix, 2, 4, 7, 27, 28, 78, 109, 125, 145, 152, 211, 212
"courtesy stigma," 7, 87, 125, 225–226
"ideal" person, 81, 214
"identity norms," 81
on institutionalization, 74
"moral career" patterns of stigmatized, 150
stigma, definition of, 3, 27, 78
Stigma: Notes on the Management of Spoiled Identity, 1, 2
"tribal" stigma, 39–40
Goodman, M. E., 194
Greek civilization, 3, 42, 45, 78

Heretics, 64–66, 69
medieval movements, 71–72
Hitler, Adolph, 105
Homosexuality
stigmatization of, 5, 66, 67, 91
Husserl, E.
"appresentation," 24

Individuality, 119–120, 219, 229–230
Infants
See Childhood
Inferiorization
See Typification
Inquisition, The, 65–66, 74
Institutionalization, 47, 74–75
de-, 125, 168
Introjection, process of, 151
Inverted reality, 71–72
Isolation, 143

Jews, Christian stigmatization of, 67–69
Jones, E. E., 28, 30, 79–80, 97
six dimensions of stigma, 28
"Just-world" theory, 19, 103, 115, 116, 125
Justice, 17–37, 46, 50
contemporary, 36–37
defined, 17
equality, 36–37
Institutionalist, 36
interrelations, 17–18
legitimation, 32–33
as nomos-building activities, 20–35
research implications, 35–37
society's conception of, 18
system, 46, 50
types of, 33
Utilitarian, 36
See also Legal systems

Kagan, J.
"discrepancy hypothesis," 26
Kant, Immanuel, 36
Katz, Irwin
ambivalence theory 127, 149
Katz, P. A., 194
Kohlberg, Lawrence, 190
Kristeva, Julia, 73

Language and stigma, 60–61, 73
Learning, three stages of, 147–148
Legal systems/mandates, 18–19, 42, 67, 70, 128–129, 146
law (PL 93-112), 128

Legal systems/mandates (*cont.*)
  law (PL 94-142), 125, 158
  See also Justice
Lerner, Melvin, 32, 34, 35, 36
  The Belief in a Just World, 32
  "just-world" theory, 125
Lewin, K.
  "negative chauvinism," 137
Liminality, regions of, 70
Little, Lester, 62
Little People of America, 91

MacLeod, Robert, 24
Mainstreaming, 126, 207
  law (PL 94-142), 128
Martin, L. G., 281, 291
Master status, 6, 86–87, 176–177,
  219
Medieval society, 42, 62–75
Mehta, Ved, 46
Mellon, Andrew, Foundation, x
Merleau-Ponty, Maurice, 21, 25
  symbolic forms, 21
Mill, John Stuart, 36
Mischel, Walter, 188
Monastic orders, 61–62
Morality, 19, 41, 53, 124–129
  ambivalence and, 127–128
Motivations, 7, 46, 75, 102–104,
  147, 167
  fear, 216, 218, 225–227
  power and, 6–7, 18, 45–48, 213,
  228–229
  self-enhancement, 19, 103, 115,
  135, 214–215, 220
  social control, 87–90
  structural inequality, 45–48
  See also Social learning

Navajo, 42
"Negative chauvinism," 137, 144
"Negative halo effect," 126
  See also Courtesy stigma
"Norm" or "normal"
  defined, 80–81, 85–86, 90
  "ideal," 81, 215
  "identity," 81, 84
  reactive, 89
  violations, 83–84

Normalization, 50–51, 128–129,
  222–225

Objectification
  See Typification

Parks, Rosa, 222
"Passing," 130–131
Peer support groups, 140–143
  "negative chauvinism," 144
Perception, 85, 107–109
Piaget, Jean, 189
  cognitive-developmental theory,
  189–191
Power, defined 45–46
  and stigma, 6–7, 45–47
Protest movement
  See Social change
Proust, Marcel 43
Psychoanalytic theory
  See Developmental issues
Pygmies, Turnbull's study of, 28

Racial prejudice, 46, 194
  childhood development of, 194–
  199
Rehabilitation Act of 1973, law (PL
  93-112), 126
Relationships, 123–144
  historical perspective, 124
  legal mandates, 128–129, 146
  "mixed," 125–127, 129–132,
  221–225
    "breakthrough," 220–221
    "courtesy stigma," 8, 87, 126,
    225–226
  defined, 124, 129
  marriages, 129
  negative aspects of, 131–132
  nonstigmatized person's behavior patterns, 126
  positive aspects of, 140–141
  sexual, 127
  stigma, meaning of and, 221–225
  between stigmatized persons,
  132–139
    avoidance, 138–139
    lateral comparison, 138–139
    social comparison, 139

Relationships (*cont.*)
  between stigmatized persons (*cont.*)
    peer support groups, 140–144
    self–esteem, 132–134
    social comparison, 134–138
    downward comparison, 135–
      138
    See also Childhood; Family
      experience
Responsibility, 228

St. John Chrysostom, 67
St. Paul, 71
Sartre, Jean-Paul, 109
Schur, E., 27, 79–81, 84
Schutz, Alfred, 20–21, 22, 23
Self-referencing, 217
Seneca, 89
Social change, 51–53, 54, 55, 61, 91
  peer support groups, 140–144
Social cognition
  See Cognition
Social comparison, 134–139, 213
  downward, 135–138
  lateral, 138–139
Social control, 87–90, 220
  defined, 87
Social identity, 145
  body image and, 48, 61–64
Social learning, 101, 145–153
  characteristics of, 148–150
  multidisciplinary perspective,
    159–160
  vs. socialization, 148
  societal assumptions, 44–45
  of stigma, 147–148, 150–153,
    159–160, 216–218
    social-independent, 152–153
    social-surrogate, 151–152
    social-survival, 150–151
  theory, 188–189
Social thought, 101–106
  cognitive perspective, 104–105
  implications, 105–106
  motivational perspective, 102–
    104, 115, 116, 125
  sociocultural perspective, 101–102
Socialization
  See Social learning

Societal evolution, 3, 4–5, 44
Society, stratified
  See Differences
"Special dispensation," 202
Special Project on Stigma, x
Stereotypes, 97, 101–102, 104, 106,
  219
  behavioral consequences of, 113–
    114
  in childhood cancer, 175–176
  cognitive consequences of, 112–
    113
  defined, 97
  morality, 125
Stigma
  acquisition, 129–130
  basis for, 27, 31, 41–42, 197,
    205, 207, 213
  as cognitive processing, 218–221
  as collective experience, 80, 85
  "courtesy," 7, 87, 126, 225–226
  definitions, x, 1, 3, 17, 19, 27–28,
    41, 60–61, 77–78, 78–80,
    163, 228
  difficulties in establishing, 1–3
  dilemma of, 212–216
  dimensions of, 28
  hidden, 50
  legitimization of, 5, 53
  as master status, 6, 86–87, 176–
    177, 219
  measuring of, 84–87
  morality, 19, 41, 53, 124–129
  origins of, 216–218
  responsibility for, 19, 34, 47, 48,
    82–83, 125, 228
  types of, 28, 77, 78
  universality of, 40–41
  See also Cancer, childhood;
    Stereotypes
*Stigma: Notes on the Management
  of Spoiled Identity (Goffman),
  ix, 2*
Stigma research
  analyses, 39
  cognitive approaches, 95–100,
    120–121
    attitudinal, 96–98
    schematic perspective, 98–100

Stigma research (cont.)
  conceptual issues, 90–91
  development of, 11–13
  future study, 230–232
  history of, ix–x, 37
  limitations on, 8–11
  multidisciplinary approach, 8–13,
    19, 56–57
  value of, 10–11, 19, 37
Stigmatization
  Christian, 61–64, 64–68, 75
  context of, 4, 22–23, 43–44, 47,
    49–50, 80, 82, 214, 215
  and deviance, 80–84
  general experience of, three fac-
    tors, 143
  interfamily, 180–181, 183–189
  methods of, 4, 74, 79–80, 88,
    125, 143, 222–223
  self-, 61–62, 147
  See also Childhood; Motivations;
    Typifications
Stigmatized individual
  attributed characteristics, 70–73
  collective behavior, 6, 51–53
  impact of stigma on, 6–8, 226
  "moral career" patterns of, 150
  normalization process, 7–8, 50–
    51, 56–61
  peer support groups, 140–144
  reactions to, 4, 19, 79–80, 87–90,
    92, 98, 111, 126, 127–128,
    220
  responsibility of, 19, 34, 47, 48,
    82, 83, 125, 222, 228–230
  self-perception, 49, 51, 97–98,
    130–131, 132–134, 177–178,
    223–225
    comparisons, 134–139
  sexuality and, 66–67, 72, 127
  social functions of, 68–70
  socialization of, 152–153

Stigmatized individual (cont.)
  structural similarities, 68–75
  transcendence, 6–8, 45, 49, 51,
    130–131, 222
  See also Relationships; Social
    Change; Social Learning
Stigmatizers
  Christian Church as, 61–75
  See also Developmental theory;
    Motivation
Stranger anxiety, 191–192, 216–
    217
Summer Institute on Stigma and In-
    terpersonal Relations, x
Szasz, Thomas, 66

Theodicy, 33
Third Lateran Council, 66
"Tribal" stigma, 39–40, 54, 56, 78
Turnbull, Collin, 29
Turner, Victor, 68
Typification, 20–23, 28–29, 79,
    104, 108–110, 219
  defined, 20
  and moral signficance, 34
  perception and, 22

"Undifferentiated family ego mass,"
    180

Value, defined, 159
Viscardi, Henry, 185
Volition, 19, 33, 229–230
  See also Responsibility

Weigert, Andrew, 20
Witchcraft
  Middle Ages, 42
  sexuality and, 72
  as social intermediary, 69–70
Women's issues, 52, 54, 61, 79